THE
MASTER

DECLAN KIDNEY
A BIOGRAPHY

THE
MASTER

DECLAN KIDNEY
A BIOGRAPHY

EDITED BY LIAM HAYES

HEROBOOKS

HEROBOOKS

PUBLISHED BY HERO BOOKS
1 WOODVILLE GREEN
LUCAN
CO. DUBLIN
IRELAND
www.herobooks.ie
Hero Books is an imprint of Umbrella Publishing

First Published 2017

A CIP record for this book is available from the British Library

ISBN 9781910827024

Printed in Ireland with Print Procedure Ltd
Cover design and typesetting: Jessica Maile
Cover photograph: Sportsfile

THE
MAN
| PART**ONE** |

THE
MASTER
| PART**TWO** |

| PART**ONE** |

THE
MAN

'Players lose you games, not tactics. There's so much crap talked about tactics by people who barely know how to win at dominoes.'
– Brian Clough

'Good coaches all have one thing in common... they work with good players.'
– Declan Kidney

IN THE DAYS before Munster claimed their second Heineken Cup in Cardiff's Millennium Stadium in May of 2008, Declan Kidney made casual mention of Brian Clough to some of the many dozens of journalists who sat in front of him that week. He was generally talking about managers and coaches he admired. Guy Noves, his opposite number in the impending final, and Robbie Deans also came up in conversation. There was nothing at all about Clough, a boozy, irascible team boss who reached the top shelf of his career with Nottingham Forest that could be associated with Kidney's personal belief in how to go about his business.

Nothing. Clough loved to run off at the mouth. Kidney never danced around the room with words in his life.

Declan Kidney instead was reminding himself and those around him of the fall, from such a perilous height, of Clough's Forest in the early 80s.

Twice, Clough's team based in a place best known for a fleet-footed Robin Hood adroitly avoiding the tackles of Nottingham's most vicious sheriff, had conquered Europe on a football field. Nottingham was the football capital of a whole continent. And, after that... freefall.

Declan Kidney certainly fancied that Munster would also win a second Europe title, when he brought Clough and Forest to the attention of those around him. He had no idea, however, that within another 12 months he would have the responsibility of conquering Europe a third time, on this occasion with Ireland in 2009.

Back in May of 2008, Kidney was aware that there was possibly only one direction for Munster to go, if they were not extremely careful, and if they took their status as Europe's No.1 for granted. After taking his leave of the Heineken Cup champions and accepting the role of Ireland head coach, he would watch Munster struggle to hold onto their elevated position.

But, after that astonishing Grand Slam triumph in his first year as an international head coach, Declan Kidney's career was soon heading back down to earth. From Europe's No.1 head coach, and the greatest handler of a team in the history of Irish rugby, there was only one direction in which he could go.

THREE YEARS OUT of four, Declan Kidney hardly put a foot wrong, or had a finger misplaced in any team selection. His midas touch was pretty much secure.

His success was based on a formidable trust in his team selections, and in the individuals on those teams. On more than one occasion, in explaining how important trust is to him, Kidney told the story of ducking down behind the steering wheel of his car so that he would avoid watching one of his players breaking one of his most sacred rules.

The story is set in his days as a schools coach. There was a cup final pending. He was fairly sure one of his players was walking down the road with a cigarette. 'If I saw someone smoking, I wasn't wasting my time training them,' Kidney explained himself to journalists. He was sitting down so low he could barely see out the windscreen. He didn't want to confirm what he thought he saw. If he did, the player in question would have to be dropped from his Pres Cork team selection.

In his first coming as Munster coach he met with the disappointment of losing two Heineken Cup finals, by one point to Northampton in 2000 and six points to Leicester in 2002. In 2006 Europe's premier trophy was clinched by virtue of a four points advantage over Biarritz. In 2008 Munster were three points in front when Nigel Owens blew his whistle for the final time.

The margins were always close. The fine line between losing and winning always remained paper-thin. The emotion that was let loose in the Munster dressing room at the beginning of that decade was high octane compared to the calmer, more disciplined approach at the end of the same decade. Second time around, Declan Kidney was also a better, more trusting coach.

In his time away from Munster, in the seasons in between the Heineken Cup finals of 2002 and 2006, Declan Kidney had learned more about himself. He had spent two years with the Irish team, as Eddie O'Sullivan's assistant coach. There was also three months at Newport Gwent Dragons without taking charge of one competitive game. Then there was nine months with Leinster that included six wins in the Heineken Cup before a quarter-final exit. In that period of time, Kidney spent a great deal of time away from Cork and outside of his comfort zone.

When he reapplied for the coaching position in Munster in 2005, he was accused of still 'having his heart in Cork'. Leinster and Ireland back row, Victor Costello would go on record several years later, saying that, 'When Declan came to Leinster, I don't think he spoke the language. I don't think he ever bought into the city thing. "High and dry" would be the wrong expression to describe how we felt. But we certainly felt disappointed in relation to what we expected from our knowledge of him. And we all felt a little let down'.

It was true, Kidney did wish to be back home.

But, as he explained in *Munster: Our Road to Glory* that was published in 2006, he did not pick the timing of his departure. He saw the job as it was advertised. Like most folk, he would always prefer to work closer to home, and he felt he had to take it. He also mentioned that perhaps 'Someone' was looking down on him and persuading him to go home. Munster as a team, and Munster as a business, had changed while Kidney was on his travels. It was a far bigger organisation than the one he had left in 2002. Over 50 people depended on the team – on a winning brand – for a living.

As a younger coach still learning his trade as a full-time professional, there is another story told of Declan Kidney. 'It was late summer of 1999,' wrote the *Irish Independent's* Vincent Hogan, 'and the squad, just back in camp, was about to do an orienteering exercise through woodland.' The same day was John Langford's first day on duty as a Munster player.

'The big Australian told Kidney he had an injured ankle and suggested he might, as such, be best advised sitting the exercise out,' continued Hogan. 'He got a short answer. "If you come back,' smiled the Munster coach, "… we'll know it's alright." The steel in Kidney is rarely articulated loudly.'

A decade later, an older and more experienced coach, would Declan Kidney dispense with the natural doubts of a schoolteacher listening to one of his pupils? Perhaps. Though the traits he developed over the course of two decades in the classroom were not entirely eroded during his 'second life' as a professional rugby coach.

❙❙❙❙❙❙❙❙❙

THE MAKING OF a 'very weird, strange and wonderful man', as once announced by Irish legend and barnstorming hooker Keith Wood, was plain sailing in the beginning. He was the son of a pirate.

Joe Kidney was born in Cobh, and worked in the Cork Dockyard that eventually became known locally as Verolme when it passed in 1957 into the hands of Dutch shipping magnet, Cornelius Verolme. Thirty-three ships were built in the dockyard and 1,500 people, including Joe, worked there until the ship building industry went under in the early 1980s. A Munster senior schools cup winner, as his son would also be, Joe was a former captain of Cobh Pirates.

His father, and not some esteemed team boss or coach in Ireland or England, was the greatest influence on Declan Kidney's career. His father was also a former winger with Dolphin, and father and son, with Declan listening intently to Joe's analysis of games, averaged three matches together every weekend in the rugby season. From seven or eight years of age, Declan played in his own match on a Saturday morning, and the pair would watch the senior team that afternoon. Sunday morning they found time to view the thirds match. Sunday afternoon the seconds match.

A lot of games for young eyes to soak up; a lot of words dropped into young ears, and so it was hardly surprising that Declan Kidney considered himself fit and ready to coach his first team at 19 years of age. He had lost a Munster senior schools final with Pres Cork by that time, and rebounded to win one. He was playing with UCC. He was playing out-half. In his playing days at Dolphin he was considered a canny No.10 with a good enough boot, but the Munster juniors was as high as he scaled the representative ladder. 'Looking back on it now,' he considered in his early days as Munster coach, 'I was probably overly harsh on myself and over analytical in what I could do. But I loved it.'

His highlights? He singled out the schools cup final, and mentioned, 'as for the club one? I suppose any time I made the team'. He had brains on the field, however. Lots of good thoughts about the game! What was the point in waiting to become an old man with a whistle? None.

After graduating from college he returned to his alma mater to coach. He also returned to teach maths and offer career advice to students. He was pointed in the direction of the under-13s. In the 1980s, Pres Cork lifted five junior cups in six years. Three senior cups, one after the other, followed smartly in the 1990s. Kidney coached all eight victories.

He oversaw an Irish Schools Triple Crown in 1993. Brought the Irish under-19s to France in 1998 for a World Cup that had not attracted the attention of some of game's superpowers. There was no New Zealand, Australian or English teams in the way. 'Why can't we win it lads?' Kidney declared. And Ireland proceeded to defeat the United States, before side-stepping South Africa after fighting back from a 17-0 deficit and earning a draw. The South Africans nicked the penalty shootout 4-3, but they still got kicked out for using an ineligible player.

A decade later, Irish team captain Shane Moore, who partnered Brian O'Driscoll in the centre, was asked by one journalist to explain Kidney's secret, and in his explanation he returned to the team dressing room before that same game against the South Africans. 'He was all, "Sure I suppose we may as well go home, we probably won't have a hope here," remembered Moore. 'And you're going, "What do you mean?" It was maybe a reverse psychology. He'd make you think and talk. Because all of a sudden you found yourself focusing on what you needed to do.'

Moore could not recall the coach shouting, or even raising his voice the whole tournament, even when everyone trooped back into the dressing room at half-time, to consider a 17-0 deficit. 'He was still absolutely calm and logical. "Why not hang onto the ball and see what you can do? Take it to them a little more, and see what they have." ' Moore and his men proceeded to do exactly that.

'I can never remember us having any fear of losing in that tournament,' the team captain continued. 'The glass was always half full. Declan always stressed the squad, so much so you felt you were going on the field with 30 people, not 15.'

In the semi-final Argentina were taken out 18-3, and in the final it was a rout against the home nation. An impeccable 18-0 scoreline. There was shock and wild celebration in clinching a World Cup, but in his memoir *The Test* Brian O'Driscoll spent time recalling something that happened distant from any of those games.

O'Driscoll explained that Kidney was pumped up for the team's first match against the United States and, at an early training session, he pulled the future Irish legend to one side and told him to stop spitting in the team huddle as he (Kidney) was talking. O'Driscoll was not even aware that he was spitting. 'Declan gets pumped up for our first match, against the US,' wrote O'Driscoll.

'Please don't spit into the middle of it,' O'Driscoll was told.

O'Driscoll apologised.

Kidney told him that if he had to spit… spit out, not in!

In his next 16 years in an Irish jersey, or Lions jersey, or any jersey for that matter, the most decorated player in this country's history never again spat in a team huddle. He also had a good long look at anyone who did.

It was O'Driscoll's first insight into a man who would be working against him and with him over the next two decades. He witnessed how Declan Kidney liked to grasp at things, real or imaginary, a possible slight, an errant insult, in order to give his team even the most minimal of psychological advantages. The day before the final in Les Sept Deniers in Toulouse, for instance, he had asked the young Irish lads to take a closer look at their team bus.

'Have you noticed how the quality of our team bus is getting worse and worse?' he asked them.

Kidney suggested that the Irish team was being treated as second best.

In between the victories by the Irish schools and the Irish under-19s, there was time spent in Division Two of the All-Ireland League as Dolphin aimed themselves at Division One and hit the bulls eye under Declan Kidney's watch.

A lot of work, a lot of experience, and all for the fun of it.

PRIVATE BOYS SCHOOLS typically like to spell out who they are, and what they represent. And the prospectus for Presentation Brothers College in Cork spells out that: THE COLLEGE GAME IS RUGBY FOOTBALL.

This code has been spelled out in capital letters over the years. There would be no point in anyone, future pupils or their parents, being confused, would there? Although seriously successful in the classroom, in addition to the rugby field, the college prospectus does not spell out its academic activities in capital letters.

The message is loud and proud because Pres Cork, built by Catholic laymen in 1878, happens to have over two dozen former pupils who have gained international status with Ireland; lads who wore the green before Tom Kiernan led the 1968 British and Irish Lions to South Africa, and since Ronan O'Gara kicked Ireland to that Grand Slam in 2009.

Pres Cork has known how to look after its pupils and its prized rugby players. Also in the college prospectus is a sentence about chaplaincy that is interesting when twinned with the coaching philosophy and methodology of the man that the college also helped make into an outstanding coach. 'Chaplaincy,' it notes, 'is about people – not structures, programmes and tables.'

Hmmm.

And it is hardly coincidence that when two of the strongest figures in European rugby were asked to put a finger on the single most important ingredient Declan Kidney mixed into an Irish Grand Slam winning team, both mentioned the word 'happy'.

Talking about the Irish teams under Warren Gatland and Eddie O'Sullivan, that preceded Declan Kidney's Ireland, Italian head coach Nick Mallet opined, 'It was a very different side then. Probably not as happy or as well organised'. Welsh coach Gatland, who watched from close up as Ireland seized the Slam right at the death in Cardiff, suggested Ireland's 'togetherness'.

Though Gatland went further. 'Declan's known a lot of those players for a long time. They look a happy side.'

❙❙❙❙❙❙❙❙❙

THE BIGGEST JOB of his life was handed over to him in the first week of May in 2008. The announcement came two and a half weeks before Munster met Toulouse in the Heineken Cup final. In thanking the IRFU for their faith in him, Declan Kidney said, 'I am delighted to have this opportunity and to be here at what is the pinnacle of my career'.

Five years earlier he was Ireland's assistant coach and, technically, a heartbeat away from the No.1 job in the game. In reality, although in close proximity to head coach Eddie O'Sullivan on the training field and in the stands, Kidney was never fully utilised according to those who watched from up close.

A dire 2007 World Cup and a poor Six Nations campaign that followed brought O'Sullivan's seven-season and 78-game reign to a halt, and he resigned. O'Sullivan was back in the job market, and in 2011 was appointed head coach to the USA. No plum international jobs, however, were offered to him in the intervening period between 2008 and 2011, despite a CV that was sensationally hot by European standards. Ireland had won three Triple Crowns in his seven years. They had beaten Australia and South Africa twice. For four consecutive years, Ireland had beaten England in the Six Nations, including a record 43-13 victory in an historic meeting in Croke Park. All of this, and something more!

Something Eddie O'Sullivan could never have expected to come his way.

But, as Declan Kidney was still standing on the field in the Millennium Stadium in the immediate aftermath of the 2009 Grand Slam triumph, he singled out the Irish coaching team preceding him as a significant part of the glittering success story.

It was Declan Kidney at his most gracious. It was also him doing what he did best, sharing equally all responsibility and glory.

If Kidney had smiled and accepted all of the plaudits and claps on the back nobody would have blamed him. Nobody would have noticed that same heady day in Cardiff, which saw Brian O'Driscoll and his predecessor as a Grand Slam hero Jack Kyle embrace pitchside, and leave the Irish sporting public with a mental snapshot that nobody had imagined possible.

But, importantly, Declan Kidney had not promised that he would bring it all back home when he took up the position at the beginning of the season, and with all of the Six Nations loot in the arms of the Irish team, he was not going to try and rewrite his cautionary words from only a few months earlier. 'There's been an expectancy given their results over the last six years,' Kidney stated on his appointment.

'There's never been a better period for Irish rugby. They've won three Triple Crowns, and were about two seconds from a Championship (in 2007, when a late French try against Scotland won the title on points difference). It's nice when people expect because it shows a belief in our ability.

'But I think you have to be realistic as well.'

As always, in setting out on his journey, Kidney surrounded himself with outstanding people in whom he held absolute faith and trust. Former international Paul McNaughton was team manager. Gert Smal was in charge of the forwards, Alan Gaffney the backs. Les Kiss had his eye on attack. However, after the first autumn of the Kidney era there was nobody certain what the 2009 Six Nations would hold for Ireland. The team was flat, moody, and off form. And unless things changed, and changed fast, there was only one man on whom all of the blame was going to be unceremoniously heaped.

When asked, in the build up to the Championship opener against France in Croke Park if an improvement in performance was around the corner and if the head coach could work some form of magic, Paul O'Connell came across all tongue-tied. 'Declan... you know, like, he's very instinctive in what he does. I think he's been doing probably what he does best over the last few months. It's very hard to put your finger on it with Declan. He's not a... if you understand what I mean? He's big into making sure people are happy, and the team is happy.'

That was true. And in camp before the Six Nations, unbeknownst to anybody outside the Irish rugby party, the head coach had already done two things.

No, he hadn't unearthed a master tactical game plan that would alter everything overnight, and neither had he drilled a new found self-belief into the heads of his players so that they would perform faultlessly.

But he had worked some magic.

And he had sought to make the team… happier.

More together… family-like.

His exact role, of course, in possibly the most famous team meeting in the history of the Irish rugby is uncertain. He was the facilitator. He wanted his players to talk. He broke them up into small groups of sixes and sevens, and asked them to talk honestly and passionately with one another. Declan Kidney asked his players to come up with some of the answers for themselves that evening in Johnstown House Hotel in Enfield in County Meath where Irish teams had convened before, many times in fact, but where never before was there such a display of brutal and disarming honesty amongst the best rugby players in this country.

THERE WAS A mounting negativity fencing in the Ireland squad as the Six Nations Championship came into view in 2009. Munster players outnumbered Leinster lads two to one. Munster were reigning European champions. Leinster were still being crudely labelled as the game's 'lady boys' by the *Sunday Independent*. Paul O'Connell as a leader on the field was overshadowing Ireland team captain, Brian O'Driscoll. But, whatever the numbers, there was a unanimous understanding that something needed to change within the team dynamic if sixteen months of underperforming was to be seriously challenged.

In Enfield, when Leinster full-back Rob Kearney asked if the Munster players had as much 'passion' for the green jersey as they had for the red jersey, a switch was certainly flicked.

On February 7 in Croke Park, tries from three of Leinster's finest, as it happened, Heaslip, O'Driscoll and D'Arcy sent the team on its way to a 30-21 victory over France. Eight days later in Stadio Flaminio Ireland took the Italians out 38-9. Thirteen days later, back in Croker, a 57th minute O'Driscoll try was just enough to edge England 14-13, and two weeks after that in Murrayfield a Heaslip try converted by Ronan O'Gara was the difference over Scotland, 22-15. On March 21 came the Grand Slam in the Millennium Stadium. Wales 15, Ireland 17.

Twelve tries in total in the 2009 Championship. Nine of them Leinster tries. Two thanks to Ulster's Tommy Bowe. One from David Wallace, not that anyone in the vicinity of Declan Kidney was parading any provincial lineage through an historic spring.

Declan Kidney's management of his team was of the highest order. His man management, however, once the words first began to tumble from Rob Kearney's mouth in Enfield, was supreme. He was strong and courageous, even as he tinkered right up to the final days leading to the showdown with the Welsh. He had made four changes before the victory over Scotland. A more ruthless streak continued to display itself as he shuffled his cards before the last game with three changes. Peter Stringer, the heartbeat of the Munster team had given a Man of the Match performance in Murrayfield. But he was gone. So too Denis Leamy and Rory Best.

'The difference between the players is so small,' noted the coach at the team announcement, explaining his reasoning was 'partly' tactical. 'The gaps are so small I wouldn't try to justify it. You've got to try to go with the chemistry and look at the game ahead of you.'

WINNING COACHES ARE always loved.

People go out of their way to thank and bestow, and parade great swathes of gratitude. As a new season dawned for Ireland, Declan Kidney, former schoolteacher and current Ireland head coach, became Dr. Kidney.

These things happen. Everyone who ever spent time in Declan Kidney's company knew that he would not feel entirely at home dressed in a scarlet robe and a gold tassled hat, but that was the dress awaiting him as he left his Ballincollig home that morning and set off for the University of Limerick and his conferring ceremony.

'It takes a special kind of person to withstand the frustrations and pressures of constant review,' read the Head of Applied Mathematics, Professor Stephen O'Brien in the university's Concert Hall. 'And it takes a truly remarkable individual to emerge from many years of intense public scrutiny as a widely acknowledged, high successful coach who enjoys the respect of players, officials, fans and media.

'Our honouree, Declan Kidney, is such a man.'

Admitting to his humbling at such an award, and sharing the same award with his team, Kidney quickly moved to address the defence of the

Six Nations and the fact that every team facing Ireland would be gunning to bring down the champions. 'But that's what you want to be checked out on,' he stated bravely, 'when you're playing sport. You to want to check out yourself against the best.

'And we will be doing that in the coming season.'

True.

‖‖▮‖‖

BEFORE THE DAWN of defending the Grand Slam, two months prior to it, Declan Kidney made the biggest decision of his time as national coach. It may also have been the most soul-searching decision of his entire career. He dropped his former pupil in Pres Cork, and his faithful Munster out-half, Ronan O'Gara. Nobody knew it at the time, but the dynamic between former teacher and pupil – the relationship between coach and celebrated No.10 – would come to also tell the story of Declan Kidney's remaining years as Ireland head coach.

Jonathan Sexton, Leinster's bullish new No.10 was instead chosen for the game against South Africa in Croke Park. Sexton's credentials were impressive. He had steered Leinster to a long awaited Heineken Cup victory in May of 2009, and he had also kicked seven goals from seven attempts on his Test debut against Fiji the previous weekend. But, still…

This was Kidney and O'Gara!

An unbreakable, dyed in the wool pairing. Kidney's rationale made some sense. His fellow Corkman was about to turn the ripe old age of 33 the following March, and how fit and able would O'Gara be when Declan Kidney prepared his team for the World Cup in 2011?

'If I don't find out more about Jonathan now, you could still be wondering come February,' explained Kidney. 'We'll know more after Saturday. I know Ronan will be disappointed but I can't play everyone all of the time. Ronan's been a perfect pro; he's taken it on the chin.'

It was a bigger call than it looked.

Ireland was seeking to stretch an unbeaten run to 11 games and complete a full calendar year without a single defeat.

'We have a squad and we need to give fellas opportunities,' rationalised the coach. 'You don't always get it right, in fact you're lucky to get it right fifty per cent of the time. But it's important we find out as much as we can about ourselves between now and the Six Nations and I need to see how Jonny will go.

'I wouldn't risk an Irish team,' Kidney enforced. "We have a chance to play the World champions in our own backyard, so you don't take risks.' Ireland duly defeated South Africa 15-10. Sexton kicked five penalty goals.

'Stunning,' wrote former England lock, Paul Ackford in *The Daily Telegraph*. 'From the swathes of mist which swirled around Croke Park, a significant message. Ireland have grown up, have accepted the responsibility that goes with being Grand Slam champions of Europe and taken it a stage further.

'They have now proved that they can mix it with the best the southern hemisphere has to offer. South Africa may have been tired after what had been an exceptional season for them, but they are never easy meat and they travelled as conquerors of the Lions and their Tri-nations rivals, Australia and New Zealand. They return home defeated, their crown very definitely askew following losses to France and now Ireland.

'The staggering fact in an intriguing, spiky contest was that it was Ireland who better maintained their composure. It was agonisingly close in the dying seconds as the Springboks threw everything at Ireland in a brave attempt to maintain their dignity.

'The Beast (Tendai Mtawarira) nearly blasted over near the corner flag, then Brian O'Driscoll almost knocked himself cold stopping Zane Kirchner during the final 'Bok attack. But before that, for long periods, it was Ireland who forced the errors from South Africa, Ireland who maintained their discipline, Ireland who played the rugby in the areas of the pitch they wanted. The quality of their game management was very, very impressive.'

REMAINING AT THE very top of the game in European rugby resulted in Declan Kidney having to make decisions in the spring of 2010 that he had never contemplated before in his career. Though defeating Italy, and then being upended by France in Paris, meant that travelling to Twickenham to meet the English was a pressure point that nobody in the Irish management team had quite contemplated at the beginning of the tournament.

Significantly, prop John Hayes became the first Irish player to win 100 caps in Twickers, and led the team out onto the field to a standing ovation. Behind him came Ronan O'Gara, who was back on the bench, and on the total of 95 caps. Kidney talked about chemistry in explaining his decision-making. 'I have to go with what I see in training,' he said.' It can affect cohesion, but everyone brings that little bit of chemistry.' Ireland won 20-16 in the home of English rugby, though on the scoreboard at the end of the evening, in order to endorse Kidney's decision, there was nothing apparent. Sexton had kicked one penalty goal from three attempts. O'Gara came on to kick one conversion.

As he always realised, the Irish coach that evening in London saw that not only was the difference between winning and losing paper thin, but the difference in selection decisions was equally so. Sexton kicked three from four penalty goals against the Welsh in week four as Ireland had a comfortable 27-12 victory in Croke Park. One week later, in the home of the Gaelic Athletic Association, the first slippage in Declan Kidney's residency as Ireland and Europe's most accomplished coach occurred.

Ireland lost 23-20 to Scotland in Croke Park, and a few hours later France defeated England 12-10. The wish to retain the Championship went through the floorboards. More than that, Kidney's Ireland showed a vulnerability that most observers considered a thing of the past, if not unthinkable.

A WORLD CUP, always defining and monumentally judgmental in the modern game, awaited in 2011. The Grand Slam of 2009 was old news. Declan Kidney was being paid to bring good news. Ireland finishing joint runners-up with France and Wales in the 2011 Six Nations Championship meant that, in effect, Kidney's team were also-rans in the spring of that same year. England were kings of Europe, but a two-point win over Italy on February 5 in the opening game of the tournament, which was earned by O'Gara coming on as a replacement and kicking a dropped goal in the 78th minute, defined everything that followed that deeply worrying afternoon in Rome.

In the final game of the Championship, Ireland welcomed England to the KO'd and refurbished Lansdowne Road for the first time, now labelled Aviva Stadium, and duly dispatched the old enemy 24-8. But, still, the World Cup awaited, now just a little impatiently.

Declan Kidney had less than two years remaining in his career as Ireland head coach.

'I AM NOT going to, with all due respect,' Declan Kidney emphasised, '… get into a discussion about comparisons between now and '07 or '03 or '99 or whichever they are. We needed the games. To me that was very apparent, and we have had the games and we haven't got the results that we wanted but we will be the better for it. I have put together teams in the past and I can see us coming together now. There is obviously work to be done but I know we needed the games and I am glad we played the games.'

Ireland's results from their World Cup preparations in the late summer of 2011 read like a wreckage report. Four defeats from four Tests, and without a try in three of those game. Worse, while Kidney's squad was walking, it remained seriously wounded.

And while Kidney made it clear with journalists that any discussion about Ireland's performance in the 2007 World Cup was not on the agenda, it remained absolutely clear and present in the minds of all Irish rugby fans. Four years earlier, Ireland ended up out of reach of the quarter-finals, a distant third in their group behind France and unbeaten Argentina. The team had made a good fist of almost losing to Georgia, and were wiped off the park by France. A bonus point against Argentina was necessary in the final game, but the South Americans also saw off Eddie O'Sullivan's troops without very much bother.

This was the giant picture at Declan Kidney's back as he discussed the impending 2011 tournament. It was what people saw as they listened to O'Sullivan's successor. And after the Grand Slam of two years earlier, the expectation was that Ireland would deliver its greatest month of rugby on the World's biggest stage.

Whatever about the team's physical limitations, there was nothing stopping Kidney from building one of his happy camps. He did so with gusto. When the squad landed in New Zealand they quickly headed for Queenstown, in the south-west of the South Island, and the adventure capital of the country.

The Irish boys tried the hilltop luge run, others jet-boated on the Shotover

River canyons, their boat emblazoned with a Tricolour. Some had an appetite for bungee jumping. 'You really do fear for your life the second you jump off,' confessed Conor Murray when he had survived the Nevis bungee jump, the highest in New Zealand, all of 134 metres above the Nevis River.

The craic was in direct contrast to the day-to-day life of the team in France four years earlier when they found themselves holed up in a hotel in an industrial estate in Bordeaux. Instead of being confined to a cement barracks, the team was queuing up for helicopter rides over Milford Sound, landing on the Mount Tutoko glacier. Kidney's World Cup squad was relaxed, enjoying itself and training hard, and then they took off for New Plymouth for their opening game of the tournament where they were loose, wasteful and unconvincing in a 22-10 victory over Eddie O'Sullivan's Americans.

The 15-6 defeat of Australia that followed in Eden Park was totally unexpected. Sean O'Brien and Stephen Ferris were immense in the back row, the pincer tackling of Paul O'Connell and Donncha O'Callaghan was roundly praised, but it was at the scrummage where Ireland excelled; Cian Healy, Rory Best and Mike Ross ripping the Aussies apart. As the team took in its monstrously sized victory, there was another surprise however. Ronan O'Gara, who had finished out the last 30 minutes and kicked two penalty goals to nail down the day's work, said in an after-match television interview that he was ready to retire. 'I'm done with Ireland in a few weeks,' he stated, surprising his team captain and his coach.

Though O'Gara was subsequently in the thick of it in wins over Russia and Italy. Only Wales, and their tough-nosed coach Warren Gatland, in Wellington's Westpac Stadium, stood between Kidney leading Ireland to a first World Cup semi-final. The country could smell that glorious 'semi', but in the second-half of the quarter-final, after Kidney's men limped in 10-10 at half-time, Wales didn't really give Ireland a sniff. A sloppy try was conceded to Mike Phillips down the short side of a ruck. Jonathan Davies found another gap in Ireland's defence for an equally soft score.

The damning performances were adding up, and some days Declan Kidney received the blame; other days his opposing number had his arm raised as a clear winner in the head-to-head battle between the two coaches.

'They (Wales) named Shane Williams on the left wing for the quarter-final,' wrote Paul Rees in *The Guardian*, 'only to switch him with George North and deploy him on the right, reckoning Ireland would have spent the week working on weighted kicks to Williams for the taller Tommy Bowe to chase, a tactic that helped them win the 2009 Grand Slam in Cardiff.

'Instead, Bowe found himself up against the rather more substantial North, while Williams was opposed by a player more his own size, Keith Earls. Before Ireland had the chance to come to terms with the switch, they were seven points down.'

FOUR MONTHS LATER, Wales came to the Aviva stadium and took their first giant stride towards winning the 2012 Six Nations Championship with Davies scoring two more tries and George North sealing the 23-21 win by crossing in the 75th minute. The remaining days of Declan Kidney's reign as Irish coach were now moving so damned swiftly. As they did so, there were more sobering defeats than ever before on the surface of everyone's memory. Ireland finished the tournament mid-table again alongside France on five points, but three behind England, and five off the winners, Wales. Warren Gatland was king of Europe alright.

Where did that leave Declan Kidney?

Facing a summer tour of New Zealand, unfortunately.

'THE TRULY FRIGHTENING aspect to this defeat is that Ireland were not particularly that bad. They have won games with worse performances than the one they gave on Saturday, but they still could not come close to their hosts, who could have racked up sixty points had it not been for some poor decisions and desperate Irish defence.'

The words written by Hugh Farrelly in the *Irish Independent* on June 11, 2012, were more prophetic than he or anyone who had witnessed Ireland's First Test 42-10 defeat in Eden Park could have imagined. In Christchurch, seven days later, Kidney and O'Driscoll and Co. responded courageously. A dropped goal in the 81st minute from Dan Carter denied Ireland an heroic draw. It finished 22-19 for the hosts. Seven days further down the road, however, in Waikato Stadium in Hamilton, came the 60 points. And a performance that ranked right up there with the 'Most Damning' in the modern history of Irish rugby.

There were nine tries.

New Zealand won the Third Test 60-0.

Fourteen days earlier, Farrelly had also written, 'Already compromised by the unavailability and retirement of a clutch of senior players, Kidney is struggling to put a team together, while his counterpart (Steve Hansen) has enough quality options to select three Test sides all capable of spanking the Irish.'

THERE WAS NO holding Ireland's troubled ground. The slippage continued. Back home, in Declan Kidney's final Championship as Ireland coach, there was a stirring Week One win in the Millennium Stadium. The cursed Welsh were thrown to the ground in front of their own. Sexton kicked six from six. Jamie Heaslip was Irish captain, taking over from Brian O'Driscoll after Declan Kidney appeared to have successfully pressed the nuclear button on that particular issue. But there was another slip coming.

And another.

A six points loss to England in Dublin. A four points loss to Scotland in Edinburgh. A draw with France in Dublin.

Then Rome.

At the end of February, after losing to England and Scotland, Declan Kidney found himself openly discussing his position as Ireland head coach with the Irish public. 'I haven't been thinking about that (my position),' he insisted at the team's midweek press conference. 'My only concern is to help this team do well. That's my reason for being here. We have a match against France next weekend and that's all I'm concentrating on. There are huge highs and lows that go with this job and last Sunday was a big low, especially after having created so much.'

On March 16, 2013, Ireland lost to Italy 22-15 at the Stadio Olimpico. The tough and even more personalised questions came thick and fast within hours. Kidney was no longer defending his position. He was assessing his career options.

'I said all along that I'd concentrate on each game as it came, and that's all I've done,' he emphasised in the 24 hours after the game. 'I wasn't thinking that this could be my last match as coach, all I was concentrating on was getting the win. I wanted to get a result, we didn't manage to do that and we'll reflect on it over the coming days and weeks.

'I have to sit down and think about whether I want a new contract,' he added. The choice was not to be his, however. And neither did it take all that long, as he'd imagined upon leaving Rome. Only two weeks.

He had to meet with the IRFU's National Team Review Group. These men were not sympathetic to the fact that Ireland were without a round dozen seasoned Test players for the Championship just dusted. Neither were they to care that the coach lost three more men in the first-half in Rome, critically all of them backs.

The historic loss to Italy left Ireland second from the bottom in the Championship, and rounded off the nation's worst Championship performance since the Five Nations Wooden Spoon of 1998. Ireland had slumped to its lowest ever position in the IRB World ranking, figuring ninth in the grid, below Samoa and Argentina, and marginally ahead of Scotland and Tonga. Ninth, in fact, would have been tenth had the Scots not slipped to a 23-16 defeat in their final Championship game.

||| ||| |||

APRIL WAS ONE day old when the position of Ireland head coach was pinned up on the World rugby noticeboard.

Declan Kidney remained contracted to the IRFU until June 30, 2013, once the tour of the United States and Canada was completed, but the IRFU took the decision to dispense with his services three months short of that date. Les Kiss was named as Ireland's interim head coach, with Gert Smal and Anthony Foley as his assistants. Leinster's double Heineken Cup winning supremo, Joe Schmidt would soon be fitting into Declan Kidney's shoes and, like the man before him, assessed on his ability to win Championships more than Triple Crowns, and more significantly his possible success in attempting to break through the formidable quarter-final barrier in a World Cup.

The writing had been on the wall. In Kidney's 20 matches as Ireland coach since winning the 2009 Grand Slam, Ireland had won nine, lost nine, and drawn two. Fifty per cent amounted, in teaching terms, to only a 'pass'.

For many months, old friends and former players had voiced on radio and admitted in newspapers that his time was up. All they asked for was that he be afforded a dignified exit. 'We would like to sincerely thank Declan for his commitment to Irish rugby,' stated IRFU chief, Philip Browne. 'His contribution and involvement across the spectrum of Irish rugby delivered age-group, provincial, Grand Slam, and Triple Crown success, and epitomises his passion, belief and commitment to the game.'

It ended with Declan Kidney doing everything in his lifetime for Irish rugby, and being able to do no more.

It also concluded as swiftly and brutally as it did for the one player Kidney had with him through that entire and often brilliant journey. Ronan O'Gara, five weeks earlier, had been left 'gutted' when told the green No.10 jersey was not his, and would never be his again.

THOUGH O'GARA remained big-hearted upon hearing of the dismissal of his old teacher and coach. 'I was omitted from the squad a few weeks ago and that's really disappointing,' he told Simon Lewis in the *Irish Examiner*, 'and then Deccie got his news yesterday and I'm sure he's hugely disappointed.

'I know the man really well and he's been there for my whole career so it would be remiss of me not to compliment him on what he's achieved.

'The last few years haven't been great but the Grand Slam has been a masterstroke, but that's the standard we need to be at. We need to be contesting Grand Slams every year and the last few years we haven't been, so in this ruthless business you get moved on for the next person and that's what's unfortunately happened to Deccie.

'I've had mixed times with him.

'I've had some great times and some challenging times with him, but I respect the man and that's exactly where I stand on the whole thing. It was only when I watched the news last night and saw Cardiff and I was the only one in the red jersey, and all the boys were in green jerseys and we were all on the stage, and that's why you play sport, and we need to get back to that stage.'

IT ENDED THAT suddenly for Declan Kidney. There was no final lap of the field. No mesmerised crowd in packed stands to wave back at. No open top bus going anywhere through Dublin or Limerick streets.

Like Ronan O'Gara, Kidney would have deserved that finale. Though he would have run a thousand miles from such a scene if he thought it any way likely. Four months later, University College Cork President, Dr Michael Murphy in a note to his staff announced the appointment of Declan Kidney as Director of Sport. He was back at his alma mater. Thirty-one years earlier he had graduated with a degree in commerce. He said he was 'really looking forward' to the new challenge in his life, adding, 'I firmly believe in a holistic approach to education and see physical activity, be it at the highest elite level or participating just for fun, to be an integral part of this experience'.

THE UNBELIEVABLE PRESSURE of being the man whom everyone else, players and staff, the IRFU and the Irish public, looked to was also at an end. It was, and remains, a level of pressure that nobody can fully appreciate, not unless they have slipped on the shoes of the head coach at an elite level.

One of the heroes in Declan Kidney's Munster days was his mighty No.8 Anthony Foley, who would graduate from an assisting role at provincial and national level, and hold down Kidney's old job at Munster with all of its myriad responsibilities and expectations.

It was a job that Foley found gripping, but immensely difficult. He stepped down from his position in the spring of 2016, assuming a coaching role within the team management of the newly installed head coach Rassie Erasmus. In October of 2016, 'Axel' Foley passed away in his Paris hotel room, the night before Munster went into European Cup battle.

'Axel' was Declan Kidney's captain in the glorious season of 2006, and he had continued to soldier as one of Kidney's lieutenants after his playing days. In an interview with Colm Kinsella in the *Limerick Leader*, in November of 2013, he spoke insightfully of his old friend's final days as Ireland head coach.

'I really enjoyed working with Deccie up there (with Ireland),' 'Axel' admitted, before cautioning, 'but it was hard at the time as well because there was a lot of pressure. The Six Nations brings its own pressure and working through two Six Nations was some experience being around the camp and involved in it.'

'Axel' was 39 years-old as he gathered his thoughts on Kidney and Ireland.

THE MASTER ▮▮ DECLAN KIDNEY: A BIOGRAPHY

He had been through the mill for so long as a player and a leader of men, scoring 39 tries for his beloved Munster in a career that spanned 13 seasons, and making 86 appearances in European competition. He won 62 caps for Ireland, scored five tries and captained his country on three occasions but, still, nothing had prepared him for the most 'unbelievable pressure' of all.

'The pressures which came around the November games last year were colossal in terms of seeding for the World Cup.

'It is something you don't experience at Munster in terms of the absolute, mind-blowing pressure that is there,' Foley concluded, adding that it was a pressure that was also absorbing.

'It is good… good to get a feel for it, good to get a taste of it.'

| PART**TWO** |

THE
MASTER

1997-1998

'If you can create the environment where players are pushing each other along, you have to watch it carefully, because players will react very differently. You don't want a fella living in fear that if he goes out on the pitch and makes one mistake that the other guy is in. It's not fair on him to do that. We're all different, with our upside and downsides. It's about learning to respect people and what they bring. We're dealing with human beings, so there's no exact science to it. But there aren't many walks of life where everybody gives everything they have to what they're doing, and when you're coaching in sport, you're privileged to see people doing that. And if the players are giving everything, you have to give them a little bit in return.'

– Declan Kidney
(February 5, 2010)

TWO WEEKS AFTER Munster had been knocked out of the Heineken Cup Declan Kidney was asked if he was willing to put his name down for the job. Except, this time it would be as a full-time head coach.

Munster's first full-time head coach.

He was asked to do a presentation the morning after Ireland had met the All Blacks on November 15, 1997. In the face of what he and everyone else had seen in Lansdowne Road the previous day, Kidney was in no doubts about the daunting prospect of professionalism. Ireland just about stayed with the visitors until half-time thanks to two tries from captain Keith Wood, but then the class of Christian Cullen, Frank Bunce, Andrew Mehrtens, Zinzan Brooke and Co. was let loose. Ireland's 14th game against the All Blacks ended with a 14th defeat, 63-15. An average sized massacre by All Blacks' standards. Malcolm O'Kelly made his debut for Ireland that afternoon, joining a group of players who held the Wooden Spoon from the Five Nations Championship in their hands. The team was coached by Brian Ashton, an Englishman who had been called in to stop the rot in Irish rugby. Ashton, however, would soon voice his regrets at ever taking on the Irish job.

O'Kelly, on the other hand, would earn 92 caps for Ireland, play in two Lions tours and three World Cups, but that afternoon in mid-November of 1997, he was a slim, innocent lion-to-be put to the slaughter.

Malcolm O'Kelly: As a first capper I was too wrapped up in my own little chasm to really respect the team we were going out against. I was so looking forward to it, it didn't matter who we were playing. We probably never had a chance of winning that match. Certainly that day the New Zealand team figured us out. In the second-half they changed their style of play. In the first-half we coped reasonably well with them (Ireland trailed 27-15 at half-time) and were very aggressive and closed them down and forced them wide.

In the second-half they went up the guts a lot more and went through the pack with great success. Suddenly they opened the game up and we were chasing shadows all of a sudden. New Zealand back then had the ability to change strategy and what they were doing. I don't remember that we had a strategy.

I was just out there playing the game that I always played, as did most of the other guys. We were 15 individuals but we didn't really have a huge strategy beyond that.

(November 16, 2016)

DECLAN KIDNEY WAS determined not to let himself down at his Munster interview, though he also knew that he had nothing to lose. He loved his teaching job at Pres Cork. He had been working there all of his adult life. Why should his working life take an about-turn, and face something completely new? He calculated that he was involved coaching 18 different teams and receiving not a penny for his labours. As a professional coach he would have one team to care for. And an awful lot of people to answer to, perhaps?

Kidney, however, had lots of good ideas about what would be good for Irish rugby, from the knees up. He had a flip chart with him when he drove up from Cork the day before. He had a presentation on an overhead projector prepared. And also a video of different teams he had trained.

When he landed at the hotel to give his presentation, however, the interview panel was not quite so prepared as the candidate entering the room. They did manage to get their hands on a board for the flip chart, and a projector was also sourced eventually. But there was no television for the video.

Nevertheless, he thought to himself that the presentation went okay. Certainly, it could have gone much worse.

He had stayed with his brother, Aidan in his house in Dublin the night before, and just before he tucked himself in for the night he decided to confirm for himself that everything was in order. He checked the acetate for the overhead. He looked over the flipchart. He inserted the video into a player to make doubly sure it was at the right point.

On the screen in front of him, instead, popped up Barney the purple dinosaur. One of Kidney's boys had changed the tape on him.

'I love you... you love me...' sang the popular cartoon character.

|| | **|** ||| |

THERE WAS SO much to learn by everybody in Irish rugby at the dawn of professionalism. Murray Kidd had become Ireland's first full-time head coach, after impressing at Garryowen and winning an All-Ireland league title with the Limerick club. The Kiwi had a no-nonsense approach to the game, but his reign ended on the eve of the Five Nations Championship in 1997 after Ireland had lost 37-29 to Italy at Lansdowne Road. In truth, there was a lot of nonsense on the loose within the game at this perilous time, and there was more to come. Ashton, with a much longer and more impressive coaching CV, was next into the hot seat and asked to put an end to a withering list of embarrassing defeats on home soil. Western Samoa, Australia, Italy and France had all been clapped off the field, victorious, by Irish teams. The IRFU had not wasted any time grabbing Ashton, a former scrum-half, who had playing styles and philosophies forged in Montferrand in France and Milan, as well as Orrel in his home country. He had been assistant English coach to Dick Greenwood in 1984. For five years Ashton and Jack Rowell ruled the English club game with Bath, winning four league titles and the cup three times. When Rowell stepped up to the English team job, Ashton won the league and cup double with Bath in 1996 before answering Ireland's call.

He lasted one season before resigning. No big reason was given by Ashton or the IRFU, though his tenure, like Kidd's, had come to a sudden halt after a defeat to Italy. He was less than one year into a six-year contract. Warren Gatland was next.

Third time lucky?

Gatland was appointed in February of 1998 and at 34 years of age had little time to build up a CV as bulky as Ashton's. He had played 17 times for the All Blacks, and amassed 140 appearances for Waikato. When asked to take charge of Ireland he was still working through his first year, of a three years contract, as Connacht's Director of Rugby. He had guided Galwegians to the Connacht Senior league title two years running, and lifted the club into the AIL second division.

Three Irish coaches in the professional era – and two of them New Zealanders!

Who'd have wanted to be an international coach at such a hurly-burly time in the game's history? In a six months period they were falling like skittles; Ashton preceded by Carel du Plessis (South Africa), Greg Smith (Australia), Jack Rowell (England) and Richie Dixon (Scotland). And who'd have wanted to be a head coach and be left selecting his Irish team with the help of two others? Irish manager Pat Whelan and Donal Lenihan formed a three-man selection committee with the head coach.

Gatland would get Ireland up and running into a whole new ball game internationally but, to begin with, despite big hearted performances and a two points defeat in the Stade de France to eventual Championship winners

France, there were four quick losses and a second Wooden Spoon awaiting him and his new Irish team once Ireland were ripped apart by England in early April.

Edmund Van Esbeck: Ashton has very specific ideas about how the game should be played and they are admirable. The problem is that such an approach was outside the compass of the talent he had available. Irish rugby has its own peculiarities and one of them is what one might call 'Irishness' or as the former Ireland coach Mick Doyle called it 'The Paddy Factor'. I do not think Brian Ashton fully understood it. Yet at the first Irish training session he took in Limerick prior to Ireland's match against France last season, he was specific in referring to it.

(The Irish Times, Feb 28, 1998)

Brian Ashton: I spoke to several people before taking the job and got some conflicting advice but I ended up making the wrong decision. My philosophy and Irish tradition are about as far away as Dublin and Bath. It didn't fit in with the Irish mentality. At the end of the day there was no way forward and no way that I could carry on.

I stayed in England because I thought the job could be done while commuting. I never got to grips with the Irish psyche, mentality.

(April 3, 1998)

THE IRFU WAS still manfully, but not very successfully, grappling with this new found professionalism. The game had officially been declared 'open' by the International Rugby Board on August 26, 1995, two months after South Africa had claimed the third World Cup. In Ireland, full-time coaches were being employed, but players were at sixes and sevens.

Some on the national team were on full-time contracts worth £25,000; others were part-timers earning £7,500, with a match fee of £700 for Heineken Cup games and £300 for Inter-provincial appearances helping them to get by. Down amongst the provinces, however, most players were awaiting the promise of contracts that might change their lives. Ireland was not alone.

After agreeing to pay out a total of £500,000 to players to cover the 1995-96 season the Scottish Rugby Union made a loss for the first time in its history. In England there was more cash splashing around the place and some Irish players found themselves playing for clubs they had hardly ever thought about before in their lives. Harlequins landed Keith Wood. David Corkery had been named as Ireland's best player at the 1995 World Cup, scoring a try in the opening game against the All Blacks and another in the destruction of Japan. He left Cork Constitution and Munster behind him and headed to Bristol.

David Corkery: They gave us weight programmes and nothing else – to get us as big and as strong as they possibly could. This might sound ridiculous but I got up to 20 stone with a 22-inch neck. But I couldn't move around the park. All of my power, flexibility, pace had all gone.

The amateur ethos was still there to a certain degree but you were playing in a professional world. In certain respects, it took about five years for it to get to the level where it should've been. So there were a lot of guinea pigs out there and I would definitely put myself in that category.

From a medical perspective, there was a physio in the club who you saw when you got injured and that was it. There were no pre-scans or post-scans or MRIs. I thought it was going to be a bit more professional but it wasn't. When I came back to the Munster set-up under Declan Kidney, it was far better. That was more an eye-opener than England. When the call came from Munster to come home, it wasn't even a thought. I saw what was happening over here and I longed to be part of that ethos, that Munster ethic. I still live and die by it. I rule my life by it to this day. To be back in it was exactly where I wanted to be.

(February 2, 2017)

BUT IT WASN'T just the IRFU that dithered and was slow in getting its head around what needed to be done if the game of rugby in Ireland was to step up to the plate of professionalism. Every man in the game had to think, and they had to change their ways. In the first week of 1997, for instance, Victor Costello was in a café in south Dublin talking to an *Irish Times* journalist about his rugby life. He should have been in the Algarve with the rest of the

Irish rugby squad, but he had been told by team manager, Pat Whelan to stay at home and get through some hard work.

Costello, who would retire in 1995 with 121 caps for Leinster and 39 for Ireland in the back row, found himself still stuck in the 'old game'. He had been a giant in his schooldays in Blackrock College, and a career in a green jersey was always going to be laid out in front of him. However, Whelan told Costello and three others that they did not need to be with the squad in Portugal for a week of warm weather training before the Championship. He told him that his fitness levels were not at the required standard, simple as that, and Costelloe had to quickly digest the conversation. He was a professional rugby player who was being told that he was not fit enough to be part of the Irish squad.

Victor Costello: I'm not happy with the situation at all. I feel ashamed that it's happened. But it's happened and I've dealt with it. I will never let it happen again.

But when Pat rang me up everything he told me was positive, not negative. He said, 'We know your qualities as an attacking forward. We need more of this in defence. To play international rugby you're defending fifty per cent of the time. You are not defending because you are not fit enough.'

He said, 'You're not going to the Algarve because all we're doing is fitness assessment and you'd be better off training.' I'm pissed off in one way and delighted in another way. I was really disappointed and I was shocked. But when he explained it, I took it for what he said.

Fitness has always been a problem. I arrived down to St Mary's when I gave up athletics and struggled from day one. But gradually, year by year, it has become less and less of a problem. Now it's caught up with me this year because I'm playing at a higher level and I'm exposed.

(January 4, 1997)

||| ‖ ||||

OVER SEVEN DAYS in November of 1995 Munster started their epic journey through the Heineken Cup. They beat Swansea by four points at home, travelled to Castres and lost by seven. They did not make it to the knockout stages of Europe's brand new competition.

They were different times indeed. Contracts for the players were still being prepared and had not been offered. And while the game was played in Thomond Park which would become a fortress, it was also played on a Wednesday afternoon. There was, in truth, an eerie silence to the whole competition. No English clubs entered. Twelve teams from five countries got on with life without them – from France there was Toulouse, Begles-Bordeaux, and Castres; from Wales there was Cardiff, Swansea and Pontypridd; Romania sent Farul Constanta; Italy sent Benetton Trevisio and Milan, and Ireland manned up with Ulster, Leinster and Munster. Jerry Holland was Munster coach that first day in Limerick when Swansea visited, and had Pat Murray to thank for a late try under the posts.

One week later, in Mazamet, in a ground that resembled a bowl with high wire fencing all around it, the French formally welcomed Munster to Europe and did their level best to gouge and kick their visitors for 80 minutes in a game which, for all the wrong reasons, remains pride of place in Munster folklore. The following season, English clubs landed into the Heineken Cup. Munster took care of Milan, got whipped by Cardiff 48-18, did a job on Wasps three days later, and then headed to France to try to make it into the knockout stages for the first time.

Wasps had already beaten Toulouse by 60 points. Second time around in France, the Munster camp rested easily the night before the game. Next day there was another riot, and a 60-19 loss. The words of captain Mick Galwey, as he stood under the posts with his team after another Toulouse try, are known by heart by all Munster fans. 'For fuck sake lads,' he exclaimed, 'can we at least keep it under 50 points?' For the second season in-a-row, Munster were merely passengers in Europe.

Getting their backsides kicked by a French team who were smarter and more cunning, and vicious into the bargain, was one part of the Munster story.

Off the field, there was a whole different story; there was a hemorrhage. The team was being bled dry. At the start of the 1997-98 season Munster had lost the services of Richard Wallace, Brian Begley, Terry Kingston, Paul McCarthy, Gabriel Fulcher, Ben Cronin, Liam Toland, John Fitzgerald, Pat

Murray, Brian Walsh and Garry Halpin. That was just a list of players who were missing from the previous season. It does not offer the totality of the team's emptying dressing room. Keith Wood, Paul Burke, David Corkery, Rob Henderson and Paul Wallace had already upped and left. 'It's a big drain,' summed up Niall O'Donovan, who was co-opted onto the Munster management team with Declan Kidney, Jerry Holland and Colm Tucker. 'You're talking about quality players,' continued O'Donovan as he faced into a new season. 'They're not easy to come by down here.'

John Bevan, the former Wales and Lions winger, had come in as coach and cried off again. Munster was not the most attractive of teams in European rugby, and neither were some of its players the happiest. The IRFU's hotch potch thinking, as they ruminated on provincial contracts, was to cut slices off the national contracts of some players, and take contracts and cars away from others. Kidney and his colleagues were at Ground Zero in the autumn of 1997.

In the Heineken Cup, Munster had Keith Wood's Harlequins, Cardiff and Bourgoin in their pool, and nobody was seriously expecting a challenge from any of the Irish teams. When told as much by Leicester's Bob Dwyer nobody in Ireland complained very loudly about the opinion of the Australian coaching genius. Wasps captain Lawrence Dallaglio, meanwhile, was demanding far tougher qualifying standards.

Bob Dwyer: There are nine sides that can win this. The French quartet, the English teams and Cardiff. But there are eleven other competitors who can spring an upset and ensure that a genuine favourite for the trophy loses out.

(September 6, 1997)

Lawrence Dallaglio: With all due respect to the Irish opposition in three of the groups, they had to win only a minimum of one match to qualify for Europe through their Irish Inter-provincial championship. That is exactly what Ulster did. They lost two of their Inter-prov games and came third on points difference above Connacht.

(September 6, 1997)

ODDS OF 100-1 were being offered against any Irish team being crowned champions of Europe. On the board of the European Rugby Cup Ltd., Ireland's representative Tom Kiernan also had his work cut out to stop representation being reduced from three to two teams. An expanded home and away format for the Heineken Cup was also thought to further diminish Irish hopes of causing some form of a surprise. In the six weeks that followed, Munster lost four of their six games, winning two of them at home, taking Bourgoin by two points and Harlequins by seven.

Once again, French soil was difficult to shake off. Away to Bourgoin, Munster were 8-6 down at half-time and still in the game, but they were ruthlessly taken apart thereafter as a cockerel joined forces on the field with the home team for the full 40 minutes. It finished 21-6. However, even though it wasn't all that apparent that glorious autumn afternoon, there were worthy individuals emerging within Munster's ranks. Alan Quinlan, only 23 years-old but a core figure on the Shannon team that had claimed a third successive All-Ireland league title, would be one to learn from the latest French visit. 'He runs straight, he runs hard, and he can unload the ball,' enthused Cardiff's Australian coach, Alex Evans. 'He's got a bit of a future.'

It was Quinlan's first European campaign. A few years earlier he was lining out for Clanwilliam. He was working as a mechanic in the garage of international amateur golfer, Arthur Pierse who helped introduce him to Shannon.

Alan Quinlan: I was a little bit nervous at the start, wondering what I was doing on the pitch with these players. I use to think about the opposition back-row but once the match started it was different. I enjoyed playing against the high profile names, guys like Laurent Cabannes. I have come a long way in a short time and it gets a bit frightening at times. I am under no illusion about the work that I have to do. I have made it to a certain standard of rugby but to make the next step requires a big improvement. I have to work on my pace off the mark, breaking from scrums and at lineouts. I think I'm fast enough but not sharp enough and that's down to concentration. That requires extra work, more training and identifying weaknesses. I know I have a lot of them.

(October 27, 1997)

ONE WEEK BEFORE Christmas in 1997 the IRFU announced that another three players had been offered national squad contracts but, amazingly, Kevin Nowlan and Reggie Corrigan, who were both playing for Ireland against Italy in Bologna the next day were overlooked. 'I am extremely disappointed and surprised,' stated Leinster manager, Jim Glennon, 'not only at the decision but also at the timing of the announcement.'

Full-back Nowlan was about to win his third cap against the Italians, while Corrigan was coming in for his second, replacing Nick Popplewell. With Leinster, both Nowlan and Corrigan remained on part-time contracts worth £7,500, plus match fees. In the same announcement Alan Quinlan and St Mary's scrum-half Conor McGuinness were offered Category 2 home-based full-time deals that provided them with a £35,000 salary, a car, a £3,000 win bonus, and a further £1,000 for every match Ireland drew. Mark McCall was offered a Category 4 contract which totaled a basic salary of £14,600 plus expenses.

McGuinness, working with KPMG chartered accountants was thrilled with his news and explained that his employers had offered him a one-year leave of absence that he had also accepted. 'I will definitely take them up on that. There is no way that you can play international rugby and hold down a full-time job,' he explained. 'The last six weeks have taught me that. I was in the office just one day a week and that simply isn't acceptable.'

In confirming his offer and acceptance, Quinlan told journalists that he would be contacting Bath and Cardiff immediately, both of whom had been chasing his signature, to let them know that he would be remaining in Ireland.

In the same IRFU press release it was announced that Declan Kidney had been appointed Director of Provincial Coaching in Munster, and was signing a three-years contract.

Declan Kidney: I am delighted to receive this honour. I was asked to let my name go forward and was quite happy to do so. As far as the new position is concerned because of commitments to the school (Pres Cork), I won't be able to take up the job on a full-time basis until February 1. Obviously I would like to thank the school for allowing me to take on this opportunity.

(December 19, 1997)

IN THE YEARS to come Kidney's body of work on Munster as a whole would be simply massive in its calculation and application. However, his work on individuals within the camp was equally inspiring. How he worked on Alan Quinlan was, perhaps, his greatest achievement of all, particularly as the flanker was of a mind to 'kill' Declan Kidney in their earliest years together.

It was the schoolteacher in the Munster coach that brought Quinlan to the critical decision that 'killing' his coach was necessary.

He was waiting for Kidney outside the dressing-room, when surprisingly Brian O'Brien, his Shannon manager, appeared instead. Quinlan confided his plan to O'Brien. He told him he was sick of the crap. He said he was going to 'bust' his (Kidney's) head. He said he was going to 'kill him', Quinlan, in his memoir *Red Blooded* in 2010, admitted telling O'Brien.

O'Brien brought Quinlan to his car, and had a chat with him for a good body of time. Quinlan explained that he could not put up with the coach's 'overbearing' and 'controlling' ways any longer. Instead of being a professional rugby player, Quinlan felt that he was back in school. Quinlan also explained his entire day that had led him to plotting Kidney's death.

It was a sunny day, and he had taken off his top and was taking a bit of sun on the pitch when Declan Kidney showed up. Everyone else was warming up and taking a lap or two. Only Quinlan was working his sun-tan. And, after that, for the rest of the session, Quinlan felt he could not catch a break with the coach. The session finally ended up with Kidney giving his flanker a piece of his mind in front of the whole gang. Quinlan told the whole story of his day in detail to O'Brien, and repeated it in his memoir.

O'Brien managed to calm him down. In his memoir, Quinlan added that he did not wait to confront his coach, and he did not believe deep down that he was ever going to 'hit him'. He wasn't really going to kill him either. Probably just abuse him verbally, Quinlan added, and thereby pay a heavy price in his career.

Quinlan admitted he had never been a man for discipline until he met Declan Kidney. He had a wild side. He was not mentally prepared to become a full-time professional rugby player, whereas Kidney was more than ready to build the greatest professional team in Irish rugby history. Quinlan felt he was seen as a messer. On a pre-season tour of Scotland he lived up to that title. He received a slap from Mick Galwey for his troubles, but did not change his ways.

The Tipperaryman and former Clanwilliam star was still struggling by the 1999-2000 season. He played in Munster's six Heineken Cup pool games, but was dropped thereafter. Kidney told him he was not applying himself properly, and Eddie Halvey was getting the nod. Quinlan did not start against Stade Francais or Toulouse as Munster made their way to the final. In his memoir, written a decade down the road, Quinlan finally understood that Kidney was protecting the player 'from himself'. He was also seeing to it, Quinlan admitted, that one of the most intoxicating careers in Irish rugby history did not go up in smoke far too early.

At the end of the summer of 2000, Quinlan met with his coach. Declan Kidney let him have it... again! Quinlan broke down in tears, finally, and explained everything about himself and his life as a rugby professional. He asked for Kidney's help, not knowing that help had already been in action for a long while. Quinlan left the meeting with only a short-term contract, and a £10,000 cut from his salary, but he still had a career, and he knew he had a coach who would see to it that the incredible explosive talent within him would shine through, and come to characterise him above anything else on the field.

1998-1999

'This is the busiest time, at least I hope it is; setting up the job, getting everything in place for the first time and getting all the preparations in place. When the matches start out on the pitch, that's the easier part.

'In the first year of professionalism the effect on the system was more noticeable. Now, the players are more in tune with taking rest and the values of rest. They're also more aware of what to eat and drink. It's more a case of them now demanding water and eating the right foods at the right time, rather than us telling them. They're aware of the needs to prepare properly, which is a big help. I'm happy with the squad's strength in depth.

We have some good young players coming through and a lot more are going to get chances earlier than they would have in years past because of the greater number of matches – take the example of Donncha O'Callaghan, our 19 years-old second row who played against Rumney. I'd like to see more of the belief coming back into Irish rugby. On the back of the trip to South Africa, and results subsequently, and the belief that a lot of the younger boys have now, I think there's a growing feeling that we're not all here just to make up the numbers.'

– Declan Kidney
(August 10, 1998)

COURTESY OF A three-years leave of absence, Declan Kidney had cut the umbilical cord with Pres Cork. When he looked around him in the Munster dressing room he had 21 full-time rugby players on his hands, compared to a total of 10 the season before when the part-timers squeezed in early morning or evening sessions to dovetail with their daily working lives. That was the up side. The down side was that some of Munster's full-timers had been demoted from international contracts. They were on less money. Cars had been taken away from them. The season ahead also looked a longer road, as in addition to the Heineken Cup, the Inter-provincial Championship was being doubled to six matches played on a home and away basis. Munster were looking at a minimum of 12 competitive matches, in addition to four friendlies. The season ahead looked at least 13-weeks long.

Welcome to the pros!

Though not all of the preparation was tick-tock. Thomond Park was unavailable for the beginning of the season, and Kidney was looking at bringing his team to Dooradoyle on Saturday afternoons, instead of Thomond on Friday evenings, for two of the Inter-pro games against Leinster and Connacht. The home venues for the Heineken Cup games were also up in the air while Munster's fortress was being reseeded.

THE FANFARE FOR the Heineken Cup was slightly muted in the late summer of 1998, following the withdrawal of the English clubs, and also Cardiff and Swansea. In Pool B, Declan Kidney had Padova, Neath and Perpignan to keep an eye on, which could hardly have been considered a 'Group of Death' or anything like it, and the reshuffle following the grand withdrawl certainly boosted Munster – having cash-strapped Neath to contend with rather than Pontypridd. Neath had just been bought out by the Welsh RFU after accumulating debts of £600,000. Their squad was also ravaged by summer departures.

Perpignan, on the other hand, had gained in muscle. The French runners-up from the previous season had added French No.8 Thomas Lievremont to their squad, in addition to the acquisition of the country's captain from the 1998 Grand Slam, Raphael Ibanez. First of all, Munster had home games against Padova and Neath in order to ensure their own bulked up professional dressing room was perfectly oiled. The two games were sandwiched by home Inter-pros against Connacht and Ulster. The fixture list played into Kidney's hands and he was thankful. 'That means we won't have to leave Munster for four weeks, which can't be bad,' he informed journalists.

Munster, however, were decidedly off-colour in the earliest weeks of the season. There were losses to Leinster and Ulster, with only a victory over Edinburgh Reivers to chew on with any satisfaction. By the middle of September, Kidney had a choice to make – earlier than he would have imagined in his first year as a professional coach. Munster needed to start winning games.

It was time to put the ball up the jumper.

That, and to order out-half Killian Keane to kick the leather off the damned thing. This resulted in a relieving 21-7 win over Connacht – a 12th successive win over their neighbours for Munster – so nothing to really talk about! It was also considered the worst game of rugby of the season, as the Shannon-dominated pack pummelled away all day long. But the Connacht fringe defence never wilted and only in the dying minutes of the game did Munster get over for their second try. Kidney had to acknowledge that the badly needed win was crafted more by a style of game about to be forgotten, rather than a game for the future. He admitted that Munster went back to basics 'a little bit,' without apologising for the win that both the coach and his team badly needed.

'I would hope that it was not too much of a retrograde step,' he added. It was Keane who had inched Munster ahead, before John Lacey, receiving his second pass of the day, worked his way over the line beyond the clutches of two Connacht tacklers on the blind side from Tomas Tierney's long pass, to score his ninth try in 10 outings in red.

Munster, and their new professional coach, were not building up an army of admirers.

THE PADOVA COACH Vittorio Munari was distinctly unimpressed on his way out of Cork. The 1,000 or so spectators who had turned up to witness a 20-13 victory probably shared his lack of enthusiasm, if not his disparaging tone. Neither the home fans nor Munari had much sympathy for Kidney's excuse that his dressing room had been crippled by a stomach bug, and that although they had intended in giving it more of a blast in the second-half with the wind at their backs, they didn't have it 'in the legs'. Up and coming out-half, Ronan O'Gara was also short of a fan base after the game in which he was judged to have lacked a commanding presence, missed tackles, and kicked with mixed results.

Munari had also contended that Peter Clohessy should have been sent off for a punch in the 10th minute of the game. The referee, David Davies and his touch judge had disagreed, believing that both men were equally at fault for the incident. It was one of many square-ups in a fractious match.

Kidney believed that he could have highlighted many other incidents, but declined to get into a 'tit for tat' with the visiting coach. A happier man was Munster captain, Mick Galwey who, tongue in cheek, did simple maths for journalists who had waited for the team to warm down.

Mick Galwey: Last week we scored one try, this week we scored two.

(September 21, 1998)

BY OCTOBER MUNSTER did look like a team that finally considered themselves a responsible professional outfit. Four victories in succession had helped. And they were geared up to give it a right go when they visited Stade Aime Giral and took on mighty Perpignan. Kidney was defiant, despite a crisis at No.9 that necessitated the selection of the promising young UCC student, Peter Stringer who had just 28 minutes as a Munster player under his belt.

Declan Kidney: We set targets at the beginning of the season, short term and long term, and despite one or two hiccups have realised many of those. The level of performance has sometimes slipped but we have refocused recently and I feel that things have improved. There is though still considerable scope to get better.

Perpignan represent a big step forward on our journey. We have concentrated on our own game rather than worrying about their ability.

(October 10, 1998)

Tony Ward: Someone suggested shortly before kick-off in Saturday's European cup clash in Perpignan that damage limitation ought to represent the extend of Munster's ambitions. It was a notion I dismissed but by half-time with the home side on fire, the passionate Catalan following at fever pitch and Munster already 29-3 behind I was having a radical reappraisal. More to the point, Declan Kidney, Jerry Holland and Niall O'Donovan were doing likewise. In all honesty there seemed no way back from a drubbing of embarrassing proportions. Munster were in a mess. The scrum was under pressure, the first-time tackling virtually non-existent, and most disturbing of all, heads uncharacteristically dropping under wave upon wave of Didier Camberabero inspired attacking.

(Irish Independent, Oct 10, 1998)

MUNSTER TRAILED BY 26 points at half-time, and had a wind at their backs on the turnaround, but everyone feared for them. It could and should have been worse. It was the pint-sized Stringer who saved two more certain tries in the first-half, in addition to servicing his No. 10 Barry Everitt brilliantly. They had been shunted mercilessly in the scrum, and destroyed on the fringes. All over the park they had been sliced open. The comeback, in the second-half, coincided with the withdrawl of the 37 years-old Didier Camberabero on 48 minutes. There were three second-half tries from Kidney's men in the second 40 minutes as they outscored the locals 21-12. 'We received a lesson in possession in the first-half,' Kidney admitted afterwards. 'It was like little boys against men for 40 minutes. We were doing the second thing before the first. They broke through easier than I expected and that was worrying.' Extremely so, as Perpignan had only really cut loose in the last 15 minutes of the half with four tries from Gregory Tutard, Patrick Furet, Alweyn Joubert and Renaud Peillard.

At half-time Kidney asked his players to talk through what had just happened. They resolved to stop turning over possession. And off first phase ball they decided to have more patience, and faith, in themselves. Their coach approved. After the game the Munster boys felt defeated and battered. Back on the team coach, Kidney informed his players that they would have a quiet night before heading home the following morning. There was to be no hitting the tiles. Instead, the coach envisaged a dip in the sea first thing in the morning before everyone headed to the airport. But then Peter Clohessy got out of his seat and strode up the bus, and grabbed the microphone. 'We're all going on the piss, as soon as we get back to the hotel!' Claw had laid down a different law for the rest of the evening. There was red wine consumed during the meal. A lot more booze followed, and some songs, as the team stuck tightly together at perhaps its most vulnerable moment. Declan Kidney watched, and understood their need.

There was nothing to take home from France, but one week later at The Gnoll, Munster took home their first ever away point in the European Cup, and they did so at the eighth attempt. It was 18-each at the finish, but Neath ravished Munster's ruck ball, and in the first-half the visitors failed in putting two successive rucks together.

Kidney retained the same line-up for the Inter-provincial showdown, and subsequent victory, against champions, Leinster at Donnybrook. Though the coach was still considered to be thinking defensively. He wanted John Kelly and Anthony Horgan on his wings. Kelly had two tries in 10 games. Horgan was on three tries in 16 games. But the prolific Shannon finisher, John Lacey, the team's leading try scorer the previous season, was well ahead of that pairing with 10 tries in 11 games.

Being top dog in Ireland was one thing. Having the loudest bark and most vicious bite in Europe was something else entirely.

|| | | ■ ■ | | | |

MUNSTER WERE PROMISING on the European stage. The same could not be said for Ireland, however, and while a third Wooden Spoon was avoided in 1999, Warren Gatland's best efforts only managed a second from last (France) placing in the Five Nations Championship. A one point defeat by England in the opening fixture was followed by a six points win over Wales in Cardiff, but England were too mean at Lansdowne Road and the Championship finished up with a pounding by 17 points from the Scots in Murrayfield. There was nothing heartening for Ireland in the international arena, but, Brian O'Driscoll was just around the corner.

And about time too.

Only once in the whole decade that was finishing up, in 1995, had Ireland managed to win two games in the Five Nations. Six times we won one game out of four, once the country managed a single point out of a draw, and there were two whitewashes. Ireland finished last in the table four times. We were second last six times. Ireland's efforts all through the long and tiring decade had been dire.

At the end of the decade, the greatest worry was that Ireland would finish up sixth in the Championship behind Italy on a regular basis. It did not work out like that. What O'Driscoll had to do with all of that on an individual basis, nobody knows.

But he had a hand in nearly everything that followed.

In the next decade, Ireland would win four out of five games in the Championship four times. Three out of five on three occasions. And we topped the Championship in 2009 with a Grand Slam. The only slump was 2008, which led to the departure of Eddie O'Sullivan, when Ireland only won two games in the spring.

Brian O'Driscoll, who would pair up with Declan Kidney as coach and captain of Ireland's Grand Slam in 2009, made his first appearance in green at Ballymore on June 12, 1999. Ireland would go do down 46-10, and they would come closer the following week at the Subiaco Oval in Perth, but despite tries from Kevin Maggs, Peter Clohessy and Justin Bishop they would again get turned over, 32-26. O'Driscoll did not cross the try line down under. That would come soon, on the Lions tour in 2001.

Brian O'Driscoll: Out of shot and charging towards me was Australia's last line of defence, the full-back Matt Burke. I clearly remember thinking I could be dead in a second if I didn't somehow dodge the massive collision coming my way.

Fortunately Burke didn't expect me to sidestep and I managed to get past him. That's when I felt really out of my depth. Suddenly I had nothing ahead but the try line, 30 metres away, so I just went for it, convinced the covering Australians would catch me. I was tackled over the line but still scored helping us to a famous win against the Wallabies – then the World champions.

On this day and throughout the series (which we eventually lost 2-1) I was just enjoying the enormity of the whole thing, bit still not quite believing I'd ever been picked. I'd watched the previous Lions tour (in South Africa in 1997) on television while finishing my final year exams in school in Dublin. If someone had told me then that I'd be involved in the next one, I'd have laughed at them.

I felt a World away from the standard of the top players, but it just goes to show how quickly things can happen when you're young. Within two years I was playing for Ireland and in another two I was here (in Australia with the Lions).

(October 24, 2016)

|||**I**|||

IT HAD BEEN plotted, and hoped, that Thomond Park would be reopened for the 20th anniversary of Munster's historic victory over the All Blacks. When that did not come to pass, it was a damaging blow to the ground's new owners, the IRFU and also to Munster's chances of defeating Perpignan and advancing to a bigger stage in European rugby. As a Munster man and their coach, Declan Kidney should have been bitterly disappointed at missing such a magnificent date, though as a Corkman there might have been some consolation that Perpignan would be coming to Musgrave Park for a European showdown.

Declan Kidney: I'm very disappointed bearing in mind the whole occasion which had been attached to this game. I was brought up on that too (Munster's 12-0 win over the All Blacks) and I am sorry we won't be playing there

(October 31, 1998)

THE WATCHING HEROES from 1978 might just have been in awe that little bit, as Munster's men from 1998 put their bodies on the line. The only people in the house, in Musgrave Park, not impressed were the French. The previously unbeaten Perpignan team reacted to the whistle of English referee, Steve Lander with churlishness and ignorance, refusing to observe the post-match handshakes. After their 13-5 defeat the only Frenchman interested in opening his mouth was the club's vice-president, Marc Beurezeau who described the referee as 'scandalous'. He was especially offended at the costly penalty count against his side. 'They were not our rules, they were his rules,' stated the indignant visitor. It was not stamping, it was rucking.'

Peter Stringer might not have agreed.

The young scrum-half finished his day's work with a six inch gash on the back of his head. Not that Kidney's men were playing the innocents after some of the most ruthless shoeing they had encountered on their European adventure to date. 'You give as good as you get,' acknowledged hooker Mark McDermott.

Declan Kidney: It was the perfect way to celebrate the occasion. We now have something that no other Munster side has, in that we are the first Munster side to qualify for the knockout stages. There'll be second and third Munster sides to do it, but we'll always be the first.

(November 2, 1998)

THE UNKNOWN AWAITED.

Munster had never won a European Cup tie in France. They had lost to Castres (12-19), to Toulouse (19-60), Bourgoin (6-21), and Perpignan (24-41). They were now destined to meet Colomiers in Stade Selery in the quarter-final of the competition. And Colomiers were as tough as Munster would get. They'd reached the semi-finals of the French Championship the previous season, losing out to Perpignan by two points, and they won the European Shield with a 100 per cent record over nine games, finishing up with a semi-final win over Stade Francais and a 45-5 rout of Agen in the decider.

On their home patch, effectively a suburb of Toulouse, they had won all eight of their European ties in front of an excited 12,000 audience. The only good news was that they were without the services of Jean-Luc Sadourny and their captain, Fabien Galthie.

It was a small consolation for a battered Munster dressing room. Over a five-weeks waiting period, Kidney had witnessed many of his pack getting a bruising from the visiting Springboks. Some had also to regroup for Shannon's opening day defeat in the AIL to Ballymena, as Anthony Foley and Co resumed their pursuit of an historic five titles in-a-row.

Anthony Foley: My main ambition is to get back into the World Cup squad and play at the highest level a player can play. The five in-a-row is also something that's never been done. It's been said to us that no team in Irish sport has ever won five All-Irelands. Kerry were beaten in the last minute, Cork and Wexford teams and whatever. It would be nice to achieve that, but it's a long way off. And also the semi-final of the European Cup.

(December 12, 1998)

THEORETICALLY, MUNSTER WERE still in the game with 10 minutes to go. But that was down to luck, a stubborn strain in Declan Kidney's team, and an impressive dose of courage. Munster were poor on the bigger stage. The quarter-final of the European Cup came, and went. Were they not tuned in? Kidney's reconnaissance mission had underlined Colomiers' brilliant driving lineout, but both half-backs were guilty of kicking out on the full. On their own ball, a couple of lineouts were also lost. The scrum creaked early.

It had all begun to fall apart as quickly as two minutes. From the very first of their lineout drives, out-half Laurent Labit invited Benjamin Lhande in off the left wing on his inside shoulder, and the pack proceeded to drive off him for Stephane Peysson to score his fourth try of the competition. Every point was precious, especially the early ones, as in those final 10 minutes Munster were still fighting, before they were forced to concede to a 23-9 scoreline.

And so ended a very successful season for Kidney and his team. They had reclaimed the Inter-provincial crown at home and dared to enter the knockout stages of the European Cup for the first time. But all they felt leaving France was misery, and disappointment. Munster had believed they would win. The coach had convinced his team, but there was an obvious disconnect in the subsequent team performance. There was also the distraction of a long lay off and international requests of his players. 'In a few days we might reflect that it was a good season,' Kidney remarked after the game, 'but right now it's very disappointing. Some people might think that's a good sign, but if we weren't disappointed now, we wouldn't have believed we could win – and we did.'

AROUND THE CORNER was Keith Wood's homecoming. It was only a brief return to Munster's red, but it was an ingredient that was beyond Declan Kidney's reach in Ireland. He and his team needed Wood home. As it turned out, Harlequins, Wood's employers were restructuring the club and its finances and they were willing to let him go, but only briefly. Whether it was a loan or a sabbatical, the single most inspirational figure in modern Irish rugby was going to be back in Declan Kidney's hands.

At the beginning of the 1999-2000 season Kidney brought his entire squad to the University of Limerick where they were asked their ambitions for the new season. It was Woody who replied, 'Winning the Heineken Cup'.

Others smiled to themselves.

One or two broke out in giggles.

Keith Wood: After the demons of the World Cup (1999 in Wales) you've no idea how important it was to me to win the Inter-pro championship and get this win here today (Heineken Cup, Saracens 34 Munster 35, Nov 29, 1999). What happened out there today was pure unadulterated guts.

(November 29, 1999)

1999-2000

'One of the things I'm glad I did this year was get one of those special trains up and down to Dublin for one of the international matches. It gave me a feel for what the Irish rugby supporters are about, which might sound like a small fella from Cork making a grandiose statement. But I think it reinforced what Irish rugby supporters are looking for in their teams. They want them to be honest and be competitive. Ulster did that last year and if Ulster hadn't won the European Cup I still think most of their supporters would have been happy with the way they played. They gave everything that their supporters wanted, and then it became a bit of an avalanche when they actually reached the final and won it. And that's what we're trying to do. I don't expect us to win. I don't expect us to lose either. But once we give it our best shot, then it will take a good team to beat us, and if we are beaten we have at least made sure that it is a very good team that beats us.'

– Declan Kidney
(December 18, 1999)

ONLY KEITH WOOD knew what to expect on game day at Vicarage Road. The degree to which Saracens had so quickly embraced the professional game, and looked to exploit it for its rich potential, was very interesting indeed. It was also massively entertaining. Every home game, Sarries put on more than a game of rugby football. The club was 124 years old at the turn of the millennium, and its founding fathers may have had a thing or two say about what they saw if they'd turned up at Vicarage Road themselves.

Those fathers were the Old Boys of the Philological School in Marylebone, London. It's said that they named their new club after Saladin's desert warriors of the 12th century who believed in their own 'endurance, enthusiasm and invincibility'. The crescent and star on the club's shirt has its roots in the flag of Ottomon, but in 1995 the club gained the financial support of businessman, Nigel Wray who had made his money initially on the stock market and property, before diversifying into mobile phones, pharmaceuticals and publishing. He also stepped into professional rugby, buying Sarries for a reported £2million, and also buying up the cream of the world's talent in Michael Lynagh, Phillipe Sella and Francois Pienaar.

By the 1999-2000 season, on and off the field, Sarries were 'all biz' and Declan Kidney needed to have a look for himself before bringing Munster there for their Heineken Cup meeting. Kidney did not miss a thing.

He was entertained, certainly, and he was also distracted. The club liked to have a fancy radio-controlled car to bring the kicking tee onto the field. They had their own team of very attractive, leggy cheerleaders called 'The Sensations'. The home team was welcomed onto the field for each half by the music from Will Smith's *Men In Black*, and at the very notion of any fisticuffs a few bars from Sly Stallone's *Rocky* were given a blast.

All of that, and supporters wearing the club's Fez hats, got the Munster coach thinking about how easily any young or old Irish rugby player might be slightly distracted and couldn't be blamed for taking his eye off the game for a second? Before heading back to London with Munster, therefore, Kidney called a special team meeting for his players. When they entered the room there was no sign of Deccie, however.

He was hiding behind a bar counter in the room.

He had asked Niall O'Donovan to commence with the analysis breakdown of the opposition.

Wood and Co then saw their coach stand up wearing a Fez hat. He had the gadget for one of his boys' radio-controlled cars in his hands, one that also fired cannonballs, and he proceeded to drive it around the room.

O'Donovan continued with the presentation.

Kidney kept up the show of driving ability. He had also seen to it that the room was adorned with photos of very attractive females. For three minutes or so he maintained his concentration and did his level best to undo the concentration of his players, he explained in '*Munster: our Road to Glory* (2006)'.

O'Donovan?

Or Deccie?

They had a choice to make about who was the most interesting person in the room. What happened in the last three minutes, Kidney suddenly asked upon stopping the car and taking the hat off his head?

He asked had they heard anything Niall had said to them?

The players had little to say for themselves. Declan Kidney informed his players that if they were in Vicarage Road they would already be 14 points behind.

IN THE NEXT six weeks Munster would meet Saracens twice. At Vicarage Road on November 28 they came away with the most unlikely of victories, 34-35 and then on January 8 in their own neck of the woods they again wrestled and barely outplayed the brilliant forces of the English club by another point. It finished 31-30. It was a splendid double triumph for Munster.

And for Declan Kidney, especially, it was irrefutable evidence of his standing in the European game. More than anyone else, in constructing the two victories he had gone head-to-head with Francois Pienaar.

The South African, who had led his country to World Cup triumph in 1995, and adorned the world stage with Nelson Mandela wearing his replica Springbok No.6 jersey, was one of the most powerful and respected brands in the game. Hollywood heartthrob, Matt Damon would play him on the big screen. Pienaar at 30 years of age had arrived in London three years earlier.

The South African, a law graduate, was determined to impress. He had been ousted from the national team in controversial circumstances for the team's tour of France and Wales in the autumn of 1999, with Gary Teichmann appointed team captain in his place.

Francois Pienaar: I am determined to challenge for my place back in the South African team and eventually go back home and put something back into South African rugby.

When I was left out of the tour squad, I realised how much South Africa still meant to me even after the World Cup final. The support for me went on for weeks and I will never complain about criticism again. I will be thrilled about going back into the South African team against the Lions next year, or even Transvaal.

However, I am committed to Saracens and you have to get over the hurt of being dropped. I am still hungry for rugby. I need rugby. Rugby does not need me.

(December 6, 1996)

BEFORE THE END of his first season in England, Pienaar was offered the role of player-coach at Saracens. It appeared to double his bullishness. After ending their time in the wilderness of the English game, Sarries had finished sixth in the Premiership the year before. With Pienaar leading in a dual capacity they were in a position to win a league and cup double in year two.

Francois Pienaar: Although I always planned to be loyal and give the club my all, I intended to spend the rest of my time at home with my wife. Becoming player-coach, however, made it a totally different ball game.

I had ideas of what professionalism should be about, and when I was given the chance I implemented them. When I was made coach I said to the team, 'I'm looking to win every single match next season'. I know they laughed behind my back at this, and it turns out we have lost three games so far this season. But I meant it. Professionalism is not just about receiving your cheque at the end of the month and putting on a good show. It's about winning.

The challenge was to find the perfect game, where we combine skill, power and ability to such an extent that others, either watching or playing, say that we are fantastic to watch. I introduced some goal-setting into the club. As the season has progressed, so our goals have become higher, but we haven't got close to our true potential yet.

Everyone's got their own locker now. We all have our washed kit laid out in front of us in the rightful place. The shower and medical facilities at the club have improved. And we have post-match, and even post-training assessments, using video and a stats library. It's difficult for me too, because I want to be one of the lads but I can't because I'm involved in hiring and firing, selecting and dropping. You have to share a laugh in the showers after a game, but players will come up to you and ask why they have been omitted?

You always want to play for your country, make no mistake, but there's a lot of talent in South Africa, and their back row in particular has gelled together very well. But this is why it's so important for me to go elsewhere and achieve. I didn't want anyone to say, 'What's Francois up to? Oh, he's gone over to England to take the money'. That, to me, would be a huge insult. I would compare any player who does that to a thief. I had as good a deal back home, but I came here for the adventure and the challenge. I'd like to think I'm proving my point.

(April 5, 1998)

THIS WAS THE man facing Kidney, and this was the suped-up club awaiting Munster in the Heineken Cup. Though Kidney had already led Munster to historic back-to-back Inter-provincial titles by the time his team were due up in Vicarage Road. They'd also taken Pontypridd most impressively, 32-10, in their opening European group game which meant that Munster were unbeaten for the season in competitive action, and had only lost twice in their previous 17 (each time on French soil). There were reasons for this.

The new arrivals, Keith Wood and John Langford were imbuing the squad with something extra and powerful, and Ronan O'Gara was growing up fast into a dependable No.10.

The biggest reason of all, however, was the more assured handling by the team's head coach. Declan Kidney looked quite at home in the professional environment, even with a Fez hat sitting on his head. There was a calmness and assurance, both new qualities, coursing the veins of his players.

On top of that, there remained Kidney's quirky habit of grabbing at any additional psychological advantage fluttering in the breeze. In the middle of the night, before the game in Vicarage Road, the fire alarm in the team hotel had gone off. Everyone had to get out of their beds at 4.0 am in the morning, as the hotel management determined whether they had a fire or some hoax on their hands. It was indeed a false alarm, but Kidney took it into his head to inform his team that the person responsible had to have some love of Saracens.

Nevertheless, it was the team's new-found personality, a calm assurance, that made all the difference in London on November 28 when they trailed Saracens 18-3, 21-9 at the break, and 34-23 with eight minutes left on the clock. It helped that the home team made a spate of forward substitutions, thinking they were on the road to victory. It also helped that little bit extra when Sarries brought in former Munster and Lions hero, Paul Wallace after 63 minutes. It was a red rag that Munster seized and held onto.

Amazingly, within seven minutes of the restart, Munster had gone in front. Killian Keane scored their first try after Pienaar had broken up the blind side of a Sarries' lineout maul without support and Alan Quinlan won the turnover. From the recycle, Mike Mullins met O'Gara's diagonal pass at pace and off-loaded with exact timing to Keane. The second try came from an O'Gara chip ahead.

Anthony Foley rucked and turned over the ball, and Mullins came from deep demanding Peter Stringer's blind side pass. It was low and inaccurate, but Mullins volleyed the ball through a gap in the Sarries defence, and gathered it on the bounce to score in the corner.

But Pienaar's men upped their game after finding themselves behind, and quickly so, with a Thierry Lacroix penalty, a Jeremy Thomson try under the posts, and a conversion and another penalty from Lacroix.

34-23, thank you, and Munster's best not good enough it appeared.

The second comeback of the half was breathtaking. Foley tapped a penalty to himself and was driven over the line. The missed conversion looked costly, and Sarries withstood two rolling mauls in the left corner.

O'Gara was held up in the tackle, but he off-loaded to Mullins and the centre threw a lengthy skip pass creating a two-to-one overlap. Jeremy Staunton finished it off. O'Gara added the points.

Declan Kidney: For the first 20 minutes we handed them the ball. The first score of the second-half was all-important and we got it. It wasn't the perfect performance. There were more try-scoring opportunities that we didn't take and a few guys in there are disappointed with their own performances, but it shows the character of the team to score four tries in the second-half against a team like Saracens.

And these are the kind of matches you live for.

(November 29, 1999)

Francois Peinaar: They (Munster) just didn't stand back, they played. Credit to their forward pack that they scored those tries at the start of the second-half. No complaints. We didn't deserve to win. The first 10 minutes of the second-half we looked like a primary school team. We just gifted them the points and there's no excuse for that. We've got a good squad and I can't understand it.

(November 29, 1999)

Keith Wood: It's an aggressive game, but there was nothing nasty there. It's rugby, not tiddlywinks. It's great to get one over the old enemy. The whole country was down after the World Cup, and it's nice to get them smiling again.

(November 29, 1999)

Tony Ward: How do you even begin to analyse a game of such intense pride and passionate quality. Take a bow Declan Kidney, Niall O'Donovan, and Brian O'Brien and everyone associated with Mick Galwey and this magnificent Munster outfit. Eight competitive wins out of eight starts this season... not to mention a certain success over the national side in Cork just prior to the World Cup.

(Irish Independent, Nov 29, 1999)

ON JANUARY 8, it was the same again. Another one point defeat for Saracens after a late O'Gara conversion sent Thomond Park wild after the two teams had gone toe-to-toe once more and ended with three tries each. The final try came in stoppage time when Wood pilfered a try after a lineout on the Sarries' line. O'Gara's kick from the touchline needed the help of an upright. The place went crazy.

Like the first game, Munster trailed 5-10 after 34 minutes, 8-17 at half-time and were 24-30 down heading into injury time, before Aussie Langford plucked the ball in the middle of the line, and Wood seized possession.

David Wallace: In the game at Vicarage Road, Paul had come on as a replacement. Himself and Claw were having a bit of a tussle at one stage and I arrived on the scene first. You don't really know what to do in that situation when you need to jump in. I umpired a bit I think from memory. It was the first season I played against Paul. The bragging rights were something you were going to hold onto though.

Sarries scored near the end to go in front. We had to work our way down the field from near our own goal-line, picking and jamming. With the last play of the game we got down there and Woody scored his try. Rog converted.

It was funny because we were training at Thomond Park the following week. For the laugh we got Rog to try and land the kick from the exact same spot again. The result was exactly the same. The ball hit off the post and went over.

(December 7, 2012)

Ronan O'Gara: I was half hoping we wouldn't get a try in the first place. There were 15,014 hoping for a try and I was thinking, 'knock it on!'

The thought cropped into my head as I put the ball down. 'What have I got myself into here?' You're the hero or you're the villain. So far I've got two out of two, but one day I'm going to be on the other side of the fence. Today Limerick was on my side and the Gods above were looking down on me.

(December 7, 2012)

Keith Wood: Days are rare in rugby when you get a ground full of absolutely manic supporters. It's different when you're on the opposition line and you're attacking, but when you're on your own line deep in doodoo, and suddenly there's 15,000 people shouting 'MUNSTER', Jesus you get out of there pretty quickly.

(December 7, 2012)

IF ANY PAIR of games helped Declan Kidney build Munster into a dynasty, it was these two victories over Saracens. For the opposition, however, the two defeats were more than gut-wrenching. They appeared to hold up Sarries in their ambitious tracks. Pienaar also never fully realised his dreams in England and only got his hands on the domestic knockout cup, never the Premiership title. Ten years into a new century, Nigel Wray's investment in the club had reached a reported £15million and the cup win in 1998 remained the only silverware on show.

While Kidney's men would advance to European finals in 2000 and 2002 and learn from twin defeats, and come back stronger to lift the ultimate trophy in the European game twice in 2006 and 2008, Saracens would have a long wait until May of 2016, when they finally could call themselves the best club team in the northern hemisphere after defeating Racing 92 in the decider.

Nigel Wray: I think that in many ways when we won the cup and were runners-up in the league, we didn't really know how we had done it. It was very early in the life of the club and the Premiership and it has taken a considerable time for us to understand what it takes to create the kind of culture you need.

(May 17, 2010)

Francois Pienaar: I played a lot of rugby matches in my career, and was fortunate to have many notable highs; Super 10, World Cup, great club occasions.

But the two games I played for Saracens against Munster in 1999 have always stood out in my memory. That may seem strange but they had a profound effect on me. Munster are never ordinary opponents to face.

(February 10, 2008)

BY THE END of 1999, Munster had gained revenge on their quarter-final conquerors the previous year by taking Colomiers in back-to-back games in December, winning by 16 points and 18 points. A first win in France was a notch on Declan Kidney's belt that was also badly needed. Despite losing to Pontypridd in their final group game, and also losing their unbeaten run into the bargain, he had steered his team back to the final eight with a certain flamboyance.

The other three Irish provinces were struggling to remove themselves from the foot of the their individual pools, and as Kidney looked back on the 12 months transformation in his dressing room he pointed to the crunching 29-12 defeat by Ulster in Ravenhill in the Inter-provincials the previous season. Kidney and his team knew that they had let themselves down that evening. It was a low point that was met with a bounce.

Physically and mentally, Munster changed. Certainly Kidney invested more trust in the ability of his players, and Munster began to show that they could win games without shoving the ball up their jumper for 80 minutes. In the away wins over Saracens and Colomiers they had scored eight scintillating tries. 'If a forward makes a mistake, it's just taken as a mistake,' he told *The Irish Times*. 'Whereas if a back makes a mistake then it's "Joe Bloggs made a complete and utter horlicks of it" and that puts an individual under pressure. But I do believe that there are more good backs in the country and our fellas are willing to have a go, and willing to take risks.'

Kidney also proclaimed by the end of the year that he had a lot of 'thinking rugby players', and that when Colomiers changed their approach his lads were able to come up with solutions. The Munster lads also knew that they had the complete and utter trust of their coach, and they were no longer afraid of working things out themselves in the heat of the battle.

Jean-Phillipe Cariat (Colomiers co-coach): A funny weekend, because of the long, long trip on Friday, because of the stadium, because of the weather and because of the changing room. The conditions were quite difficult for us. Munster adapted to them better than we did, perhaps because they are used to playing in these kind of conditions.

(December 20, 1999)

Henri Auriol (Colomiers co-coach): I was quite surprised by the quality of the Munster backs, and I have been generally with the Irish and British backs this season, with their speed and explosiveness.

(December 20, 1999)

||||▌|||

AND THE QUALITY of backs in Irish rugby was about to get even better. In the spring of 2000, Declan Kidney was on Ireland duty, in addition to Munster watch; as coach of Ireland A he guided his charges to a boosting Triple Crown. In November of the same year, South Africa came to Thomond Park to meet Kidney's Irish side. Mick O'Driscoll was mighty, snatching five Springbok throws, and Alan Quinlan, Victor Costello and David Wallace showed themselves ready for honours higher than the 'A's', but importantly there were three tries to admire from Justin Bishop, Mike Mullins and Tom Tierney.

Irish supporters needed to see this. They needed to know that internationally their team was not a lost cause. Of course, they had no idea that Brian O'Driscoll in full fight was just around the corner.

The UCD and Ireland under-21 centre had made his debut in the summer tour of Australia in 1999, though working some immediate magic was really beyond him. In the Championship that had ended just a couple of months earlier, Ireland had only managed three tries in 320 minutes, all of which came from turnovers. The pressure was on Warren Gatland to call up young lads from the under-21 squad. Shane Horgan's name was often quoted. So too O'Driscoll's after Ireland assistant-coach Philip Danaher watched the 20 year-old score 26 points for UCD in Division Three of the All-Ireland League.

Brian O'Driscoll: I don't pay that much heed to what is being said. I mean Warren Gatland doesn't pick a team from newspaper clippings. It's nice to hear people think you have the ability but I mean, I won't be getting carried away by it.

To be honest I wonder what I have done to get this publicity. I feel that you should have to earn a reputation and I don't think I've done that yet. I think that Shane Horgan deserves it a great deal more than I do. He's proved it at higher levels.

I was out for three months of the season with a knee injury, didn't play for Leinster and had one hairy performance for the under-21s against Wales. I was replaced that day and it really hurt. I was very disappointed and desperately wanted to prove a point in the next match against England, which I think I did. In Division 3 you get more space at outside centre and get to gallop. You are more involved at inside centre. I like to think I can play both, that I'm not just a bosh merchant.

(March 31, 1999)

THE 1999 WORLD Cup had left the team and their supporters red-faced, both departing Lens after losing to Argentina 28-24, the tournament at an end, and no Irish team about to show up in Lansdowne Road for the much anticipated quarter-final against France. O'Driscoll was present, but he was still a boy. But growing up fast. Very fast, and his magnificent hat-trick of tries in the Stade de France was only a matter of months away in the very first Six Nations Championship.

Gatland's Ireland were in the slipstream of Kidney's Munster, and there were repeated calls for Ireland to pick up the pieces and learn from a province that had immense courage when looking for the ball, and some charm on the ball.

The first Championship of a whole new century began with a reminder of the past as England reached the sum total of 50 points at Twickenham in the opening game, and tries from Kevin Maggs and Mick Galwey looked puny in a 50-18 defeat. O'Driscoll got his first Championship try in the double scores (44-22) win over the Scots at Lansdowne Road, another at the old stadium in a rout of the Italians (60-13), and then came the Triple Whammy in Paris that ended a losing run of 15 games against the French and recorded Ireland's first win in Paris in 28 years.

Ireland may have been late arriving, but on March 18 they finally showed up and officially joined the likes of Ulster and Munster as a professional outfit. With the win in Paris, and a third place finish in the Championship table, came talk of contracts and money as well.

O'Driscoll, same as approximately 90 players plying their trade for province or country, was almost out of contract. The IRFU needed to tidy up the whole lot of them by June 1. Newspaper talk had O'Driscoll's earning power in the bracket of £150,000-£200,000. English and French teams had their eye on him.

Castres and Toulouse were showing an interest, meanwhile, in Munster's double act behind the scrum, Peter Stringer and Ronan O'Gara. Winning was good, but it came at a cost, and the IRFU (same as Munster and Ireland) now needed to speedily pull up their socks.

|||| ■ ||||

FOR THE FIRST time Munster supporters were about to become hot under the collar about tickets. The Munster Branch had made the decision that their clubs should receive the lion's share for the European Cup quarter-final against Stade Francais, and only 2,000 tickets were made available to the public from a total capacity of 13,342. For the first time too, men were showing up and forming queues at midnight, with flasks and temporary bedding on their person.

Those who made it into Thomond Park to witness a first historic knockout European win also saw one of Declan Kidney's masterly performances. The coach scripted the game and a 27-10 win to perfection, beginning with the finest of homework on Stade's lineout. The choice of Eddie Halvey aided Munster in targeting the dodgy French throwing at the front of the line, and in the middle of the line John Langford also worked brilliantly. Kidney also nullified his opponent's running game with an expertly organised defensive pattern. On top of all that, he made sure his men were in the mood to ruck the visitors right off the park.

Stade were 12-0 down before they knew it, and heading for the back door. Toulouse away was next in the semis.

Alan Quinlan: The Stade game was brilliant but we didn't feel any pressure. There was no mention of, 'this is the first ever Heineken Cup knockout game in Thomond Park'. We just saw it as a huge opportunity. We won a lot easier than I thought we would actually.

(October 18, 2014)

THE MUNSTER PLAYERS had never enjoyed their lives as rugby players as much before. They felt protected by their coach, who remained a private man, but gave them so much of himself. 'You'd never want to miss a training session,' remarked John O'Neill to reporters, 'because there's always something interesting in them. The talking is done beforehand; they're short, sharp, to the point and interesting.' Eddie Halvey said that he had never known a spirit like it as the team prepared for their semi-final in Toulouse. 'We're always having a laugh, but the work is done and done well at the same time. I can honestly say it's the best camp I have ever known.'

Though Munster were enjoying themselves without all of the accoutrements of professional life. The team, for starters, did not own a scrummaging machine. That 'small' problem was alleviated by using the machine at the University of Limerick, but before the semi-final the college had moved it because their season was over, and Kidney had to bring his men out to Annacotty to do some scrummaging there. The machine there was rusty, however, and didn't hold. And Kidney did not have enough fit forwards to stand on the other end of it.

At the opposite end of the field a local was cutting grass with his tractor. He took a break when asked, and lit up a cigarette. The tractor was positioned at one end of the machine and Munster scrummaged.

If there was any chance of Munster taking their new-found status in rugby life too seriously, moments like this helped everyone to pinch themselves. They laughed off the incident, and one of the 'suits' on the team asked what the media would make of it if they found out that Munster were shoving against a 'Massey Ferguson'? With a serious face, John Hayes, the farmer amongst them corrected him.

'That was a John Deere.'

Declan Kidney mused to the media in the lead-in to the semi-final, asking if anyone really expected Munster to defeat such a French powerhouse, though he did let it slip that he wanted his team to go hunting more for tries.

Toulouse, meanwhile, were eyeing up the scrum. They named their reserve props, Cedric Soulette and Luigi Esposito on the bench. Kidney chose Marcus Horan only as reserve cover even though he fully realised that the home team would throw the kitchen sink at it for the last 20 or 30 minutes.

Though Munster had no fear of the last quarter, as they soldiered to a thrilling 31-25 victory and made it into their first European final. They got rid of anything bordering on anxiety or fear long before then. They did do before the game ever began by heading to the shaded end of the ground for their warm-up, and to where the most faithful and nosiest of home support could be found. Soaking up the hostility and forgetting about it just as quickly was step one to victory.

Step two was more of a surprise to the team and its management. At half-time, rather than take the long walk through the Stade Lescure to the dressing rooms, the Toulouse players sat down in the cool shade of the tunnel. As the Munster team stepped around them, one or two looked slumped on the ground. 'They looked shattered,' stated Peter Clohessy afterwards.

Kidney had been surprised that Toulouse had chosen to play with the wind in the first-half. He knew they wished to score early and often, and break Munster's back by half-time. It didn't happen. The wariness in the Munster camp of the sweltering, humid conditions had resulted in 240 1.5 litres of water being transported with the team from home. Another 120 were bought locally. Kidney had his team throwing back the water for two days solid. As they waited in their dressing room and talked at half-time, Munster looked perfectly hydrated and strong.

There was no sign that they would break.

Instead, Toulouse appeared suspect in the mental strength department. After Mike Mullins had been sin-binned, Toulouse had opted to kick three points from under the posts to make it 18-14 against opposition who would have been without an eighth forward or a seventh back at a scrum under their posts. 'In the modern game,' Kidney mentioned afterwards, 'that's when you go for seven points.' In the 10 minutes Mullins was off the field, Munster outscored Toulouse 3-0.

Munster were the team ready and more wanting, and after the hour mark their physical and mental game showed up in perfect harmony. They had a scrum just outside their 22. In the next 91 seconds of breathtaking rugby the ball was played through 16 pairs of hands before Ronan O'Gara touched down.

'I've never screamed louder or longer for a pass,' the out-half confessed. Jason Holland's intercept try followed to finish off Toulouse. The team stoutly defended. Before too long Declan Kidney, of all men, shaking his head vigorously and trying to avoid the adulation, was lifted into the air and was being carried around shoulder-high.

Mick Galwey: To come here and win is what dreams are made of, it's what the European Cup is all about. It's the greatest day I've ever had in a Munster jersey. We're not as good as the 1978 team yet but if we go on and win this maybe we'll be put in the same bracket.

(May 8, 2000)

Warren Gatland: I thought it was an outstanding victory, a great result for Munster and Irish rugby. I think it proved for once and all that Ireland teams can now travel to France with justifiable confidence of winning. In the past there was a case whereby teams were in awe of the French opposition; matches were lost before you stepped out on the pitch.

(May 8, 2000)

IT WAS A season of seasons.

A season when Munster took on the richest team in Europe and defeated them home and away! And a season when Declan Kidney brought his team to France and defied Munster's inner demons who were so full of doubt.

A season too when, back home, they had travelled the much shorter journey north to Belfast and humbled Ulster in front of their own supporters for the first time in two decades.

More than any of that, it was a season when Munster, team and supporters, found one voice. It was a voice of the team first. Then it became the voice of the province. As the players and management celebrated in their dressing room in the bowels of Stade Lescure, and champagne was sprayed from bottles, everyone joined in the song that team manager, Brian O'Brien first introduced to them in Belfast four months before.

Stand up and fight until you hear the bell,
Stand toe to toe, trade blow for blow…

IT'S A SONG within a musical that doesn't turn out so swell for Carmen Jones herself. The 1943 Broadway musical was crafted by Georges Bizet, but the lyrics and book were written by Oscar Hammerstein II. *Stan' Up and Fight*, also known as *March of the Toreadors*, found even more widespread fame 11 years later when Austrian-Hungarian director Otto Preminger adapted it for the big screen and asked Dorothy Dandridge and Harry Belafonte to star.

In the movie Carmen has her 'cards' read to her, revealing the nine of spades – The Card of Death. And Carmen, a parachute maker in the Second World War, dies at the end of the movie at the hands of Joe, an air force man who becomes besotted with her, loses her, and ends up strangling her.

It's the movie's final act, and in the final act of the Heineken Cup in 2000, and again in 2002, Munster would also meet with tragic endings. Halfway through the decade most of Munster's audience, even their most devout supporters, believed that Declan Kidney and his team had mysteriously been handed the nine of spades.

Declan Kidney: It's important that if you give something your best shot, that you accept the result at the end of it.

(May 29, 2000)

Mick Galwey: It's obviously very disappointing for everyone, and no one can point a finger at Ronan, he got us this far all year. We're not going to look and say that Ronan missed the last penalty. We just felt that as a team we didn't perform on the day. That's been our attitude all year; we play as a team and nobody can blame anybody else.

(May 29, 2000)

Declan Kidney: We should feel proud. We have given it our best shot throughout the season. We knew that it would take a good side to beat us and

Northampton are a very good side. There is no disgrace in that. It's to hold yourself up and to acknowledge this that is important. In the same way that you accept victory, you must accept defeat.

(May 29, 2000)

Mick Galwey: We weren't believing all we were hearing or reading. There was a big expectation but, as for the favourites' tag, we knew we were playing over here at Twickenham where the Irish haven't had great success. We felt personally that we were underdogs because we have a lot of respect for Northampton and we knew that they were going to come good today.

They have had a tough season, now they have got their reward. I felt that we had to play the game in their half in the second-half (Munster led 8-6) and take our chances. It didn't work out that way. They came back at us very strongly. You know they carried the ball and defended very well. They did not allow us dictate the game.

(May 29, 2000)

Declan Kidney: In a one point game like that (Northampton won 9-8) you are talking about the narrowest of margins between victory and defeat. They are an exceptionally physically strong side.

(May 29, 2000)

Mick Galwey: At the very end we gathered in a circle, we were almost numb at that stage. We said we would go over to the crowd. We almost went over apologising for not winning the game. They were on their feet and gave the team a great lift. They probably feel a little bit sorry for us, as we feel for them.

(May 29, 2000)

THE EMOTION THAT engulfed team and supporters in the home of English rugby that afternoon was the leftover from the previous night. Truth is, Kidney had watched his team swimming in emotion for far too long before the kick-off. It was, of course, a game his team might still have won.

Northampton were formidable opponents and Pat Lam and his teammates had outscrummaged them for the 80 minutes, and they were also under intense pressure in the lineout. As a consequence Peter Stringer was so often getting man and ball, and at the base of the scrum Anthony Foley was picking up morsels. Referee Joel Dume might also have been kinder, and in the final quarter he harshly sin-binned Munster captain, Mick Galwey for 10 vital minutes.

But Munster still might have won!

On a day that delivered a blustery wind, and a greasy ball on a greasy surface, Paul Grayson kicked penalties in the 2nd, 38th and 48th minutes to win it for Northampton. O'Gara kicked one penalty wide that might have put Munster back in front, and right at the death after a large dollop of luck brought Munster back into striking range a second time, he struck what appeared to the perfect kick but watched the ball get fractionally blown off course right at the last seconds.

KEITH WOOD SAW what Munster needed to do to correct things before their next final, though he would not be around for the next loss or the twin victories that followed. The day before the final the team bus had been caught up in London traffic getting to the ground for their run-out, and again coming back. The team, he resolved, played the match against Northampton for too long in their heads. He thought it left everyone edgy. The team was far too excited by the event awaiting them.

And at the team meeting the night before the game, every last man had been tipped over the edge. Mick Galwey's final speech in the hotel came almost 24 hours too early. The players drained themselves of vital energy. They were listening to 'Gaillimh', their captain. They were surrounded by faxes on the walls wishing them well. Some of the lads had tears in their eyes.

Others were letting them spill out.

It proved a costly evening for the coach and his team.

2000-2001

'I know what I can bring to it. I know what I brought to it over the years, I know that I've been in holes before like this and I know how to get out of them, but I think now is the time to sit back and reflect and let's take a look at things. In terms of doom and gloom, and there'll be a lot of that, in a strange way over the coming year we'll benefit from what we've gone through here (Six Nations Championship, 2012-2013) with the fellas coming through, and that's what we must remember.'

– Declan Kidney
(March 18, 2013)

MISSING THE KICK that might have won Munster a first Heineken Cup was not something that a young tyro like Ronan O'Gara was going to be allowed to forget in the Munster dressing room, or out on the training field as elder statesmen on the team took turns to try their luck with the exact same kick. More than one forward succeeded too.

And Declan Kidney did not attempt to shield his brilliant new No.10 from the guillotine-like humor that characterised the Munster camp.

O'Gara had been a first season wonder. A Championship points record in his first start for Ireland when his six penalties and six conversions helped humble Italy, 60-13. That, and his guiding hand in the Heineken Cup semi-final victory in Bordeaux, might have teed up most players for a fall from grace in a more pressurised and demanding Year Two.

'I've seen the kick a few times now and 'Axel' (Anthony Foley) won't let me forget it,' the 23 year-old informed *The Irish Times*. 'Every day of the week nearly, it's mentioned. I've no problem living with that, it was a hard kick. On the day I didn't get it, on another day I might have. But sure that's sport. I'll probably find myself in situations like that again, please God, in the next seven years or so.'

To fortify himself further, he repeated the wisdom of his coach.

'In the words of Deccie, "winners fall and they get straight back up, losers fall and stay down". So that's the attitude I would take. You look at somebody like Woody. He's had one or two upsets, and people bitched about him once or twice, and he's probably the best rugby player in the world.'

But, still, someone would take the ball at the end of a training session and tell O'Gara that he was in Twickers! The kick would be duly lined up for that same someone to have a lash at the posts.

That was the Munster way. Always had been. As a squad accustomed to the schoolteacher-cum-professional coach amongst them, they needed to let off steam. Kidney, it should be noted, allowed his players this 'steam' time.

When the time came for him to hang up his boots, team captain Anthony Foley reflected in his memoir, *Axel* what he would miss most... the day-to-day craic and the banter, even the vicious slagging in the dressing-room. Every player knew that once they crossed the gates of the University of Limerick it was best to leave all feelings... all sensitivity, behind them. Otherwise, a man might not survive that room!

So-called big names parachuting into the Munster camp especially were nice, easy targets. And none bigger or larger than former All Black record try scorer, Dougie Howlett. The winger had not even been formally introduced to his future teammates when he found himself singled out. A couple of months earlier he had been in a spot of bother with the British police when he did a dance on a couple of cars at Heathrow Airport. It was an 'international incident' as Howlett insisted on making a public apology to the whole of New Zealand through his website.

Remorse did not save him from the tongue of Alan Quinlan, who spotted him watching the team train from the sideline.

'PLEASE STEP AWAY FROM THE VEHICLES,' Quinlan announced very loudly, with the whole squad listening.

Foley saw the team's caustic tongue as a caring tool. There was never any point in awkward silences amongst a group of men who had to bare their souls and face all of their fears and self-doubts together every single weekend. Foley was one of the most merciless in handing out the abuse. Though he was also a prime target, because of his slight speech impediment.

'We'll have to thet out our thtall early doorth,' he'd hear others imitating him, always making sure to begin with, that their captain was within listening distance. Nobody talked behind anyone's back. All verbal charges were full-frontal, and announced in advance. Foley even got worked over about how he breathed. He had received so many breaks to his nose over the years and never had the time to go and see a specialist.

The team christened him 'Darth Vader'.

‖‖‖▮▮‖‖‖

WINNING THE INTERPROVINCIAL Championship in September 2000 allowed Munster to look forward, not back at where they had fallen in London. Kidney, unusually, was extra loud and clear in making his feelings known after the title was clinched in Musgrave Park with a 29-21 victory over Ulster.

Declan Kidney: I'm extremely proud to be associated with them. They've made their bit of history today. I don't know if people realise how difficult it can be to get going again. I've held my whist until now but of the last four teams to lose the European Cup final, we're the first to win our National Championship the following season. It just shows the mental strength of these players to be able to do that.

(September 30, 2000)

ONE MONTH LATER, Kidney watched his men labour for possession in the Stade Pierre Antoine. Castres, captained by Ireland's Jeremy Davidsson, led 20-9 at half-time but a brace of penalties from O'Gara and a Dominic Crotty try brought it level. The home team stretched into a six points lead. Munster responded with two more tries, the first from Anthony Horgan. The second came from a move started in their own 22 and was finished off by O'Gara, for a three-point victory.

Declan Kidney: Rugby is becoming more chess-like now. Give yourself 10 minutes to get a score, give yourself another 10 minutes to get a score, and then have the calmness to go for the tries.

(October 16, 2000)

O'GARA'S FINGERS WERE on those chess pieces too. Travelling to Bath and losing for the first time all season left Munster looking a little off the pace on their journey straight back to the knockout stages, and the new year began with a trip to Wales, to the impregnable fortress of Rodney Parade. It was a ground that Kidney would get to know a little better a couple more years down the road when he held down the job of Newport coach for only a few short months. In January of 2001 it was not a place that issued a warm welcome. One defeat in their preceding 20 matches, over a 14 months period, were very simple and daunting statistics in Newport's favour, and when Kidney's men fell 15-0 behind by the end of the first quarter, it looked an impossible equation for the coach or his men to work out successfully.

How did Munster manage to win the second-half by an astonishing 29-3 margin? Kidney mentioned honesty. Newport captain, Gary Teichmann mentioned Munster's confidence and spirit. Ronan O'Gara mentioned fearlessness. The out-half had just completed his most immaculate performance in a red jersey by setting a Munster record of 29 points.

Gary Teichmann: They are playing with a lot of confidence and spirit. I think they know what the tournament's about, and how to win away from home. It'll be important for them to get a home quarter-final, but they've got the ability (to win the cup) definitely.

(January 15, 2001)

Ronan O'Gara: I was in the groove tonight. Once I got my set-up right, I was confident that I was going to get them over. You get knocked for certain things but I knew I was always capable of a performance like this. I've got to keep it at that level now. There's an awful lot to play for personally this season so why not go for it? Who else is out there to be honest? The bigger the challenge, the better the team. There's a huge appetite there with the likes of Gaillimh and Claw coming to the end and a good youth injection and a few of us are playing at international level, so the Heineken Cup probably isn't as big a step up as it might have been in the past.

(January 15, 2001)

|| | **|** || |

THE CAREERS OF Declan Kidney and Ronan O'Gara were hand-in-hand. Nobody knew Rog as well as his former teacher and coach, for what seemed like forever, at Pres Cork, Munster and Ireland over two decades. But, back in the early weeks and months of 2001, and by the end of the summer after touring Australia with the British and Irish Lions, and keeping company with Neil Jenkins of Wales and England's Jonny Wilkinson, the Corkman definitely came of age. He was no longer one of Kidney's kids.

Wilkinson, if not his absolute hero, became his guide on the international stage, O'Gara admitted in *Munster: Our Road To Glory (Penguin, 2006)*. On the 2001 Lions tour O'Gara had watched the other man's work ethic first hand and tapped into what he had seen. O'Gara also wished to be the best in the world. In the same publication, O'Gara remembered being in a bar with some of his teammates not too long after losing the Heineken Cup final to Northampton. He was in the bathroom and knew there was a guy looking at him. The guy asked how he knew O'Gara?

O'Gara responded he was not sure.

'Oh yeah, I remember,' the guy responded. 'You're the wanker that missed the kick against Northampton.'

O'Gara would quickly grow into the man who stood on the bridge of Irish rugby. He wanted to be on that bridge. He wanted to be the best. He knew whom to trust. He understood who mattered most around him. When he looked at the opposition he was not afraid to stand even taller on that bridge, with or without the more diplomatic, more cautious Declan Kidney always for company.

Ronan O'Gara: We no longer suffer from being beaten before we even travel to England or Europe any more. That's the level we're at in Munster. We expect to win when we go over there. It's the same with Ireland. I've played against England six times and won four of those matches. That's not surprising to me because, between the walls of our dressing room, we always expect to beat England. But the English public and their team have a hard time believing that. They still assume they should come out on top every time because, apparently, the natural order in rugby is that England are the greatest. It's probably down to the way they've been brought up.

All the old clichés about us being the gallant losers or the plucky Irish is absolute nonsense. I honestly think that, both for Munster and Ireland, we've got more talented players than the English in many positions. Maybe that will surprise a few people in England – but our Celtic League is looked down upon because it isn't covered by Sky Sports. I watch some Premiership rugby and I have to switch off the sound because I wonder if I'm seeing the same game. Their commentators are enthusing about the quality and excitement and I'm just like, 'Oh, my God.'

Sky do an incredible job in dramatising the whole of English rugby, but the way they hype these English players is unbelievable. I've toured with some of the players they're now saying are the best in England – and it just doesn't make sense. We all talk about the English players so this is the general opinion in Irish dressing rooms. Some of the people they are trying to put on a pedestal just don't deserve to be there.

(October 17, 2006)

O'GARA ALSO GREW as a No.10 and a kicker who was responsible for the winning of games. In Brendan Fanning's excellent examination of Irish rugby's journey into professionalism, *From There To Here (Gill and Macmillan, 2007)*, O'Gara elaborated on his growing expectation of himself. 'I'd be lying if I said that up to this year, goal-kicking didn't occupy ninety per cent of my thoughts going into a game,' he confessed. 'Fear of failure, fear of letting the team down. And that's a different pressure. Obviously in the quarters and semi-final and final especially, I felt pressure. But I never doubted my technique whereas, in previous years, of course I had worries about it. This year, once I've hit the pitch, I've clicked into routine mode.'

Ronan O'Gara would outgrow his coach, and also Kidney's team, by becoming his own man. He demonstrated that in 2009 when choosing to keep his hands deep in his pockets upon meeting Queen Elizabeth II in Belfast. His decision met with mixed reaction, though views of his hand placement and general posture drew extreme comments from every quarter. A Grand Slam had been brought home to Ireland by then. But commentators did not forget or forgive him, and a year later when Ireland faced the French, Kevin Myers of the *Irish Independent* saw fit to comment that O'Gara was as ill-equipped to handle the powerful French centre, Mathieu Bastareaud 'as Kate Moss'. The observation drew blood and the Irish No.10 responded with a personal letter to the same newspaper. However, even within the corridors of the *Independent*, opinion was divided.

Vincent Hogan: O'Gara may not be everyone's idea of a cuddly toy. He can be waspish and, on occasion, seem a mite self-absorbed. Yet his achievements in the game have been extraordinary. He has been at the Irish console for four Triple Crowns and a Grand Slam, just as he has been the Munster pivot for two European Cup victories. He is the top points-scorer in Six Nations history and a man who has been at the epicenter of just about every positive Irish rugby story of the past decade. That decade has been embroidered by the kind of success that, frankly, goes against Myers' assertion of a group 'comfortable with failure'. So if O'Gara feels antagonised by commentary designed – it would seem – to belittle him, does that make him precious? Or merely human?

(Irish Independent, February 27, 2010)

THERE REMAINED A vulnerability in Declan Kidney's out-half at the beginning of the same decade as the title of Europe's No.1 team was still being chased down a little frantically, though Munster had secured their favoured home draw for their quarter-final against Biarritz at the end of January, 2001. Leinster were also into the last eight, and having encountered the same French side twice in their pool, coach Matt Williams was in generous mood. He was also right in his assertion of how the game would go. He got O'Gara's input about bang on (with the out-half kicking 23 points in the 38-29 win), but had not imagined Anthony Foley rampaging through for a hat-trick of tries. It was a compelling victory, though it had its deficiencies.

Matt Williams: I sent Dec (Declan Kidney) all the tapes as soon as we got back (from France) last week. I honestly believe that Munster will beat them by about 20 points. Their back play is solid rather than exceptional and I would expect Ronan O'Gara to have a bigger influence on the game than his counterpart.

(The Irish Times, January 24, 2001)

Mick Galwey: That was probably the toughest game we've ever played in the Heineken Cup in Thomond Park and that's a credit to Biarritz. For them to score four tries and (us) to come out on top, you have to be happy with it.

(January 29, 2001)

Declan Kidney: The expectation levels for the Munster team are now way over the top. There was a lot of mental pressure on the lads today and they overcame that and all credit to them. In many ways coming here for Biarritz was like us going to Bordeaux for the Toulouse match last year. There isn't any reason why we can't be beaten here and all we can do is make it as difficult as possible for all visiting teams.

(January 29, 2001)

Franco Botica (Biarritz out-half): I think the crowd was fantastic. We had no problem with that. We were motivated by all the things that were said about us by the players from Leinster. I think he (O'Gara) is an excellent player, an excellent kicker. He can kick the ball, he can run, he's very gifted and he's played very well today. He certainly kicked better than me today, that's for sure.

(January 29, 2001)

⫼⫼

THERE WERE SO many good and lousy reasons why Munster lost their Heineken Cup semi-final by a single point, 16-15 to Stade Francais in Lille on April 21. Getting on the wrong end of the balls coming out of the bowl at the semi-final draw in Dublin's Sugar Bowl was just the start. But former Munster and Ireland hero, and Lions manager, Donal Lenihan could hardly be blamed for that – for pitting his old team against the French, whom they had beaten 27-10 in the last eight at Thomond Park a year before. And letting the French have home advantage! Lenihan was merely the bearer of bad news.

There were all variety of reasons. Bad luck. Tough luck when the Foot and Mouth epidemic robbed the team of games, and deprived the team of some of their players who had squeezed in game time with their clubs to get themselves up to the speed of the Heineken Cup and lucked out with injuries. There was coaching from Declan Kidney that had still not evolved to the requisite level. And then, finally, there was the team's out-half who still missed crucial kicks at goal.

All in all, lots of good and lousy reasons.

To begin with, however, Kidney felt only for his team's followers when the semi-final draw was made.

Declan Kidney: That's the biggest regret of the away draw. The supporters are the ones who helped to get us this far, that's the big pity. I am disappointed for the players because it is their families that go to the matches too. That's the greatest disappointment. This is our final and we have to go to France to see how we get on. I suppose if you look at the stats, they have been favourites for the competition for a long time. When we played them last year they were missing a few backrow players and the fact that it is over in France will probably mean a 15 to 20-point swing from last year's game.

(February 8, 2001)

John Connolly (Stade Francais coach): I saw them against Biarritz and they played very well and I'm good friends with Peter Clohessy (he coached Claw while he was at Queensland Reds) and he's going to send me over some tapes, so that's good, he'll help. I'm going to send him a law book in return. They are a good side, eight or nine Test players, with the young guys like Ronan O'Gara growing in confidence. You don't make the final and the semi-final and have the record they do, week in and week out, without being a very fine side.

(February 8, 2001)

THE RIVAL COACHES were kind-hearted, diplomatic and in the case of Claw, Connolly was mischievously tongue in cheek about his old friendship. These were their kinder game faces.

Kidney, actually, had problems far beyond the damaged pockets of his supporters. Alan Quinlan would join David Wallace on the injured list after suffering a fractured thumb in helping Shannon defeat Young Munster. Anthony Foley had injured his knee, though less severely. All hands were on deck and Kidney was left to talk about Dion O'Cuinneagain. The 28 year-old back rower with 19 Irish caps had missed much of the season with a broken hand and hadn't been named amongst Ulster's 30-man squad for the competition, thus leaving him open to Munster selection. Also, O'Cuinneagain was in South Africa completing the final year of his medical studies.

Declan Kidney: He's working very hard and has difficulty getting time off from his studies. Dion hasn't played a match since last September and won't be able to between now and the semi-final so it would be a huge ask of him. We'll wait and see. A lot can happen in the next three weeks and the guys who have been training with the squad deserve the first crack at the whip, so we'll see how they go with their clubs.

(March 27, 2001)

AS THE SEMI-FINAL came into sight, the fact remained that it had been 11 weeks since Munster's quarter-final win over Biarritz, and the team had only four training sessions in that time. Amongst the walking wounded was Ronan O'Gara who was nursing a bruised hip. However, like others, Rog was keenly aware that Munster's final warm up game for the Heineken Cup semi-final was a shop window for Lions selection with Lenihan eagle-eyed alongside coach Graham Henry and Andy Robinson.

Ronan O'Gara: To be honest, yes! There's no point in saying otherwise when virtually every fella is thinking about it. It's like a mini Irish trial for the Lions. People mightn't say it but we all know it. But if Munster do well, hopefully the rest will look after itself. The team comes first on Friday (Munster v Rest of Ireland, Thomond Park), individuals are secondary. That's been the secret to our success. When we pull together as a team the individual rewards take care of themselves.

(April 11, 2001)

THE RIVAL COACHES continued to talk. But Kidney knew in his heart his team needed a perfect implementation of everything they had been told and trained for. And they needed O'Gara spotless with his kicking, if they were to be sure of having another shot at winning their first European trophy.

Declan Kidney: We're a year further down the road and hopefully the experience we gained both on and off the pitch will help us to deal with it. But it's always a fresh challenge. Last year I described it as a journey which nobody knew where it was going to take us. To be back this year is just like a dream.

(April 19, 2001)

John Connolly: It (the ground) doesn't give Stade Francais any advantage. It might as well be on the moon as far as we're concerned. I hear that Munster will be bringing 10,000 and I reckon we had that many for the visit of Swansea in the European Cup but our following is nowhere near as passionate as that for the clubs in the south (of France)

(April 20, 2001)

CONNOLLY WAS ONLY one year into his position, but his squad was four years at work, and the team's owner was seven years into his investment. Max Guazzini, a radio entrepreneur, and thought to be one of the 20 wealthiest men in Paris, had watched Stade win the equivalent of the French fourth division in his first 12 months. They bridged a 90-year gap when defeating Toulouse for the National Championship three years later. They had then won the French cup, and the Championship once again. Stade Francais were on their own roll.

Guazzini listened to his coach toy with the media, and with Munstermen. Declan Kidney also listened and knew he was up against a master chess player.

John Connolly: Stade were played off the park (last year) and couldn't even win the toss. Stade had a very strong back line last year but I'm not sure if the set-up we have this year is any stronger. Our team has an awful lot to turn around from last season. There are two ways we can look at that game. They can be more determined and positive, or they can be negative and allow Munster to take control.

(April 20, 2001)

LIKE ALL KNOCKOUT games the 2001 Heineken Cup semi-final came down to fine margins. In the run-in to the game memories sharpened.

Anthony Foley: As this game gets closer the wounds from last year have started to open again. The hurt is starting to come back out. You look at the score, 9-8 and think 'Jeez… one kick', but then you realise you've got a chance again this year. If you get a second chance to rectify something that didn't go the way you felt it should have gone, you take it.

(April 22, 2001)

WORD GAMES WERE over. But there was an unprepared look to the Munster pack. David Wallace hadn't played in nine weeks. Donncha O'Callaghan was making his European debut. Foley had one and a half games in that same nine weeks. Behind the pack, Peter Stringer had two and a half games, O'Gara only three, in that same damning time-span.

Munster would lose because they were not good enough. Bad luck and lousy luck of course played a part, but so too did their coach who had failed to overcome the daunting odds. Declan Kidney would have to learn from a stinging 16-15 loss to John Connolly's Stade Francais.

They were 16-6 in arrears at half-time. Six of those points were needlessly coughed up by trying to run the ball out of defence leaving Jason Holland and John Hayes isolated and then penalised for not releasing. That hurt. So too did Munster coughing up a dozen of their own lineouts and scrums. In addition, Ronan O'Gara's three missed penalties – one into the wind, one from halfway almost, and the third a kick that looked to have curled inside a far upright before being hesitantly decreed wide. There was also a try that John O'Neill was certain he had grounded but was ruled against by the referee.

All of it, a question of misfortune?

The ERC had not deemed the game worthy of a fourth official, a spokesman for the organisers attempting to explain… 'one of the reasons being because of the various different stadia. Some have the capacity to do it, others don't. It also involves the presence or otherwise of television'. Privately, one ERC official admitted that the cost of a TMO, reckoned to be in the £15,000-20,000 bracket, was simply prohibitive.

Bad luck?

Lousy luck?

Coaching not quite at the highest level?

A kicker without a perfectly chilled bloodstream?

O'Gara kicked points in the 49th and 71st and 79th minutes in the second-half to bring Munster to within one single point. But once again, O'Gara learned that it was easy enough to kick them when a game looked lost. An entirely different story with a game on the line.

2001-2002

'I just gave them back their own words. They knew what to do. They're an intelligent group, and they did it. I sound a bit like an echo really.'

– Declan Kidney
(April 29, 2002)

MICK GALWEY HAD played in all 36 of Munster's European games. 'It's a good record to have,' he joked with journalists. 'I've been lucky to stay healthy and avoid injuries during the last six years, and it's important not to be dropped.' The Kerryman who had become a Munsterman first and foremost knew it had been a long hard road. His journey was almost finished and as he looked ahead to another season, and looked behind him, he cited defeats more quickly than victories. Defeats hurt. Defeats strengthened a team.

Galwey talked about the 60-19 loss to Toulouse in Munster's second European campaign all those years ago and, still, stressed to those listening to him that going into that game the team had believed that they could win.

'I suppose we were naïve,' he admitted. 'They just came at us 100 miles an hour on a warm day in the south of France.'

Six years later, the belief in Galwey and his men had grown.

But there is a powerful self-belief in every team.

And then there is an *absolute* belief.

An *absolute* belief within a team that it can not lose. Munster were not there yet. Declan Kidney had a team with the biggest heart in the world. And that, perhaps, was Munster's greatest strength, and weakness.

Mick Galwey: We've underachieved a little maybe, we haven't won any major competition. Okay, we've won the Interpros a few times and okay we've scored some victories and some moral wins, but we've nothing to show for it. All of the lads know that there is more potential in the squad. I do believe that Munster will win the Heineken Cup. I just hope I'll be around for it, that it happens sooner rather than later. Some teams are just meant to win things, like Kerry in the All-Ireland, or Kilkenny, they will win another All-Ireland before long.

Every year the Munster team is better. We're catching up with the likes of Leicester and Stade Francais. They may have bigger budgets but what we have is special. Our day will come.

(September 29, 2001)

GALWEY WOULD NEVER get his giant hands on the Heineken Cup. By the close of the 2001-2002 season there was another European final. Leicester stood between Kidney's team and their destiny. The likes of Mick Galwey believed that it was Munster's turn, but none of them, and not their coach, understood that winners do not take turns.

Winners have an absolute belief that presents itself when it matters most.

Though their captain was right. Munster were building. They had lost Keith Wood and Eddie Halvey the year before, but they were gaining. John Langford was returning from Australia for one more shot, and he was bringing with him his fellow countryman, Jim Williams, a man who knew what it took to win on the world stage and also in the Super 12 with ACT Brumbies. Williams would feel at home within weeks.

Jim Williams: One of the reasons I came here to Munster was that they have been so consistent in the European Cup and in the Interpros and everything. It's been fantastic from a personal viewpoint. There are not as many staff involved (in Munster), like personal trainers and stuff like that, but on the whole there is not a great difference. In terms of the way the game is played, conditions do play a part in how the football game goes. Obviously, you don't get a chance to play French sides and Welsh teams back home and it is considerably different playing these types of sides. Playing against teams from South Africa and New Zealand the game is very quick and the physical side of things isn't as great but over here, it is very physical.

It's a little more physical in the tight as well as out wide. It does make for a much tougher game sometimes.

(December 15, 2001)

WILLIAMS WAS ONE new face. There were more fresh faces taking up room around the place: Paul O'Connell, Conor Mahony, Conrad O'Sullivan, Mossie Lawlor, Martin Cahill, Peter Malone, Denis Leamy, and Frank Murphy. One or two amongst them would have a belief that would surpass Mick Galwey's, and would indeed become *absolute*.

Declan Kidney would have choices to make like never before in a new season, and with the IRFU deciding to offer full-time contracts to 30 players in each province, he knew there would be a new, stronger dynamic at work within the squad. 'This season we will have good back-up,' he outlined. 'And this will allow an opportunity to rest players without hopefully affecting the team's performances.' The pool stage in another European campaign would go to plan, pretty much, for him as Munster lost one in six and finished behind Castres, and ahead of Harlequins (and an emotional Keith Wood) and Bridgend. Only a loss to Leinster, one week before Christmas, when the men in blue demonstrated a greater killer instinct at the death of the Celtic League final, was a legitimate source of worry.

It was three months work that led Munster straight back, face-to-face with Stade Francais whom they would play in the quarter-final at Stade Jean Bouin.

Keith Wood: I am a Munsterman, but I have been at Quins for five years and I feel strongly about the club. It'll be a strange afternoon, but I am very, very excited.

(October 6, 2001)

Keith Wood: Munster played very low-error rugby. They had great defence, time after time, and then pounced on our mistakes. It's clinical rugby, which Munster is fully capable of doing.

(October 8, 2001)

‖‖ ▮ ▮ ‖‖

SUDDENLY, DECLAN KIDNEY was a far busier man than he had ever imagined at the start of the season. He was 41 years-old with a young family. He had Munster under his wing, and in the first week of December he was appointed assistant-coach to the Irish team. He agreed to see out Munster's season and work under Eddie O'Sullivan. The man out of the picture was Warren Gatland.

Gatland was ousted, swiftly in the end, to bring a halt to a three and a half years reign that took in 38 games. The end also came soon enough after a disrupted Six Nations Championship was finally concluded and one that saw Ireland, despite going down lamely to the Scots, win four Championship games. Ireland had inflicted England with their only defeat in 15, and their biggest haul since the Grand Slam of 1948 actually would have left Gatland's team as champions had the rules of the European Cup applied.

Irish rugby was becoming cold-blooded. More was being demanded of coaches. More and more, as O'Sullivan would discover, and after him Declan Kidney! But, first there was the thorny matter of O'Sullivan and Kidney seeking to build a winning partnership as national coaches.

Philip Browne (IRFU Chief Executive): We fully acknowledge the progress that has been made to date. Inevitably it was a very difficult decision and not taken lightly. It's disappointing for Warren and difficult for us.

(December 1, 2001)

IN HIS MEMOIR, *Never Die Wondering* (2009) Eddie O'Sullivan looked back and supposed the arrangement (twinning himself and Declan Kidney) had been 'an artificial one'. O'Sullivan understood both men were ambitious, and he wondered if the Union had ever thought through exactly how they might work together. O'Sullivan thought the working relationship was difficult for both men. He further admitted that he was suspicious, from day one, that such would be the case.

KIDNEY AND O'SULLIVAN had different thoughts on the game that turned out to be difficult to contain on the same page. O'Sullivan was also a Munster man, and like his new assistant a half-back in his playing days, but his working relationship with Kidney would not turn out to be the greatest double-act in the history of Irish rugby.

They also presented themselves differently. Kidney still looked like a schoolteacher. O'Sullivan looked fit as a fiddle, and long before the game ever had thoughts of turning professional he had earned himself the monicker 'Beach Boy' within the Garryowen squad because of his interest in building up muscle. A meeting with Tony Ward had gravitated him towards Garryowen. His first club was his home town club, Youghal, and he had studied physical education, maths and science at Thomond College, before breaking into the Munster squad and reaching the summit of his representative career, one Ireland B cap. 'I didn't have a problem with that,' he admitted to journalists, 'I thought Crossan and Ringland were marvellous wingers. I just came along at the wrong time maybe.'

Coaching, like it was for Declan Kidney, was in O'Sullivan's blood during his own playing days. Before becoming one of the first IRFU Development Officers in 1989 he was already doing his bit in his adopted county, in Monivea in Galway. In '89 George Hook asked him to assist with Connacht, and he had remained involved with the province as assistant or head coach for the next six years. In his final year out West he also took up the role as Blackrock head coach. His CV would include the US Eagles and assistant to Warren Gatland in Ireland. He'd been in a No.2 role for many years, and therefore stressed to journalists that he would be able to work with Declan Kidney as his No.2.

Eddie O'Sullivan: There is a tradition in coaching in Europe that there's only one voice on the field and when one person is talking only one person can talk and when you interject as a coach you're undermining the leader. I don't buy into that at all. I used to buy into it because I was brought up that way, but America showed me that if everybody is contributing it's better.

(January 19, 2002)

HE HAD HELPED Gatland get the Irish team to third place in the Championship two years previously, and to second place the year before. From day one, the pressure was on Eddie O'Sullivan to continue the climb. Six tries and a 54-10 trouncing of Wales in the opening game of the 2002 Championship reflected well on Eddie and his team on the sideline with him. The lineouts reflected well on Niall O'Donovan, the backs effective running game on Kidney, and the defence on Mike Ford. It was a good first day in the office for Eddie and his 13 official helpers. Afterwards, flanked by his captain, Mick Galwey, Kidney and manager Brian O'Brien, the new Irish boss reflected on the victory and his team's first try, when David Wallace combined with Geordan Murphy. Was it dreamt up on the training field by himself and his new assistant?

Eddie O'Sullivan: I'd have taken 1-0 at ten to two this afternoon, the way the wind was blowing. We do practice things you know. It was all done on the training ground. It was a good trailer. You put guys in holes and run trailers off them.

(February 4, 2002)

THIRTEEN DAYS LATER it was Ireland on the opposite end of a massacre. England 45, Ireland 11. Two years of hard work, that totaled eight Championship wins out of 10 and just five defeats in 13 games, looked tiny in Twickenham as Clive Woodward's team, on their way to winning the World Cup soon enough, put on an all-singing, all-dancing display of rugby football. Six unanswered tries. And a Jonny Wilkinson masterclass.

Mick Galwey: It was a hard lesson for us. Every one of our players to a man had to put up their hands and say that they didn't perform. The best team won by a long shot. It's now a test of the team to see what it's made of in responding to this defeat.

(February 17, 2002)

Declan Kidney: This game can be a bit of an emotional roller-coaster. In the same way when you can't get carried away when you win a match, you can't allow yourself to get overly depressed if you lose a match.

(February 17, 2002)

WITHIN THE NEXT month the 35 year-old Galwey would be dropped for the 15th time in his 41-match Test career. It was a big call for O'Sullivan, an even bigger decision to stand over for Declan Kidney and Niall O'Donovan as they watched their Munster leader (and winning Irish captain) getting the heave-ho. Three Brian O'Driscoll tries saw a 43-22 win over Scotland, that was followed by a double scores victory against the Italians, quickly followed by Galwey's demotion, and followed again by the returning Irish captain, Keith Wood scoring the solitary points in a 44-5 loss in the Stade de France that positioned Ireland all alone, and back in third place in the Championship table. A headline in *The Irish Times* read, '**Gatland Not To Blame For This Season**.' The sub-heading read, '**Far from raising the bar, the new management team has seen it lowered in the Championship**.' The media had taken its gloves off.

In June Ireland headed to New Zealand for two Tests in a brief tour. A brave enough 15-6 loss in Dunedin in which O'Sullivan suddenly asked his men to play a blitz defence and 'go after the All Blacks like mad dogs' had almost worked, except Ronan O'Gara missed four kicks at goal, and Ireland slipped up twice in defence. The next Saturday, in Auckland, the dogs were sent home whimpering with a 40-8 loss, but the home team had help from Alan Quinlan who was sent onto the field with 20 minutes remaining and one score between the teams, and duly stamped on an opponent in the first ruck he met and received a yellow card.

Mick Galwey: It's disappointing to be left out after being captain of a winning team but that's the way the cookie crumbles. In fairness to the management, they let me know where I stand. There were times in the past when I felt I could have done a better job than the player who I was replaced with but I know I'm not going to last forever and I don't have any problem about Paul O'Connell being picked. He's the future of Irish rugby and if there is consolation, that's it.

(March 15, 2002)

||||█|█||||

ROB HENDERSON HAD left England and the Premiership behind him at the end of the previous season, and signed up with Kidney and his men in Munster for three years. He was 29 years-old. He knew what he wanted. And he knew what he would be getting from the Munster coach. Like, he'd get to watch the movie, *The Lion King* with his new teammates as they drove to the ground a couple of hours before vital European knockout games. Kidney especially fancied one scene in the movie. In it a monkey hits a lion over the head with a stick.

'Ow, what's that for?' asks the lion.

The monkey replies, 'It doesn't matter, it's in the past. The past can hurt, but you can either run from it or learn from it.'

Anthony Foley and the lads in Munster had grown to expect nothing less from their coach, or his way of turning events on their heads, especially events that looked to have the potential to poke the Munster team in the eye.

Foley called it 'Kidneyisms'.

Rob Henderson: The timing is right. I've won leagues and cups with Wasps, but this offers me the chance to try something new with a good squad, who have good back-up staff and a good coach. It's the perfect opportunity. I'm playing well and hopefully I can help bring some success to the team and they can bring some to me. I think it's a fabulous move and I'm really looking forward to it.

(April 10, 2001)

WHILE HE WAS predisposed to *The Lion King*, Kidney also had a choice of inspirational material aimed at his players. This included stronger stuff, such as Marianne Williamson's... *Return to Love, Reflections on the Principles of 'A Course in Miracles'* (Harper Paperbacks, 1996).

'Our deepest fear is not that we are inadequate. Our deepest fear is that we are powerful beyond measure. It is our light, not our darkness, that most frightens us. We ask ourselves, Who am I to be brilliant, gorgeous, talented, fabulous? Actually, who are you not to be? You are a child of God. Your playing small does not serve the world. There's nothing enlightened about shrinking so that other people won't feel insecure around you. We are all meant to shine, as children do. We were born to make manifest the glory of God that is within us. It's not just in some of us; it's in everyone.'

Williamson's lines – which appear in a famous speech in the movie *Coach Carter* – were kept by Kidney until the hours before his team faced Biarritz and duly claimed their first European title.

KIDNEYISMS WERE IN rich supply in the spring of 2002, as Munster found themselves with back-to-back trips to France in the quarter-final and semi-final of the Heineken Cup. The quarter-final was Game Three against Stade Francais in the same number of years, and the scoreline stood at 1-1. More than that, it looked the defining game in the respective careers of the opposing coaches. Each had narrowly failed to already win a European Cup, and both Kidney and Stade's John Connolly were about to vacate their respective positions at season's end. Before their semi-final, Munster actually got around to naming Declan Kidney's successor, 55 years-old Leinster assistant Alan Gaffney.

Alan Gaffney: I've had two great years at Leinster, and they've been the best guys I've ever worked with in rugby in terms of administration, management and players. I mean that sincerely, it was very difficult to leave, but it's a great opportunity and a great honour to be asked to coach Munster. Munster have probably been the highest performing team in Europe over the last three or four years. It's a very tall mountain, but they're not far from the top of it. It's going to be a challenge and Declan will be a hard act to follow.

(April 18, 2002)

Christophe Juillet (Stade Francais captain): Munster will want revenge for last year's semi-final in Lille, but we too have a bad taste in our mouth after losing out in last year's final so we very much want to get back there to put our record straight.

I find Munster have opened up their game a lot more this season which has weakened them somewhat. Last year they played a very tight game and it was more difficult to play against them. Last season our game was largely based around the set-piece and defence whereas this year we have used our backs well and scored a lot of tries.

(January 26, 2002)

MUNSTER LED 16-3 at the interval in Stade Jean Bouin after enjoying the benefit of a near gale that blew down the pitch. Nobody wearing a red jersey amongst the 12,000 packed crowd was certain that it was enough. In fact, it looked insufficient. The home team, in Diedo Dominguez, had a kicker who could close his eyes and bang them over from 60 metres. Kidney gathered his players around him in the dressing room. 'Do you want to try to defend the lead, or attack?' he asked them. Munster's subsequent defence was Alamo-like, certainly, but they only allowed Stade three try scoring chances and blotted each of them out. It was 16-14 at the finish – a late finish as referee Nigel Whitehouse played 45 minutes in the second-half.

Declan Kidney: The team decided that they would attack and that takes courage. Ultimately that is how we won the game. We tried to control possession and apart from a couple of lapses of concentration we didn't give them too much encouragement.

(January 28, 2002)

Anthony Foley: The discipline was awesome. We could not afford to give away any penalties in the second-half against someone (Dominguez) who could kick them from his own 10-metre line. We played as a unit. Everyone stepped forward and did what was required. We put up with the sly punches, the sly digs. We kept our cool, focused on what we wanted to achieve and produced our best performance for a long time.

(January 28, 2002)

BY THE END of April, it was boiling in the south of France. Castres awaited in the semi-final in Beziers. Kidney had his team locked up in their own private chateau, though the coach referred to it as a house really, 'a B and B'. It was a B and B with enough drinking water to fill an Olympic-sized swimming pool. And cold towels were in plentiful supply every hour of the day. The team's kit manager, Noel 'Buddha' Healy had set off several days before anyone else in his red van emblazoned with MUNSTER RUGBY. And there was more colour on its way as Kidney had had a word with sponsors, Bank of Ireland who had issued all supporters leaving Cork and Shannon with red berets and baseball caps.

Declan Kidney: We chose (the chateau) because it has air conditioning and because we were trying to get the right food and nutritional requirements, carbohydrates mostly. Every country has its own style of food and this chateau was willing to accommodate us. Other hotels are more geared towards holidays and we didn't want a holiday mode.

(April 26, 2002)

THE 25-17 VICTORY over Castres, in the fifth meeting between the teams in under 18 months, was a coming of age afternoon for Donncha O'Callaghan, who until then, had more people believing in him every time he wore the white of Cork Constitution in the AIL, than Munster's proud red. He was sent into the game by Kidney after 15 minutes, and commenced the greatest hour of his young life for his province. An injury to Jim Williams got him back into the squad 22. Then a belt to Anthony Foley got him onto the field. There he joined Paul O'Connell, who was also lucky to be playing. A shoulder injury had left him in some doubt, but the day before the game Kidney made up his mind to find out for himself about O'Connell. He took him out to the field personally for a fitness test.

Kidney ordered two quick press-ups.

O'Connell managed one.

Kidney told him that he would not be doing press-ups in the game anyhow, and ordered him to hit a tackle bag. O'Connell needed to impress at the second attempt. He hit the bag hard. His head came up and struck the coach on the face. Turned out one of Kidney's front teeth had been knocked out of his mouth.

Kidney picked up the tooth.

He put the tooth in his pocket and told O'Connell he was ready to play against Castres the next day.

Donncha O'Callaghan: You see Gaillimh crying at half-time as he was speaking to us, that would shake you to the bones. You see a fella like that, who it means so much to, you have to give it everything. It was quite funny to find myself out there, that early in the game. Then there was the sin-binning (of Peter Clohessy) so I was back off, so I really had to keep a level head on the whole thing. The play was broken up a lot as well and I was lucky that little things went my way. The lads were very good too in helping me out. I grabbed a hold of Quinny (at the final whistle) and it was quite weird. I was holding him and thinking, 'I could be beating the daylights out of him next week in the AIL final.

(April 29, 2002)

Mick Galwey: It's going to be heavy stuff. It's going to be emotional stuff, and I'm emotional at the best of times, so I don't want to think about that. I know that when we're in there, that's the way it's going to be, but at the same time we can't get carried away with that either. We have to keep steady heads, because we're going to have play better than we have ever done before, it's as simple as that. We don't have to hide from that. It's a fact.

(May 25, 2002)

||||■|■||||

THE 2002 HEINEKEN Cup final is remembered only for Neil Back's cheap infringement at the bitter end when he knocked the ball out of Peter Stringer's hands as he was about to roll it into a Munster scrum. What happened before that incident has been long forgotten.

All of it forgotten, everything that had led to Leicester's 15-9 advantage – and making the Tigers only the second team to lift the trophy twice. Two penalties from O'Gara had Munster off to a perfect start and winning 6-0 after 20 minutes. A timely dummy from Tim Stimpson allowed Geordan Murphy in for the first of Leicester's two tries. The conversion sailed wide. Munster dominated, but their lineout was dreadful. The scrum was doing better and after Leicester were penalised for not binding, O'Gara stretched the lead to 9-5. When O'Gara missed his man, Austin Healy in front of the posts and Stimpson added the points, Leicester got their noses in front. Leicester collapsed another scrum but O'Gara failed to level up the game. Stimpson kicked three more points. And that's how it stood when Neil Back acted.

Neil Back: I'm quite at peace with myself. That's part of the professional game. That wasn't the turning point, that wasn't the way we won it. We scored two fantastic tries so we deserved to win. Obviously it was a risk. I weighed it up and fortunately it went our way. I did what I felt was necessary to secure possession for Leicester when we were under extreme pressure at the end and I used all my experience of playing club and international football to ensure we won the game. I'm not a cheat. I'm a very committed player and if anyone called me a cheat I would be very upset. I've played first-class rugby for over a decade, you learn things along the way. I don't think you should make a big issue out of it. We won the contest and that's what it was all about. I think if you ask any back row player, they have all done it in their career. I don't make a habit of it, but it was the right thing to do.

(May 27, 2002)

Peter Stringer: It's something that I've never really come across. The ball was hit out of my hand as I was putting it into the scrum. The referee didn't see it but we were disappointed as a whole losing the final. It was one decision that went against us but as a whole it just didn't go our way on the day. I thought the touch judge (Joel Dume) might have seen it but obviously he didn't. It's one of these things that you don't expect. You automatically assume you'll be allowed to put the ball into a scrum.

(May 27, 2002)

Declan Kidney: No comment, really. No, I don't have... no comment.

(May 27, 2002)

Dean Richards: At the end of the day it was a decision by Neil, who I believe to be a winner. You may cast him as a cheat, but if you do you're going to cast anybody who gave away a penalty today as a cheat. Was it any different to the way Clohessy was scrummaging? Neil Back made a decision for Leicester rugby and I have no problem with that. At the end of the day it was part of the winning process for us.

(May 27, 2002)

Martin Johnson: I don't really know what happened, the ball just seemed to shoot back to our half and I was glad to see it.

(May 27, 2002)

Neil Back: In a way, I wish I hadn't done it. I have to be honest about it. I don't like people thinking that I'm a cheat. I don't want that slur. I'm not a cheat. I had a lot of mail over that incident, mostly negative. There were letters saying I was a cheat. Some of them from Leicester fans, which was a bit hurtful. If people wanted to make me feel bad about what happened, they have. That's disappointing and I know it upset my wife, Alison. If I thought there was any possible way of redressing it, I would consider it. I regret it, because I don't like to think that, because of that one incident, there are people who think I'm a cheat. It has tarnished my reputation. In making any judgment, I would hope that people will evaluate me over my whole career and not label me on that one moment. It happened spontaneously. I weighed the options up in a split-second and did what I did.

(January 27, 2009)

2002-2003

'We have a brilliant natural resource with an awful lot of rugby players in the country. In fact I think in the country overall we're unbelievable how many sports people we turn out for the size of us, yet we can be very harsh on one another and criticising one another. But if you have such a good natural resource you need to take care of it and not abuse it, so that it doesn't turn sour.'

Declan Kidney
(May 6, 2000)

EDDIE O'SULLIVAN AND Declan Kidney parted company after the 2004 Six Nations. O'Sullivan admitted in his autobiography, *Never Die Wondering* that the two of them were never going to go in history as inseparable as 'Clough and Taylor' or 'Redgrave and Pinsent'. He knew that their marriage had been 'arranged' and that this was the flaw in the beginning that had always kept them apart. O'Sullivan came to understand and honestly admit that it was probably unfair on both men.

WHEN EDDIE O'SULLIVAN began collaborating with Vincent Hogan of the *Irish Independent* on his memoir nobody in Ireland imagined that a Grand

Slam was about to land. The book was published in the autumn of 2009, a handful of months after Declan Kidney delivered to the IRFU and the people of Ireland a first such momentous 'Slam' after a 61 years wait. It wasn't the best of timing for Eddie. His seven years and his Triple Crown successes – and his Championship near-misses – were swept away by the tsunami of emotion that followed Kidney's achievement in the spring of 2009 of finally delivering the big one. Declan Kidney, of course, while he was still on the field, minutes after his team had clinched the title with a clean sweep, was big-hearted in remembering what Eddie had done. It was Kidney at his most stylish, side-stepping his role as national hero.

CHAPTER 19 OF O'Sullivan's memoir was titled 'DECLAN AND ME' and, while only five pages long, it told a story of two good men in an uncomfortable working relationship. O'Sullivan was at pains to make known on page one of the chapter that there never had been any 'profound' difference between the two men. Though on page two he suggested a divide in their personalities. He found Kidney 'forensic in discussion' and willing to tease 'arguments out exhaustively' and determined to reach a targeted bottom line no matter the growing impatience of others in the room. O'Sullivan found him bright and brilliantly organised and, very simply, 'not suited out to be a number two'.

On the training field, there was another problem. Kidney's official role within the management team was to coach the backline. But O'Sullivan's favoured job of all in his multi-layered role as head coach was also coaching the backline. After the 2003 World Cup O'Sullivan finally took the tough decision to go to their bosses, the IRFU, and tell them that his partnership with Kidney was not working.

The pair did not socialise together, which was no big deal. But in his chapter on their working relationship O'Sullivan did come clean on page three and confessed that he found Kidney 'draining'. O'Sullivan wanted to take more control, be more hands-on. He wanted to let his number two go. He actually made his views known to Kidney before the 2004 Six Nations, even though Kidney's contract with the IRFU ran until the following July. The Union acted upon O'Sullivan's wishes.

In February Declan Kidney was offered the job of 'Performance Manager, Age Grade Rugby'. Effectively more of a schoolteacher behind a desk, and a strange career move for one of the top coaches in the European game. Kidney declined. He remained O'Sullivan's assistant for the 2004 Championship – and, in those final months, their working relationship was under more strain than ever in their two seasons spent glued together.

On page four of the same chapter O'Sullivan explained that Kidney sought a meeting with him immediately after the conclusion of the 2004 Championship, and on page five – the last page of the chapter – O'Sullivan admitted that 'some of what I said was diplomatic, some wasn't'.

|||▐▌▐▌|||

BACK HOME IN Munster there was a Heineken Cup to be wrestled with and, in the absence of Declan Kidney and Niall O'Donovan, a real estate businessman from Sydney had lots of shoes to try and fill. Alan Gaffney's primary gifts were different to Kidney. In his five years in charge Kidney had been 'The Master' as much as 'The Coach', always looking to work minds, and primarily getting players to work their own minds in a way that might never have occurred to them before. Gaffney's genius was coaching individual skills.

Alan Gaffney: Mate, I think the Leinster guys are absolutely right, because they (Munster) are great guys. They've got a lot of fun in them, a lot of craic, but when it's got to be done they just do the job. A few things have got to be twigged or changed here and there, but they know where they want to be. They have been close to the mountain top, and they want to get there. They've still got the desire.

(August 24, 2002)

Gaffney, or 'Gaff', had to buy into the Munster ethos as quickly as possible, but finding the secret ingredients was not all that simple. He asked Mick Galwey what was the Munster X-factor?

Galwey replied that he had absolutely no idea.

But it didn't take a prized gumshoe to get to work on what Declan Kidney had achieved in the dressing room in his five years. Gaffney got to work. As the son of a bookmaker, and after growing into a man on the more hard-nosed rugby league paddocks, he did not slouch in getting to grips with his team's character.

Gaffney was also an out-half, like his predecessor, serving Randwick through the 1960s and 70s, though injuries curtailed his achievements and he drifted away from the game. Real estate became his life. And it remained so until famed Australian coach Bob Dwyer lured Gaffney back into the game, and into coaching Randwick, where he remained for 13 years. He then assisted Matt Williams at New South Wales, but remained on a part-time basis, still tending to his 'house' business.

At the turn of the millennium, Williams talked Gaffney into making the trek to Leinster and leaving two grown up children back home in Sydney.

Alan Gaffney: I was getting absolutely sick of what I'd been doing in Sydney for 30-odd years. We had to be successful (in Ireland) or I'd be tipped out and I didn't know what I'd go back to, but it's worked out really well.

(August 24, 2002)

MUNSTER WAS IN Aussie hands, on and off the field in Kidney's absence. Aussie coach and Aussie captain! Though one of those pairs of hands was of Declan Kidney's making.

Jim Williams was a former winger, and a king of the back row, as Kidney discovered when he had spent some time down under in 2001 watching The Lions, and making it his business to go and see the ACT Brumbies play the visitors in Canberra. Together, Gaffney and Williams steered Munster through to the quarter-finals of the Heineken Cup in 2003 the hardest way – out on the road.

Munster had shared top spot in their pool with Perpignan and Gloucester, but earned a seventh seeding for the knockouts. There, they met Leicester Tigers in Welford Road. In the absence of Declan Kidney, revenge of some description was on offer for the heartbreaking loss in the final the year before. A 20-7 victory propelled Munster into the last four, and to Toulouse where they would again have their European dream left dangling after a single point (13-12) defeat.

ALAN GAFFNEY WOULD try everything he knew to win the big one for Munster. His second season had a five points quarter-final win over old enemies Stade Francais (37-32) and a five points loss (32-37) to Wasps in Lansdowne Road. Year Three would come to a halt in the quarter-finals when Biarritz stood strong over a 19-10 scoreline in San Sebastian.

It was time for Gaffney to head home. He took up an offer to be part of the Australian coaching staff. He had one trophy to show for his three years in Munster. But as his players did a lap of honour after beating Llanelli Scarlets in the Celtic League final, Shaun Payne had a word with Anthony Foley.

'This doesn't feel right,' commented Payne, 'we're parading the wrong trophy.'

❘❘❘❘❘❘❘❘❘❘

NIALL O'DONOVAN had to get used to the new regime on the national stage as well. Like Declan Kidney he had to remove his Munster hat. That hat had been such a tight, perfect fit for both men. But now 'Niallo', as he was known within the Munster family, was Ireland forwards coach. The pair of them had so little time to get to grips with their responsibilities during the 2002 Six Nations, but at the start of a whole new season only Ireland was their responsibility.

Niall O'Donovan: It's a huge difference from what I had been accustomed. Winning at club and provincial level doesn't prepare you for this. At national level you are far more in the limelight. There is a lot more focus on you. The big difference is trying to get used to that. Everything is analysed in far greater detail and when things go wrong, as the lineouts did for a while last season, the focus can be very damaging. It was like a domino effect. The lineouts were criticised, the hookers got uptight, you were trying to get them to relax and all the while hoping you came out the far side. You know that the problems can be rectified, it's just a question of having the time and space to do it.

There was no way that I could simply come in and start changing everything around immediately. I actually tried not to change too much, just to concentrate on getting things right. For some of the games it came right, in others it most definitely did not. I'd say the tour to New Zealand was the first time that all of us coaches could work with the players on an individual basis and on a unit basis as well.

Last season was a funny season for me in the sense that I was still involved with Munster. I was really double jobbing up until the end of May. Doing both last season was a strain on both teams and me. This job on its own is demanding so to try and piggy-back something on top, it just wasn't on really.

(November 22, 2002)

WHATEVER ELSE, THE Irish head coach and his number two did get to see the World together. Ireland's defeat in the 1999 World Cup play-off against Argentina in Lens meant that the team had to pre-qualify for the 2003 tournament. Amongst other places, Eddie O'Sullivan and Declan Kidney got to travel to Siberia together.

They had to cross seven time zones to get to Krasnoyarsk, Russia's chosen venue, but a place more familiar as a junction on the chuckling Trans-Siberian Railway. For the 14 hours in the air, everyone, coaches and their players, were squeezed into an elderly jet chartered by the IRFU, knees against chins.

Ireland won 35-3, but only raced away from the home team in the final quarter. Keith Wood had nailed one of the tries as usual, but he had also damaged a disc in his neck and on the return flight west he was deeply uncomfortable. That was the bad news from Siberia. There was also good news.

Ireland was about to get a new captain who was going to stick around as the team's leader for a long time. The following week Ireland defeated Georgia 63-14 at Lansdowne Road. In the autumn series, Australia, Fiji and Argentina looked like serious opposition for O'Sullivan, Kidney, O'Donovan and Co, but the past was the past as the team was named for the first game and Brian O'Driscoll became the youngest Irish captain since Rob Saunders led the country out against France in 1991.

Despite his 30 caps, and the experience of a Lions tour, O'Driscoll explained that his only duty as captain before then had been UCD's under-20s.

Brian O'Driscoll: I had a few talks with Eddie about it, and whether I was comfortable about it or not. Essentially I thought about it over the weekend and spoke to my father about it, and I thought it was too good an opportunity to pass up. The role of the team captain is to talk when you need to, not to talk for the sake of it, and I'll certainly be adopting that approach.

(November 6, 2002)

IRELAND HAD NOT beaten one of the southern hemisphere big three since 1979, but O'Driscoll and his men managed that against the Aussies (18-9), and also scalped Fiji (64-17) and looming World Cup foe Argentina (16-7). After the first of those wins the team jogged and walked a lap of honour to U2's *Beautiful Day*.

All seemed so good for Irish rugby. In 25 attempts Ireland had not beaten the game's superpowers. Australia alone had reeled off 11 successive victories until Ronan O'Gara out-gunned Matt Burke six penalties to three.

Eddie Jones (Australia coach): We knew that at Lansdowne Road the sun was not going to be bearing down on our backs but in those conditions our skill levels let us down. We have had two games in the wet this year, the other was against the All Blacks in Christchurch, when we have struggled.

(November 11, 2002)

Brian O'Driscoll: I spoke to Keith (Wood) after the game and he was delighted and at least we have buried that tag of nearly-men. We nearly beat New Zealand this summer, and South Africa two years ago, but this will give us a lot of confidence and self-belief.

(November 11, 2002)

THE SIX NATIONS that followed saw Ireland continue to gallop. A 36-6 win over the Scots at Murrayfield was followed seven days later with a 37-13 win over Italy in Rome. David Humphreys was holding the No.10 jersey over Ronan O'Gara's head and he kicked four penalties as the French were squeezed out at Lansdowne Road (15-12). A one point (25-24) win over Wales in Cardiff, with O'Gara sweeping in for a late appearance and a winning dropped-goal, set up a crunch decider against Martin Johnson's World Cup winners to-be in Dublin.

Ronan O'Gara: With 15 minutes to go Declan (Kidney) told me to warm up. It's an awful place to be because at least if you start a match you're into a match straight away. After 60 minutes you're as nervous as anyone in the stand. But you've got to keep that out of your mind because I may go onto the pitch and it's not easy coming on like that, especially warming up and stopping, and warming up and stopping. It was a dodgy scoreline at that stage.

We were ahead by a point and they got an excellent drop-goal from long range, to be fair to them. I looked over and Drico couldn't talk he was so wrecked, so I badgered the referee to find out how much was left and he said two minutes. Which doesn't give you an awful lot of time, especially when they're at home and they were so pumped. I didn't expect it so quickly but with Strings inside you, you're always going to get the ball. I just struck it ahead. I was nearly directly in front. It kind of got shot halfway through its flight but it managed to stay on course to fall the right side from our point of view.

(March 24, 2003)

ON MARCH 30, Ireland had to rethink.

About mostly everything, beginning where to stand on the field for the national anthem after Martin Johnson decided that England should be boss for the whole day. President Mary McAleese was allowed no carpet to walk on to welcome both sides. Five tries were contained in the English win (42-6). But Ireland should have been a happy enough camp that evening. There was so much to build on from the 2002-2003 season.

Eight wins in total. Except, all was not as well or as unified as it appeared from the outside.

2003-2004

'I don't know anything about any article. I'm getting ready for a hugely important match on Saturday. It's a brilliant day for Paul O'Connell and I suppose the people who wrote that don't really know me, do they? I'd have to think hard about my life, but I'm not sure I've resigned from anything yet. I took on a job and I'll do it to the best of my ability.'

– Declan Kidney
(February 12, 2004)

BEFORE A BALL was spun 'down under' in the 2003 World Cup, Eddie O'Sullivan was handed a new four-year contract by the IRFU to take him through to the following tournament in France, in 2007. He was also given the freedom to choose his own back-up staff. It was no surprise that Declan Kidney was not on that list. By February of 2004, and a week before Ireland commenced the Six Nations Championship with a costly defeat (35-17) to France, Kidney's future in the game was up for discussion in newspapers and on radio. Almost round the clock.

There were rumours of his resignation from the national management team, which he quickly dispelled. 'I'm not going to go into a public debate about my future,' he stressed in a statement to the media, 'because I'm in negotiations with the Union and meetings have happened there.'

It transpired that the IRFU was creating a brand new spanking role in the game, one of a Performance Manager for Age Grade rugby, and they had designs on Kidney filling the position.

Declan Kidney: While obviously disappointed my current contract is not being renewed, I appreciate the offer of this new position from the Union. However, the offer in question is not a coaching position as such, therefore, while considering it, I will now be looking at all options open to me. In the meantime I will as usual be concentrating on fulfilling my obligations to the best of my ability in the best interest of the team.

(February 17, 2004)

Philip Browne (IRFU CEO): Declan would, of course, always be considered for any front-line coaching role that might become available in Irish rugby and in which he might be interested.

(February 17, 2004)

HIS FUTURE REMAINED the talk of the rugby town. Alan Gaffney and Michael Bradley looked more than secure in their head positions in Munster and Connacht, but South African Alan Solomons was not renewing his contract at Ulster. Gary Ella was closing out the first season of his three-year contract in Leinster but player disquiet had that head coaching position up in the air at the same time. Amongst clubs in England and Wales, it was a typical end of season merry-go-round. Leicester Tigers, it was murmured, had Kidney on their short-list and, with Dean Richards departed, heads turned when the Irish assistant-coach turned up in the middle of March at Welford Road to watch Geordan Murphy make a comeback from injury.

Kidney remained on the job with Ireland, excelling in his role and avoiding any distraction as best he could, and doing as much as anyone in Eddie O'Sullivan's management circle to see to it that Ireland's rich vein of form did not buckle after the disappointment of losing to the French. Four wins would indeed leave Ireland at French heels and in second place in the Championship's final standings, with Kidney's backline scoring 13 out of Ireland's total of 17 tries in the campaign. A famous win over England and a first Triple Crown in two decades were definitely his to share.

David Jenkins (Gwent Dragons CEO): Declan was a guest of ours for the Blues game. He came down to run the rule over the set-up and he is obviously a coach of the highest calibre. We are looking at a head coach with his reputation working with a young up-and-coming coach.

(April 20, 2004)

KIDNEY HAD BEEN in Newport to watch the Dragons defeat the Cardiff Blues and met with Jenkins and club owner, Tony Brown. A two-year contract was in the offing. In the first week of May 2004, the Dragons released an excited statement announcing the appointment. But Declan Kidney would never oversee his new Welsh team in a single competitive match.

Declan Kidney: I am very excited to be here, and I am relishing the task before me. Rugby in Gwent has very strong traditions, there is a great structure at the club and the players possess the ability to achieve great things. It is up to me to bring that out of them, and I will be working hard to do so. I have been very impressed with what I've seen, and there is a great base here to work from.

(May 7, 2004)

Tony Brown: I had no qualms about going outside Wales for a coach. Declan has a huge pedigree and hopefully we've got a man to move things forward.

(April 20, 2004)

IRFU BOSS PHILIP Browne spoke up the same day, outlining that the union had had protracted talks with Kidney and were keen for him to remain involved in Irish rugby. The Union said they respected his decision but press officer, John Redmond also briefed the media in explaining that Kidney, even though he was not taking up his position in Wales until August 1, would not be part of the Irish management team during their two Test tour of South Africa in June. Redmond also clarified that the position of assistant Ireland coach no longer existed.

Meanwhile, however, more than one man within the Leinster camp was flabbergasted that Declan Kidney had escaped the hands of the IRFU. Leinster wanted a new coach. Ella had not fitted into the job vacated by Matt Williams. They wanted Kidney still. And before the month of May was out, there was more talk all around town of the Dragons and Leinster possibly needing to agree on a compensation package. The talk was backed up by meetings, and fast action, and Declan Kidney was soon preparing another statement about his future as a coach.

Declan Kidney: I'd like to stress that Gwent Dragons have been brilliant in facilitating me. I was very happy and very excited about the challenge there. The unfortunate demise of the Warriors had a silver lining for the Dragons in that six or seven players were coming on board, many of them internationals. But the Leinster offer meant that I could be closer to my family. I had a duty to inform them (the Dragons) of this offer, and Tony Brown and their board understood the personal side of this dilemma. I had no problem in fulfilling my contract there but their understanding attitude was brilliant. They are extraordinarily good people.

I am looking forward to reacquainting myself with a lot of players who I've known from underage, the A team, and with the Ireland team over the last two and a half years. The few there I don't know are very exciting prospects, or else they wouldn't be there.

(May 27, 2004)

Mick Dawson (Leinster CEO): I assume he will have his own ideas and we've put a few names in the loop for him as well. Deccie is an outstanding coach with huge experience of the domestic, club and international game. Having secured the services of all our international players for the coming season, and with the number of quality young players coming through the system, I believe that Declan's expertise will help Leinster move forward.

(May 27, 2004)

Reggie Corrigan (Leinster captain): There's been a lot of talk going on with Leinster in the last couple of weeks, and speculation and everything else, and the decision was made earlier in the week that Gary (Ella) wouldn't be continuing with us anymore, so that left us in limbo a little bit as to who we were going to get. It was a bit of a nervy time and everyone was wondering, but now that it's been announced that it's somebody of Declan Kidney's calibre, it's unbelievable. I can't imagine anyone in the squad who wouldn't be happy with that decision. Most people have worked with him, they've had him at underage level. I think it's going to be a massive lift with the whole squad. Everyone will have the ultimate respect for him because he's been to two finals already and we'll be drawing on all his experience to try and get there.

(May 27, 2004)

ON AUGUST 20, 2004, a Friday evening in Castle Avenue, Declan Kidney's reign as Leinster coach began with a 16-13 win over Worcester thanks to tries from Shane Jennings and Clontarf full-back Dave Hewitt. Kidney and Leinster, however, was a marriage that would not last all that long.

‖‖▮‖‖

THE IRISH MANAGEMENT team was not shy in asking some remarkable people to visit their camp in the months prior to the 2003 World Cup finals. Sir Ranulph Fiennes, the famed explorer turned up in the team's Citywest Hotel base to talk to the players about all sorts of things, like being the first man to trek to the North and South Poles, being the first man to make the walk across the continent of Antarctica by foot, and about how sometimes men have to take charge of their own lives in different ways. His chat included mention of tidying up his finger stumps (his fingers having partially been lost through frostbite) in his own garden shed with a blade. Marvin Hagler, undisputed middleweight champ of the World for seven years in the 1980s, and a warrior who had gone toe-to-toe with Roberto Duran, Sugar Ray Leonard and Thomas 'Hitman' Hearns, also showed up and knocked some of the Irish players off their chairs with delight.

Hagler made sure the Irishmen sitting in front of him remembered, despite being star-struck, at least a few words from his mouth. 'STARVE THE DOUBT... FEED THE FAITH' he repeatedly told them.

Indeed, such memorable morsels of wisdom, were straight from the Declan Kidney pocketbook. One of Kidney's specials was mention of ice and fire.

Keep the brain 'on ice'.

Keep 'the fire' in the belly.

THE SUMMER PLANS in 2003 included a visit down under in June to play Australia, which was memorable to begin with for Frankie Sheahan failing a drugs test – the Munster hooker, an asthmatic, had levels of salbutamol in his system from using his ventolin inhaler which were too high and he had to return straight home and fight a two-year ban down to an acceptable three months. Ireland got thrashed 45-16 in a Test against the Aussies, and then Eddie O'Sullivan sent most of his first-choice players home.

The rest of the gang, and their management, embarked on more 'memories' and a trek through Tonga (40-19 to Ireland) and Samoa (40-14 to Ireland) that was remembered more for bad hotels, sickening food, and boiling temperatures than anything else. In the fine-tuning for the World Cup, however, O'Sullivan and Kidney watched their team beat Wales by 23 points, Italy by 56 points and Scotland by 19 points. Not for the first time, and certainly not the last, tails were up as Ireland set off to conquer the world in the autumn of 2003, expectations were high, and nobody dared imagine that a fall from a great height was around the corner. Ireland expected to beat Romania and Namibia. The Argentinians in Adelaide were considered the crunch opponents in order to secure a quarter-final place. Then Australia awaited.

Before departure the IRFU had seen fit to award O'Sullivan with a new contract which he considered a 'great shot in the arm' and a 'timely boost' for the team and the whole of the travelling party. The Union had not extended the same courtesy to either Kidney or forwards coach Niall O'Donovan.

With a World Cup awaiting, the Irish assistant coaches looked more vulnerable to results than the head coach.

Eddie O'Sullivan: The position would be that everyone will be up for review anyway at the end of this cycle. What Philip (Browne) has told me is that we'll wait till after the World Cup and into the new year, and we'll sit down and review the management situation. That's the position, he's the chief executive and that's what he wants to do.

I don't think it will be my decision but I think as the head coach I would have an input into what happens. Things have gone well, and I have to say that I'm very happy with the work we've achieved, and again there's decisions for the people who are on the staff as well; where they see their roles. So it's kind of an open door really.

(September 23, 2003)

AS THE DAYS counted down to the World Cup opening game against Romania in Gosford, Declan Kidney, even from his role as an assistant, had to work out in his head how to thread pool games and arrive fresh 'n' ready for a quarter-final. In the World Cup of 2003, getting to the last eight was a must for everyone in the Irish management team. The dream was to get to the last four for the first time in Irish rugby history. How to thread those early games, and then duly thread a quarter-final spot into the bargain, would prove an impossible task in 2003, just as it would again for O'Sullivan in 2007, and also for Kidney when he led Ireland into the 2011 tournament.

They were different men, and their styles and personalities were poles apart, but O'Sullivan and Kidney had the same dilemma. Though before the first game in 2003, they already had different thoughts.

Eddie O'Sullivan: I've used the old cliché of taking one game at a time, but there's four hurdles to be jumped in this pool and you can bet your bottom dollar that if you're looking at the third hurdle when you're jumping the first one you'll fall on your face.

(October 6, 2003)

Declan Kidney: You'll try and hold back something. You'll see what you have to use to get to wherever you have to go, and then see whatever else you have up your sleeve after that. But I don't think that makes us different to any other side. It will come down to whoever defends the best, but the referees will obviously have a part to play in that as well. The penalty count in all matches now is reducing. I think on average it is now about 22 to 24 penalties a match, so if eight of those are shots at goal then it might be the side who is scoring the tries that's going to come out on top.

They're (referees) quite consistent now, there's only going to be a certain number of referees (16) refereeing the matches, right through to the final stages, so everybody is going to get to know what to expect from them and we're not going to go out testing referees like we used to before. As a result, that will probably reduce the penalties.

(October 6, 2003)

Eddie O'Sullivan: We'll always struggle to produce 10 world-class players, but there was a time when Ireland struggled to produce 15 international players. Now we know we can produce 20 to 25 international players and sprinkled amongst those you're going to get a handful of World-class players. And that's what has probably made Irish rugby step forward in the last number of years.

(October 6, 2003)

Declan Kidney: All sides are coming from a background where they haven't been able to play a match for four weeks beforehand. So there's lots of anxiety, as Eddie (O'Sullivan) said, within the camp and fellas are going to have to keep that under control, but that's going to be the same for all teams. I think if you look at any World Cup, be it football or rugby, the first round (of matches) can be a small bit hit or miss but we're hoping to hit. We'll have to wait and see but that's our aim.

(October 8, 2003)

Eddie O'Sullivan: There's a sense of relief now that the team has been named and this is the line-up that's going into the first game, but with that comes pressure. So the sense of pressure is all on the guys who've been picked now to deliver a performance. They're the lucky 15 at the moment and it's a funny mixture. It's the first game of a World Cup so there's a lot of emotion there on top of a lot of hard work.

It's the people business that we are in, whether it's a company or a rugby team, it's pretty much the same. You've got to get everybody rowing the boat in the same direction, and have the same goals and aspirations. It's something within an Irish rugby team that you never have to work too hard at to be honest with you. In my experience of Irish rugby teams, whether it's going well or it's not going well, everybody puts their shoulder to the wheel and gets on with it.

(October 8, 2003)

SUCH WAS THE truth in the autumn of 2003, and getting on with it and putting their shoulders equally to the wheel was what Eddie O'Sullivan and Declan Kidney did. The Pumas were indeed beaten (16-15) but only thanks to an Alan Quinlan try and Ronan O'Gara dutifully coming off the bench late and nailing a penalty in true blue Rog style. In the Telstra Dome, as Ireland fought out an enthralling battle with the host nation, there were two routes to the semi-finals. The winners would meet Scotland. The losers got France. Ireland lost by a point to Australia (17-16). In the last eight, O'Sullivan and Kidney watched their team heroically score three tries in the second-half against the French and lose 43-21.

Brian O'Driscoll: I've been involved in three World Cups and I've got one quarter-final out of it. I wouldn't say that's anything to shout about and I don't want to finish my career having not achieved on the biggest stage. There's your motivation for me. I can't speak for everyone else, people have motivations for different reasons, but that's mine and I want to finish my last World Cup on a high and do something no other Irish side has done.

(August 31, 2011)

2004-2005

'I think that's a word (underachieved) that has been bandied about alright but who is anybody to say what anybody else does with their lives? Sometimes in this country we give teams different tags, (but) I haven't seen any players not try their best. And once every player tries their best that's all you can ask of them. They're (Leinster) a very good group to work with and that's what I'm looking forward to.'

– Declan Kidney
(August 4, 2004)

IN THE FIRST week of August, in his new Leinster t-shirt, and with a gold harp sitting over his heart, Declan Kidney posed with his new management team on his first week of duty in blue. The four men standing behind him, all of them with their arms folded across their chests, as they posed for photographs at the start of a new season, were all true blue Leinster men. Kidney with a broad smile on his face brought this to everyone's attention.

'A lot of Leinster fellas there!' he quipped. 'It wasn't just a question of them jumping on board. I think they all have Leinster at heart and I think that is a great starting base. Then if you add in the amount of experience they all have in the game, and the different areas where their experience comes from, once again I think I'm very fortunate to have them helping me to help the players to reach their full potential.'

Standing directly behind Kidney was Paul McNaughton, a former Greystones, Wanderers, Leinster and Irish inside centre. Behind him was Bobby Byrne, a former tight head prop, and a UCD, Blackrock College and Terenure College captain. Behind him was Gerry Murphy, a former Irish coach, who had also coached Wanderers and Clontarf. And, finally, behind him stood Roly Meates, another former national coach who, simply put, was a legend and known as Mr Leinster.

The 2004-2005 season would be successful. Leinster would rout everyone in their Heineken Cup pool, going unbeaten in Europe for the first time, and even though they came a cropper in their quarter-final against Leicester, it was still a breakthrough season. Except for what happened after that game against the Tigers in Lansdowne Road.

Declan Kidney was heading home!

Paul McNaughton: Because of either Munster's insistence, or whatever, that applications had to be in the Wednesday before the European Cup quarter-finals, or the European Challenge Cup semi-finals, and that the interviews had to be held the Tuesday after those games, it was a shambles. People may have different feelings about Declan going, but the whole process with details leaked publicly, and the nature of our defeat to Leicester exacerbated this.

There's every likelihood the new coach will be an overseas coach. The emphasis will be on getting the right person, rather than on getting a person quickly.

(April 16, 2005)

KIDNEY WAS LEFT looking into his own heart when he made the decision near the close of the season that he wanted his old job in Munster back – a job being vacated by Alan Gaffney. But at the start of the season he had also being looking into his heart. In his first two months in charge of Leinster he had to meet his two former clubs, Munster and Gwent Dragons in quick succession.

First up was Munster, in Donnybrook, in the middle of September in the Celtic League.

On September 20, 2004, Declan Kidney prepared a Leinster team to defeat his beloved Munster. He succeeded.

Leinster won 17-15.

The game was played in Leinster's new home, in Donnybrook, which despite a refurbishment was soon too small to attend to the team's needs in the professional era. But it was an historic evening as the blues defeated the reds for the first time in seven attempts.

Declan Kidney: Munster's positivity was incredible. Perhaps because it's early in the season we capitalised on one or two errors they made and got 14 points. After that we just hung in there really. It was an extraordinary result. I've a huge amount of pride in the men I'm working with but I know Munster are going in the right direction as well. They were only one or two passes away from cutting us open. We have to be able to retain the ball longer and play through a few phases, and we will not survive with the kind of penalty count we had against us in the second-half. To use a golfing analogy, which would be appropriate this weekend, we were in and out of the rough all day but managed to sink a few crucial putts.

(September 20, 2004)

Alan Gaffney: It's very frustrating. We spoke beforehand about being precise and not trying to force things, and then we went out and did exactly the opposite.

(September 20, 2004)

MUNSTER'S SET PIECES were spot on, and that resulted in more than enough possession. Territory and opportunity were not problems either. Munster, perhaps, just tried too damned hard in Donnybrook against their old coach and master. They made 14 turnovers in the first 40 minutes alone.

From one such mistake Christian Warner grabbed the ball, Brian O'Meara took possession from the recycle, Leinster went wide and Gary Brown took a Ben Gissing pass. Brown broke through the visitor's cover, stepped inside Christian Cullen and touched down. Brown was on fire all evening. Denis Hickie, introduced in the 11th minute after a 10-month absence, was just as hot. Munster had nobody to compare, and Paul Burke positioned himself far too deep, and was too slow in letting the ball work.

Less than two weeks later, Kidney had the Dragons in his sights – and a return to his former 'residence' in Rodney Parade.

Declan Kidney: I'm looking forward to going back actually. They're very good people in Newport, Jim McCreedy, the manager there, and the players I met, and Andy Marinos and especially Tony Brown. He rang me eight or nine days ago and said he was looking forward to us meeting up again. Tony Brown was very generous in facilitating my move here, he knew it was for family reasons and that I'd worked with the players here before.

(October 1, 2004)

Ian Gough (Dragons' lock): There are no hard feelings. He's a good guy and we can appreciate the reason he had for going back. He was man enough to tell us all face to face, which is a hard thing to do.

(October 1, 2004)

||||‖|||

MEETINGS BETWEEN LEINSTER and the Dragons had a habit of being liberal affairs. The season before the two games between them had resulted in 18 tries and a whopping 144 points. That whet the appetite, as did the prospect of Brian O'Driscoll going up against the Dragons' recalled outside centre, Percy Montgomery. Plus, since branding themselves as the Dragons, the Welsh side had won 12 out 12 of their home games. Whereas just under half of the Leinster team were playing their first game of the season in blue, and it bloody well showed. The Dragons laid down the law in a 34-13 victory, and the home team's coach, former rugby league guru Chris Anderson, made sure there was precious little room for O'Driscoll and Co to breathe. Two weeks later when Leinster suffered another reverse in Wales, going down

11-3 to the Ospreys, their new coach was in the mood to call a spade a spade.

Declan Kidney: We were poor and we lost. We were naïve, and that's the thing we have to sort out. We just struggled in most facets. We let them run at us. It wasn't a game of huge quality. There was a lot of chess being played, but of a poor standard really. It's another game under our belt but we just need to wise up and smarten up – but it's only games that will do that for us. I do believe that the whole thing will come together but there's a lot of things that will have to happen before we become a good side.

(October 16, 2004)

DECLAN KIDNEY NEVERTHELESS led Leinster into Europe with some serious intent and in winning all six of their pool games they totted up a points total of 257, a tidy sum and 108 points ahead of nearest challengers Bath. Leinster only conceded 100 points. It had started at the end of October with a 25-9 win in Treviso where O'Driscoll and the Leinster backs seemed to lack cohesion. Instead there were lots of solo thrusts, not that Kidney was unimpressed – for their first try Denis Hickie set off from inside his own 22, took his man on the outside and made 50 metres before looking inside for O'Driscoll who scored under the posts. Brian O'Meara looked hot and cold at No.9, but the star of the evening, and the rising star for the remainder of the campaign in Kidney's eyes was New Zealander David Holwell. In taking Bath 30-11 there were tries from Hickie, Gordon D'Arcy and Shane Horgan, but again Holwell was the centre of the show. He kicked five from five opportunities with the placed ball, two of which were close to the touchline and another from 45 metres. He was unanimously praised for his distribution, vision, tactical brain, courage in the tackle, and general workrate.

It was mostly all about Holwell for the 2004-2005 season, and the Argentinian Leinster had signed from Bristol on a four year contract, Felipe Contepomi would not take up the duties as 'General' for another 12 months.

The 27 year-old, however, still took every opportunity he got to show that Leinster were on the money. When Bourgoin came to Dublin (after losing 22-12 to Bath at the Recreation Ground) Contepomi let loose faster than anyone else, and alongside O'Driscoll in the centre, he ran in three tries in a rip-roaring 92-17 demolition of the French. There were 13 tries in all. Holwell and Horgan had two tries each, and Miller, Costello, Hickie, Jennings, Gissing and Brown also ran them in!

Twelve of the tries were converted by Holwell (eight), and Contepomi and O'Meara (two each). Holwell kicked one penalty.

Pascal Pape (Bourgoin second row): It's obvious that the defeat was very bad and that we didn't play to our normal standards. But it is important not to forget that we faced a quasi-Ireland side in Leinster whose play was of the highest standard. Since the finish of the match we have thought of nothing else but to take our revenge and show our true worth as a team. Bourgoin can play a lot better than that. I am counting on our supporters, that in these difficult moments, we have need of them and their support. I promise them a great game of rugby against a great team and we will give our maximum.

(December 10, 2004)

ONLY 3,000 PEOPLE turned up for the return game in Stade Pierre Rajon. Leinster won 26-23, but needed an O'Driscoll try three minutes from time, converted by Holwell, to make it through.

A loss to Munster, 19-13, was unhelpful as Leinster turned into a new year and sought to move even further up the gears in their efforts to land a first European title. It was Munster's 13th win in 14 outings. Both Leinster and Munster had the heads down, but both would fall far short of the finish line, both exiting in the quarter-final. Leinster to Leicester in a cool and somber Lansdowne Road, Munster to Biarritz in the heat of San Sebastian.

LEINSTER'S DEFEAT WAS damning, and the entire week or so was confusing. Sooner than anyone expected, Kidney would step down as coach with immediate effect as his future back in Munster became a sure thing.

Kidney had gambled on his team selection against the Tigers. He was not a gambling man by nature and his 'roll' on this occasion didn't work – he had plumped for Ciaran Potts and Keith Gleeson in his backrow, but early enough in the second-half both were replaced by Costello and Jennings. D'Arcy was also sprung from the bench, but by then Leinster were chasing a lost contest. Almost the entire first-half had been played in Leinster's half. The top seeds played like rank amateurs. They racked up 11 penalties and a yellow card as their discipline became non-existent. The visitors' first try in the 38th minute summed up the whole day.

Holwell hit the post with a penalty, Leicester cleared the ball long, Leinster turned over their own lineout, Leicester worked several phases as they swept into Leinster's half, Leicester loaded their blindside outside the Leinster 22, Contepomi was hopelessly outnumbered, he bought Ollie Smith's dummy, and Potts looked in reverse gear as he chased after Smith who scored the game's opening try.

It was 16-3 at half-time. Leinster were in trouble on the field. Declan Kidney was being out-coached in the stand, and whenever Leinster did manage to hold onto the ball the Leicester defence was ruthless and machine-like in aggressively drifting to O'Driscoll and Girvan Dempsey in the outside channels.

Declan Kidney: That's the way life is. It's just one of the things you get on with. We want everybody to go well in this country. We've a small group of players who are being asked to do an awful lot and we just need to broaden that base. They've (Leicester) been playing together over a long period of time. They play with one another right through the season. They have that bit of cohesiveness. They're just a good team. There is no shame whatsoever losing to a good team and that's what happened to us today.

(April 4, 2005)

John Wells (Leicester coach): The first-half was tremendous. There's no other word for it. I don't think Leinster got out of their own half or if they did it was just fleetingly.

(April 4, 2005)

IT WAS EVENTUALLY revealed that there had been 20 applications for the Munster job. In the end it came down to two individuals – Leinster coach

Declan Kidney and Connacht coach Michael Bradley – who were the only two interviewed. On April 8 it was made known that Kidney was successful.

Mick Dawson (Leinster Chief Executive): Though disappointed to see Declan leave, I understand his reasons and I would like to take this opportunity to wish him well in the future. Leinster would like to acknowledge the success of a campaign which has seen the side secure a home Heineken Cup quarter-final and a third place position in the Celtic League. Declan will stand down with immediate effect.

(April 8, 2005)

Garrett Fitzgerald (Munster Chief Executive): Firstly I would like to thank all those who expressed an interest in the position. It is obviously a very important role and I am delighted that Declan has opted to accept it. In my opinion he is an outstanding coach, whose record at the highest European level speaks for itself. Despite the fact that his family are based in Cork and that he has been away from them for long periods over the last three years, I know it can't have been an easy decision for him to decide to change roles within the IRFU. However, we found ourselves in a similar position to Leinster three years ago when we lost him to the national squad so his return is a welcome development.

(April 8, 2005)

Mick Dawson: The players return for pre-season training in late June, but we'd hope to have someone in place by the middle of next month. In terms of the players and contracts all the decisions made prior to Declan's departure stand. At this point in time we have 26 or 27 players contracted for next season and have three or four left to fill.

(April 21, 2005)

2005-2006

'The line between this happening and winning is so thin, that I know the exact reversal can happen in the return fixture. I really enjoyed last year and I know the character and the quality of them (Leinster), that they'll bounce straight back, and I'm glad that we're not playing them next week. Everybody is getting carried away with the Heineken Cup. We've a huge task to try and challenge the Guinness teams in the cup, because they're run as a commercial enterprise. Our job is to supply the Irish side and that's very necessary, and two or three fellas put their hands up and said (tonight)… 'in a few years time maybe you'll take a look at me'.

– Declan Kidney
(October 10, 2005)

MICHAEL CHEIKA DIDN'T know Declan Kidney from Adam, and didn't appear in any rush to find out about his predecessor in the Leinster hot seat.

But it was also a question for Kidney of… Michael Who?

Cheika, indeed, was a choice well from left field by the Leinster supremos.

The 38 year-old was of Lebanese extraction, his father emigrating to Australia in 1950, and it was 'down under' that Cheika, or 'Cheiks' to his players, made a name for himself, though his exploits had not sent ripples through world rugby.

He was New South Wales Coach of the Year in 2004-2005 after guiding Randwick to the Premiership title. He also seemed destined for the new Super 14 franchise in Perth, but turned down a role there as an assistant when beaten to the top job by former All Blacks coach, John Mitchell.

Luckily for Leinster, Cheika liked travelling the world. And with him to Ireland he was bringing his own assistant, former Wallabies' No. 10, Andrew Knox.

Cheika had spent valuable time in his early career playing 'footy' in France and Italy, before returning home fluent in both languages and ready to captain Randwick to a Premiership title. At the age of 33 he stopped playing mid-season and took up an offer to return to Italy and coach Padova. Then he about-turned to Australia again, where he also had a fashion business, importing and distributing, with offices in London, Hong Kong and Sydney. His business had a staff of 30. Michael Cheika did not take up the Leinster head coach job because he needed it.

He took it up because he wanted a fresh challenge. 'My business experience has shown me that you have to understand all your employees,' he told the Irish media on his arrival. '… and what they are doing. When you've to make a decision, you make it. Sometimes, that's hard. Yeah, I'm decisive. I think I know how to make decisions and be confident in them. But I'm not saying they're always right.'

Michael Cheika, who was about to become Declan Kidney's closest opponent and most difficult opponent, also had a reputation for getting hot under his collar. And he didn't like to lose very much. He was the perfect choice to tear off the 'losers' tag from Leinster's big toe. Five weeks into his first season in Dublin, his players were making it known that they were being flogged.

Michael Cheika: We've been training them very hard physically. That's with an objective to try and control tempo, to play controlled games at our own tempo. Yeah, they (the players) said it has been harder than any other pre-season. Maybe, though, it's just longer. In every football season the great thing is there is a new start. Every time you lose a game you know there is another one around the corner. I don't mean to be too philosophical. If there is a hangover, I don't see any of it. The players have taken on the work ethic. No questions.

Enthusiastic? Yeah.

Wouldn't want any more from them.

There was an obvious connection here. I knew Alan Gaffney very well. I knew Gary Ella. I dunno the last coach here and no, I wasn't aware at the time at what was going on at the end of the season.

That part is something of the past. Whatever happened, happened. I've seen a real hunger here. Players want to achieve. Whether that's because of the past, I dunno. I think as a footballer, if you don't want to achieve, you can't do anything. We try to bottle that approach in paying attention to detail, making sure the players are prepared enough to get them to where they want to go.

(July 30, 2005)

CHEIKA STRESSED THAT he wanted to achieve. In his early chats with Brian O'Driscoll he explained that he had a league title in his sights by year two, and a Heineken Cup by year three.

O'Driscoll was excited.

He spoke of fun returning to the training ground. He talked about 'new voices, new ideas', in his autobiography *The Test*, and a higher level of coaching than he had been handed in some time in the province. He was also enthused to get more game time with the Argentinian, Felipe Contepomi – never one of Kidney's first choices.

Michael Cheika: People have put confidence in me to come and take up a position. I'm not going to let them down. We bring a certain skill level to the table. We work on making the small parts of the players' game better. Fine details so that they can perform better under pressure. I want to teach everyone in the squad something new. I want to make them better and I want them to do it consistently.

(July 30, 2005)

FIRST BLOOD, HOWEVER, belonged to Declan Kidney. In early October, Cheika, Knoxy and Co made the trip down to Cork where in Musgrave Park they were turned over in what some newspapers termed a 'thrashing'. After three successive wins it was a sobering evening for the pair of Aussies. A sizeable portion of the 8,000 watching were chanting 'EAASSYYYY.... EAASSYYYY' long before the end. The final scoreline was a record Leinster defeat, 33-9. Though, of course, Kidney was not partaking of that celebratory mood himself.

Munster had lost Trevor Halstead and John Hayes on the day of the game, with Barry Murphy and Federico Pucciarello coming in. Twenty-two year-old Tomas O'Leary, nipping at Peter Stringer's heels, took his chance in his second start. He sniped adventurously all day.

Though, Contepomi accused his opponents of running off at the mouth as well and accused them of lacking respect, and lacking a basic education in the manly rules of the game. It wasn't the major moment of the match, but it was to be remembered for many years. It occurred in the 38th minute. Contepomi addressed a penalty kick from 30 metres out, after play had been brought back 50 metres, much to the crowd's annoyance, when the touch judge took a particular view of Alan Quinlan's actions. As he prepared, the ball fell over on Contepomi in the stiff breeze and a pack of Munster players rushed forward. Included in the number was Ronan O'Gara, which did not go down well at all with the Leinster No.10.

The referee, Simon McDowell took the decision that the ball could be reset. The crowd's annoyance did handstands. Some Munster players were additionally stirred by the noise around them. The referee's decision on a penalty kick was absolutely correct. But as Brian O'Meara held the ball for Contepomi, the Leinster kicker was further distracted by a gang of Munstermen again encroaching the 10 metres.

The Munster players were pointing to their wrists. They felt Contepomi was acting the lad, taking far too much time out of the clock. The crowd now responded to the Munster team. Contepomi pushed his kick wide. Musgrave Park went absolutely ballistic with delight.

Contepomi would never forget, or feel forgiving.

Michael Cheika: We gave them the ball far too much, which got them in the game, and you can't do that. If you give good teams opportunities they'll take them, and that's what they did. Our handling mistakes let us down more than anything. We've got to take something away from this game and make sure we add it to our repertoire so that it doesn't happen again.

(October 10, 2005)

Felipe Contepomi: I don't mind the crowd booing or shouting when you are going to take a kick, but the players? That's a lack of respect. It's difficult to speak when you lose because that didn't change the result. Munster were a much better side than us, but it really frustrated me in the first-half when I had a penalty, the (Munster) players were shouting when I was going to kick. It's a lack of education or something. It's strange that their coach (Declan Kidney) is actually a teacher. Maybe he could put some of his knowledge into the players as well.

(October 10, 2005)

Anthony Foley: That's a little strange. Obviously it's not nice when something like that happens. We have a code of silence for place-kickers but that happened at a stage of the game when the players and the crowd were getting frustrated with some of the decisions, and you want to put pressure on the opposition. I'm not sure what was said to him. I was standing under the posts. We were exposed to that last season when Paul Volley of Castres was swearing and shouting at Rog as he was kicking. It's not something you want to see in the game. We were not too happy about how long he was taking with his kicks, but I'm sure that it was a one-off occasion.

(October 10, 2005)

|||**I**||||

IN THE FIRST week of the new year, Cheika made it 1-1 in his battle with Kidney and left everything in the balance between the two teams until they would meet three months further down the road in the middle of April, in the biggest game in the history of Irish rugby, in the Heineken Cup semi-final at Lansdowne Road.

It was five tries to nil in the first meeting between the teams in Musgrave Park. In Leinster's 35-23 return victory, once again tempers flared and both Reggie Corrigan and Contepomi were binned for a time. Though the Argentinian displayed his true genius by the end and converted his two late tries for a 25-points haul and some fresh, sweet revenge. Leinster looked closer to the complete team that could possibly fight for European honours on the day. Munster, in comparison, looked and played like half a team and depended massively on the work ethic and ball-carrying of their pack, a charge that faced Kidney after the game.

Michael Cheika: There's no getting away from it, they smashed us up in Musgrave Park, and we know it. We talked about it, not revenge, but getting back what we gave away there. But the world's not changing because we won here today. We've got to keep producing that week in, week out, against all teams if we want to go where we want to go. It was good to have that win but, mate... they could have won it, and we couldn't have won down in Musgrave Park. So we need to keep things in perspective.

(January 2, 2006)

Declan Kidney: We know that in most aspects we didn't perform as well as we can. There's no doubt that the boys wanted it, but we probably just have to play with our heads up a small bit more. Our heart is huge – we just have to make sure it doesn't create such anxiety that it stymies our thought process out on the pitch. Every team plays to its strengths. Maybe some people want us to play a different way but I don't know a team in the world that doesn't play to its strengths.

(January 2, 2006)

BACK HOME IN Munster, Declan Kidney employed the exact same approach to life on and off the field as he did in his first tenure as coach. He had no wish to stand out in front, not unless it was absolutely imperative and for the good of his team. Such an act, for instance, was not at all necessary when Munster produced a 76-page programme for the European Cup quarter-final against Perpignan in Lansdowne Road. Other important people were up front in the publication. Closer to the back there was a profile of every one of Munster's 38 squad members. The name of the Director of Coaching (Kidney) appeared only once, further back, listed amongst the 20 or so members of the Munster management team.

Typically under-stated Kidney.

And that is how he measured up against Michael Cheika – the former career guidance teacher going chest-to-chest with the fashion empire builder. When their teams met, Kidney was happy to be on the pitch pre-game, tipping around in his tracksuit and returning errant balls to players. Cheika looked happier in his Italian shoes and a fine woolen sweater.

Sitting in front of the media, Kidney had always given the impression that it was a part of his job that had to be endured more than anything else. Cheika, in the spotlight, seemed to grow in form and always appeared to quietly enjoy himself, and swashbuckling with awkward questions did not inconvenience him in the slightest.

Cheika wished from his Leinster team a flamboyance, a style and panache. Kidney wished for strength, conviction, and if Munster were not enticing spectators to the edges of their seats with an engagement of risk dotting their play then he was not going to apologise.

By the end of January, 2006, doing it their own individual and very different ways on the field, Leinster and Munster had made it through to the last eight in Europe. Cheika's men got there by beating Bath 35-23 at The Rec and putting on a pulsating display for their own travelling supporters and the home crowd. Forwards and backs interlinked with what seemed abandon. Felipe Contepomi was mesmeric. Brian O'Driscoll was absolutely commanding. Together they were responsible for a length-of-the-pitch try following a quick Contepomi tap inside his own 22 that sparked a whirlwind 21 points inside the opening 18 minutes of the game. Leinster left almost everyone feeling thankful.

That number included the Munster boss, Declan Kidney who was quickly on the phone to his opposite number in Leinster with a thank you. Cheika recounted their conversation later. 'No worries mate... a bottle of red wine on its way to you with a red ribbon!' The result had left Leinster taking on Toulouse away from home. If they had not denied Bath a late try and bonus point, then Munster would have been heading to The Rec for their quarter-final.

Instead, they had Perpignan on precious home soil.

Brian O'Driscoll: When it comes to the crunch you want as many Irish teams in the quarter-finals as possible. It's not about begrudgery and if we helped Munster get a home quarter-final, so much the better. We played some great rugby, but we played some smart rugby too. That's the pleasing thing. Both sides ran out of gas a bit towards the end but I hope that our performance proved some of our doubters wrong.

(January 23, 2006)

Michael Cheika: We were working for our Munster brothers all the time. Hey look, in all seriousness, the more Irish teams involved the better. It's better for us, a lot of my team are going to be playing international football and they want to be playing at the top level and we may run into each other later on. If we helped them get a home quarter-final that's good.

(January 23, 2006)

A COUPLE OF days later the dreamy prospect of an All-Ireland Heineken Cup final in Cardiff's Millennium Stadium on May 20 went by the wayside. The draw decreed that if Munster and Leinster overcame Perpignan and Toulouse respectively on April 1 they would be meeting one another in Lansdowne Road three weeks later.

Declan Kidney: It doesn't really bother us in one sense, because we're not there yet. Other than that, we would have preferred if there was the carrot of a home semi-final although, either way, if we beat Perpignan we'd be playing a very confident Leinster team or the team who have won it twice in the last three years. But a week ago we'd have taken it.

(January 25, 2006)

||‖‖||

MUNSTER'S EUROPEAN CAMPAIGN had got off to a rocky start the previous October when they lost by double scores (27-13) at Edgeley Park and felt the full force of Sale's battering rams, Sebastien Chabal, Jason White, Andrew Sheridan and Sebastien Bruno. It was the last physical thumping they were on the receiving end of, doubling up victories over the Dragons, before extracting revenge over the Sharks at the opposite end of the pool games. Like Michael Cheika, Declan Kidney knew his men were ready for the very best that Europe had to offer when the Heineken Cup resumed after the Six Nations. In the quarter-final Perpignan were a 'handful' at times, and Munster were 'far from vintage' in the estimation of Paul O'Connell amongst others. On a blustery and rainswept Lansdowne Road, the French wanted a war. And Munster obliged. O'Connell scored the first try of the afternoon in the 20th minute when Jerry Flannery broke off a maul and ran at the Perpignan defence before O'Connell took Christophe Manas' low tackle and scored on the blindside. Kidney's men were 13-10 in front early in the second-half and what they had, they were determined to hold, and when the Catalans decided on a close range lineout off a penalty Munster made an early 'last stand'. O'Connell led the resistance as the Munster pack drilled the French maul back and drove them sideways over the touchline.

It was now Munster v Leinster.

Declan Kidney v Michael Cheika.

One last time in the 2005-2006 season.

Declan Kidney: The draw is that we're away. Leinster are at home. It's being played in Dublin. We're away.

(April 3, 2006)

A GAME OF inches was expected, and Declan Kidney was immediately into gaining every tiny psychological advantage he could get for his men. While Leinster did have home advantage, that did not necessarily mean that they would get to prepare in their own dressing-room. Tournament rules insisted on a toss of a coin to decide who sat in that particular room. Kidney won the toss.

Leinster had to remove their sign from the door of the 'HOME' room.

LIKE GOOD OLD country boys, like an old-fashioned GAA team on its way to an All-Ireland final, Munster made their way to Lansdowne Road slowly the day before the game. Kidney's schoolmaster touch had his boys looking at their watches, and assembling as though they were on a particular mission. From 8.45 am the Cork based lads began arriving at Kent Station for their 9.15 am train to Dublin. Meanwhile, the Limerick-based lads were in the Kilmurray Lodge by 9.0 am for their 9.20 am coach to Limerick Junction. There the two groups would form one Munster.

Anthony Foley: The whole day was good. The preparation was good. Everyone seemed focused. There had been a lot of pressure, but once we got together on the train fellas got into their old routines. Some played cards, some played Scrabble, others listened to music. It seemed like there was a comfort in numbers. Once we're all together, we're all in the same boat, so to speak.

(April 24, 2006)

THE NEXT DAY, it was more of the same, as the meticulousness of Declan Kidney's management held the group tightly together. Sunday lunch was at 11.30 am. The players then headed back to their rooms to prepare their bags. At 1.15 pm, strictly keeping with custom, there was the all-important 10-minute team meeting. Kidney would speak. And Foley. But Paul O'Connell was also now given time by the coach to help set heads straight in the vital final hours before kick-off. From the two agonising European final defeats, Kidney, like everyone, had learned. Emotion had a firm lid on it.

No tears, No bubbling over.

THE KIDNEY PLAN worked a treat from start to finish, and there was the added bonus of some luck, like when Malcolm O'Kelly dropped the ball from the kick-off and it bounced into the arms of Donncha O'Callaghan. From there, luck was not necessary. Munster bullied. O'Connell directed and O'Gara sliced Leinster open. In reply there was so little for Leinster to do. O'Kelly and

Bryce Williams could not get their hands on any ball. Kidney had seen where so many of Leinster's tries had come from lineout ball from the back, and he decided to put a stop to that deft Cheika trick. Forced to throw to the front of the line, Contepomi was left under constant pressure. Overall, Kidney's muscle smothered Cheika's craft from start to finish. Munster hit the tackle area hard and quickly to clear out ruck ball. Leinster could not slow it down. O'Driscoll and D'Arcy were unable to work turnovers. Contepomi was starved. To make absolutely sure, Kidney had installed David Wallace in midfield to snuff out any daylight in the red line for O'Driscoll and his two fleet-footed buddies to enjoy.

For O'Gara, the triumph over Contepomi was to be treasured. He had been listening to analysts and supporters talking about the craftsmanship of the Argentinian all season it seemed.

O'Gara knocked over the game's first penalty after two minutes. Two minutes later he converted Leamy's try off a rolling maul. Contepomi brought it back to 10-3, but O'Gara stretched it out to 13-3, and then 16-3, and his final flourish was yet to come. Munster went for Leinster's jugular.

All of the hard work done, O'Gara scampered through and handed off O'Kelly before touching down for his try, waving his fist in the air, and leaping the advertising hoardings in his celebrations. An intercept try by Trevor Halstead, picking off Guy Easterby's pass to D'Arcy, ensured the largest European Cup semi-final win in eight years.

Munster 30, Leinster 6.

Michael Cheika never did explain how he spent the rest of that Sunday evening, but some of his players admitted that they needed a quick drink. O'Driscoll felt embarrassed more than anything else. Himself, Denis Hickie and Shane Horgan stopped at an off-licence on their way home from the ground and grabbed a bottle of gin and some tonic water.

Declan Kidney watched his crew retire to a pub across the road from Heuston Station, before getting their train south. Once there, the evening recommenced in Jerry Flannery's establishment on Catherine Street. Fla's pub had been mentioned in a TV interview by O'Connell earlier. The place was hopping. Twenty of Kidney's man, nevertheless, remained in a tight fist in a wood-panelled snug. They sang, and they drank their beer, and let all of the emotion flow, knowing that everything would be bottled up once again by their coach 24 hours later as he zeroed in on a first European title. The Kidney job was not even half done, even if they had landed in another final. That was another lesson the coaches and their players now knew by heart.

Munster had to be smarter in everything they did; and smarter than they had ever been before. Twelve days out from the final Kidney gathered together Jim Williams, Brian Hickey, Tony McGahan and Graham Steadman, his 'think-tank' and four hours later there were reams of paper and a great assortment of ideas. Too many, in truth. Kidney wanted to condense everything down into a 15 minute overview of what had to be done. That's what his players needed. Straight messaging, no detours, absolutely nothing that might leave them in any doubt – and too much information was worse than too little in Kidney's estimation.

When the nuts and bolts were on paper, he took the 'game plan' to his more senior players and let them chew on it first of all. Once they bought in on it, he had a plan ready for the entire squad. The opening 20 minutes were going to be crucial, in Kidney's estimation. That's when Biarritz liked to bury the opposition if they could. Kidney had also made other observations. Biarritz had a habit of leaving their short side a little bit exposed. They crowded the middle instead. They loved their pressure.

Munster needed to pressure the French first.

On the Tuesday of final week, when the players trotted out onto the field at Musgrave Park they found themselves surrounded by loud speakers.

Declan Kidney would not have been able to sleep at night if he had not covered every little something, anything! He had decided to give the lads a sense of how loud it was going to be in the Millennium Stadium with the roof closed. He had asked for five tracks lasting 23 minutes to be cut. On top of that he had asked for crowd noise – as noisy as it could get.

He was asked by his helpers what sort of music he had in mind? He replied... 'loud'... the first track was a live version of the U2 hit *Where The Streets Have No Name*. After that it was *Thunderstruck* by AC/DC, then *Welcome To The Jungle* by Guns 'n' Roses. It was noisy alright, but most of the Munster players were not amused.

They felt Kidney was laying on the message too thick. Rob Henderson told him that his choice of music was 'crap'. Everyone was uptight that week.

Ronan O'Gara was recovering from food poisoning.

He had worked under Declan Kidney as a coach for 15 years, and he was used to the coach's teachings, and his mind games. But Rog said nothing. He thought that Kidney was as 'cranky' as the players as the days counted down so slowly. Everyone was nervous. Uptight, as they concentrated on winning, and tried valiantly not to even think of what it would like to be to lose a third European final. Munster flew out to Wales on the Friday, a day later than they had departed their homes for the final in 2002.

Kidney wanted them relaxed and in their own environment as long as possible. He had timed every single journey for the 48 hours ahead of them... airport, ground, hotel... and back again.

ON THE AFTERNOON of Friday, May 19, in the media centre of the Millennium Stadium in Cardiff, Anthony Foley steadfastly reused the requests of the attending scrum of photographers to lift the Heineken Cup with the Biarritz captain, Thomas Lievremont. If the Frenchman wanted to lift it, that was fine with the Munster captain. But he would not lay a finger on the trophy himself. Foley did not believe that a captain should lay a finger on a trophy until he and his team had earned the right to do so.

Declan Kidney had his team take up house in the Vale of Glamorgan Hotel, a home from home for Kidney and Co at this stage. They had stayed there before the 2002 final, and had returned to take in the hospitality and privacy before a more recent outing against Ospreys. Foley was in room 101, alone, as captain's usually had it. Others were not so lucky.

Donncha O'Callaghan and Marcus Horan were sharing in room 110 down the corridor. It was a fine room. Normal size for two grown men, except... outside the room someone in the Munster ranks had parked a ping-pong table. The table would attract all-comers through the evening and into the early hours. Kidney was told about the problem, but he decided that there were just some things that his players had to deal with on their own, and O'Callaghan, freaky about his sleep or not, would have to get by.

It rained the night before the game. And despite Kidney's expert preparations, Rog did not get all the kicking time he wished for earlier in the day. He only got to kick into one end of the ground, before Munster were moved on by officials. Rog had that on his mind. In his own room, Kidney was receiving text messages by the dozen. He wanted to reply to them all, but soon he needed to go for a walk around the car park, to get some time to himself to think, and also to see if there was any player who needed a final chat?

Back in his room, he took up the book that every member of the party had been given by the supporters' club and that contained good luck messages from so many caring people.

Some of the messages in the players' heads were clearer, and more to the point, than others. One of them up on the wall in the team room had been approved by team management, like all of the others. It was from Peter Clohessy.

'BEST OF LUCK AND SOW IT INTO THOSE FRENCH BASTARDS'

Kidney's immediate opponent was Patrice Lagisquet, a clearcut winner in rugby circles, although after failing to land the big one in 2006, and falling back in France after that, he would be let-go after a failed season for Biarritz. Three times in the five years prior to 2006 he had claimed the French Championship, and the cup once, and the former winger who had represented his country 46 times was generating the same sort of momentum on the sideline as he did out on the pitch. In his 10 years on the wing for Bayonne he had claimed the nickname... The Bayonne Express.

Like always, at the very top of the game when a major battle presented itself on the pitch an equally dramatic head-to-head was about to be enacted close to one side of the contest.

Munster v Biarritz?

Kidney v Lagisquet?

Also in the corner of the Biarritz head coach was the phenomenal former French full-back, the great Serge Blanco. It was his dream to build something big and memorable for the people of the Basque country. Lagisquet was his dream-maker, even if he had done such damage in the name of Biarritz' neighbours and greatest of enemies for those 10 years. Lagisquet, however, had ended his playing career one mile down the road from Bayonne, in the colours of the team he was now moulding into outstanding champions.

There was another illustrious person in the Biarritz corner, however, their 'sugar daddy'... Serge Kampf, one of the 10 wealthiest men in France, who was in the business of selling human intelligence, such as computer support. Biarritz had Kampf's money, Blanco's vision, and Lagisquet's genius.

All told, a formidable opposition for the former teacher from Pres Cork who had never worn the Irish jersey.

Kidney's primary job, in addition to affording his own men a stage on which they would express themselves and become Europe's No.1 team, was to deny Lagisquet (and devalue Kampf's spend). He had to get to grips with their out-half Julien Peyrelongue, their lock Jerome Thion and, of course, the irrepressible Dimitri Yachvili who needed more attention than anybody – same as Lagisquet was sure to spend more of his time thinking about Munster out-half, Ronan O'Gara than anybody else in red.

Thomas Castaignede (French star and newspaper columnist): What's certain is that Biarritz will have to raise their game if they are to lift the trophy for the first time. On the weekend's showing, the only area they might have a slight edge is in the scrum. Munster's lineout is dynamic and well organised, and their backs were perfect yesterday: not one mistake, wings who can burst through anywhere, an ice-cool full-back and no hiccups when Rob Henderson came on at centre. Biarritz have been criticised for a lack of ambition but they didn't show their true colours on Saturday due to the conditions. They are a team who adapt to the opposition and the weather. The week after they played Sale in the quarter-final they adopted a far more open style in beating Toulouse. In Cardiff, with the Millennium Stadium roof closed against the weather, we may see the face they show in the French Championship and, indeed, the kind of rugby they created in beating Saracens at home in the pool stage.

(April 24, 2006)

Colin Noon (Biarritz prop): Biarritz folk are very passionate, about their food, lifestyle and Basque identity, but most of all about rugby. That's what makes the area such a wonderful place to live. They know how to relax and enjoy themselves... but at the end of the day they still win trophies. The warm-ups consist of a 10-minute jog, then some of the lads just start throwing the ball around. I have never encountered that kind of relaxed working environment before. Nine or 10 balls might be knocked on during a session but you don't get screamed at. If that happened in the UK you'd be on the ground doing push-ups. All of this has a great impact on team morale because we're all treated like humans instead of robots. The supporters are a really passionate bunch and the big thing is the bond between the club and the supporters – they don't just turn up for the game at the weekend; you'll find loads of them watching you in training or they'll be hanging about at the club later asking you about scrummaging.

But the one big difference that I've encountered is the amount of time spent on video analysis. Patrice (Lagisquet) and Jacques (Delmas) probably spend five hours a week with us on it and I've certainly never been involved in a club that spends so much time in analysing the opposition.

(May 15, 2006)

ANTHONY FOLEY LOST the toss, which meant Munster would be receiving the kick-off. The team generally liked to chase and tear into the opposition. Again, the plan in the minds of the players would have to be altered slightly, but great teams always needed to be on their toes, ready to do it themselves when the moment demanded... make it happen themselves! That's how Declan Kidney always wanted it to be.

On message, but independent of spirit when absolutely necessary.

As Julien Peyrelongue kicked off, the Munster coach was sitting up in the stand – in the front row, in the middle tier of the front row with a view suitable for visiting royalty. His trusted assistant Jim Williams was pitchside. The remainder of his coaching staff sat either side of Kidney. They all wore a mic each. Kidney wanted to hear what everyone had to say at all times, but warned them... ' don't give me so much that I can't handle it'.

Payne and Wallace failed to hear each other call in the noise. Kidney watched the ball being turned over. The ERC had made their decision to shut the roof. The Stadium was as deafening as he had feared it would be. U2, Guns 'n' Roses and AC/DC indeed. One minute later everyone in the ground in a red shirt was stunned to silence, however, as Philippe Bidabe the Biarritz centre made little of O'Gara's tackle and expertly raced down the left touchline before just getting down in the corner.

O'GARA'S PENALTY ON seven minutes brought it back to 7-3. Next time, Munster got a penalty, Kidney's demand for 'pressure' was foremost in Anthony Foley's mind. Captain and coach had agreed to have Biarritz chase the game. Kidney had made that clear for the previous four weeks. Biarritz were front runners. Like all French teams, they were prone to lose some discipline if they were not out front. But, if they were where they liked to be in a game, they had Yachvili's boot to keep them there, and keep controlling the scoreboard.

Munster kicked into the corner twice. Damien Traille grabbed O'Gara's chip behind his line and Biarritz earned a 22 drop out. Kidney, potentially, had watched his lads throw points away. But he had also watched Foley and his team make a decisive statement in the face of the French.

George Hook (RTE analyst): Well, the extraordinary thing here, I think, is that Munster are displaying a strange attitude towards kicking goals. They turned down a certain six points earlier on. It's all very well to say they're 10-all now, but I think they need to take the points.

(RTE, May 20, 2006)

Ryle Nugent (RTE commentator): Here comes the decision now. And it is… well, it's to go down the line again. It's brave, but the question is… at the end of 80 minutes will it prove to have been foolhardy?

(RTE, May 20, 2006)

IT WAS A day when Munster would not nurse regrets. On 17 minutes O'Gara ran back a clearance from Peyrelongue. Flannery off-loaded to O'Connell. Munster were making the game happen. The ball was swung left. Biarritz were at sixes and sevens. Munster squeezed. Biarritz felt the pressure. Trevor Halstead used his pace to gather an O'Gara pass and break through two tacklers. He touched down. O'Gara converted.

Munster 10, Biarritz 7.

Munster had taken charge of the afternoon.

Midway through the half Yachvili kicked three points, but it was independence of spirit, sheer courage, and pupils willing to listen to their master, that saw to it that Munster did not delay in taking the game by the scruff of the neck in the next 10 minutes. It was a hold they would not let go of either. Putting the ball into the scrum, Peter Stringer had noticed room on the blindside. It was a secret he kept to himself. The Munster scrum was rock solid. Stringer had the ball back in his hands and was running. Foley took off after him, waiting for his No.9 to be tackled, waiting for the referee's whistle, not certain what was about to happen next? Stringer dived over. O'Gara converted. And O'Gara kicked three more points on 42 minutes.

Munster 20, Biarritz 10.

There was only one team chasing in the second-half. And even though Biarritz brought the game back to 20-19, they had to work hard, and they had to be frantic in that workrate. Off a scrum, Halstead took an O'Gara pass and piled over the gain-line. Biartritz erred. O'Gara kicked another three.

Munster 23, Biarritz 19.

Biarritz had been pulling on an elasticated rope trying to get themselves back into the game, and get back out front.

Peter Stringer: I could see the winger (Sereli Bobo) was standing slightly behind the scrum so when the ball went to Anthony's feet at the back I turned and guessed, and hoped, he would work infield – from the analysis we had done on them. Thankfully when I picked he wasn't standing in my way.

(May 22, 2006)

Kevin Mitchell (writer): You knew which way the fight was going physically by the movement on the bench. When Federico Pucciariello came on for Marcus Horan in the 63rd minute, he was Munster's first replacement; Biarritz already had four fresh men on for their wounded. When Benjamin Noirot followed soon afterwards, taking over the hooking duties from Benoit August, Munster had seen off four of the Biarritz pack, including the captain Lievremont, with quarter of an hour to go. Betsen was still there, the most gnarled of warhorses and obviously nursing the odd bruise. He emerged ever more slowly from each ruck. Ruthlessness, indeed.

(The Guardian, May 21, 2006)

Declan Kidney: I heard Ronan quoted after the semi-final that you had to be in the dressing-room really to try and understand what it means to everybody. It's definitely about the players. Without a shadow of a doubt, they won it. It's not just the players. It's the players' partners, their families. The next-door neighbour. It's everybody. If goodwill was ever going to win a competition, this was the one it was going to win.

(May 21, 2006)

Donncha O'Callaghan: It wasn't the prettiest of finals, they normally aren't. We'll just look at parts of it and wonder how we managed to hold them out. We said all week we wanted to perform, we wanted to go well. That was the thing we learned from the last two finals. You have to go and win finals; we did that to a degree. We scored two tries; Strings' was a beauty, a fine individual effort.

(May 22, 2006)

Jim Williams: There is a lot of relief. If I can make a comparison the first time the Brumbies won the Super 12. There was a sigh of relief first after winning it, but then we moved on. Toulouse and Leicester are the targets now. To see who can win it the most times? That's the drive that's got to be there. To be successful all the time; Paul O'Connell said it after the semi-final… this can't be it. The last seven or eight minutes were excruciating. You'd much rather be a player because you're out there in the thick of it, but when you're on the sideline and expecting the team to do things it's a little bit frustrating. To the same point, they have trained hard all year and they executed the game plan to the letter. That was the most pleasing thing from a coaching perspective.

(May 22, 2006)

Patrice Lagisquet: Munster played with a really high intensity. Our kicking let us down in the second-half when three returning kicks went straight back to Munster players. I also can't condone players for losing their heads in a game. There should have been more support for the ball on the ground. We were lucky to score a try very early on in the game and then we just kept hitting up the defence. We kept getting ball that wasn't playable. The game came down to Munster's kicking and our errors. We lost this game maybe due to a lack of calm and serenity between the team. We worked hard to get this style. Munster had lost two finals; they knew what they needed to do in order to win today. They deserved it after playing so intelligently over the years and throughout the tournament.

(May 22, 2006)

THE JOB DONE, Anthony Foley could not wait to finally get his hands on the trophy that he had denied himself a day earlier. But when he finally got to carry the trophy around with him, after the presentation, he found himself sharing it with players present, and past. Like Mick Galwey; men who had worked to make Munster an institution, but who had to make way for younger, stronger Munstermen to complete the journey.

'You'd think after 10 seasons playing in this tournament, and seven seasons after our first final defeat, I'd be willing to wait a few more minutes to get my hands on this bloody trophy, but the delay, as everyone else collects their medals from the ERC chairman, Jean-Pierre Lux, is killing me,' Foley wrote in his memoir, *Axel*. ' I'm also a bit put out that they won't let me bring Deccie up on onto the platform to accept the cup. Typically, he's happy to hold back. The trophy is heavier than I thought it would be but it feels like the noise would lift it anyway – none of our supporters appear to have left the building.'

DECLAN KIDNEY DID not stay in the shadows all weekend. At Shannon airport, where an estimated 5,000 Munster fans patiently awaited their heroes at 12.30 am, the head coach offered up a rare and wonderful sight.

He led a rendition of *Stand Up and Fight,* his voice finally breaking as he closed to a finish.

2006-2007

'This is a fresh competition. Everybody starts on a clean sheet, let's see how we go. All we can judge ourselves on is ourselves. The players have been disappointed with what's gone on, fairly critical. We have to keep a handle on that, and put a reality on getting things right. And 90 per cent of it they know themselves. It was great winning, but now we'll find out if we're the type of people who want to win it again. Maybe once would have been nice back in 2000, but not after the last six years.'

– Declan Kidney
(October 21, 2006)

MIDWAY THROUGH THE season in which they defended their European title, Declan Kidney found himself centre stage, a single spotlight hitting him. It was not a scenario he would have cooked up for himself in December of 2006. The Munster coach would have chosen to be in control of the spotlight, if given a choice. But it was out of his hands as he was declared Philips Manager of the Year.

Worse for Kidney! It happened to be the 25th anniversary of the Philips awards and therefore all of the great and the mighty, those who had been voted No.1 before him down through all of those years, were in attendance. All except former Ireland soccer supremo, Jack Charlton who had been forced to cry off.

The award was always going to be his. Twice in the year he had been voted Manager of the Month, in April and May, as Munster barreled to their first European title. But Kidney, on stage with RTE's Des Cahill, award in hand, was typically self-effacing. 'I feel like a fraud really,' he began.

'I'd like to accept this on behalf of all the people I work with. Brian O'Brien (former Munster and Ireland manager) once said you are only as successful as the people you work with want you to be. The players deserve the credit. It's always good to work with good players.

'It helps.'

Cahill asked Deccie if he felt 'joy or relief' when the full time whistle sounded in the Millennium Stadium the previous May, and the long cherished European title was coming home to the people of Munster?

'Yes', replied Kidney.

However, if he thought that short-changing his interviewer with answers would help him, the Munster and future Ireland head coach was mistaken. He would be back in the spotlight, voted the greatest and the mightiest all over again, soon enough.

IN THE 2003-2004 season, Arsenal football club went unbeaten. Arsene Wenger's fabulous team was labelled 'The Invincibles' as in the 38 games they played, 26 were victories and 12 were draws. In the season that followed The Gunners would defeat Middlesborough and thereby equal Nottingham Forest's total of 42 league games unbeaten. They went one better with a home win over Blackburn Rovers next time out, and the run by Wenger's team extended itself for six more matches before it ended in a controversial 2-0 loss to Manchester United. It was sensational stuff. But Arsenal were still unable to defend their title successfully – finishing runners-up and eight points behind Chelsea in the 2004-2005 season.

Holding onto a hard won title, no matter how desperately a team may have wished to do so, was never easy. Arsene Wenger in his long haul managerial career at Arsenal never managed to do so. Lots of outstanding coaches had found it incredibly difficult to remain near perfect in back-to-back seasons.

Munster's hopes of remaining at the top of the European rugby mountain were dealt a blow in the summer of 2006 when the draw for the 2006-2007 Heineken Cup pools were announced. Kidney found out that in his first game defending the trophy he would be bringing his team to Welford Road, the home of Leicester Tigers, twice winners of the same trophy – significantly winning the pair of them on the trot at the beginning of the decade.

The good news for Munster was that Kidney had overseen a seamless change of captaincy; Paul O'Connell taking the role over from Anthony Foley. That should have had everyone in high spirits, and plotting an even more successful future, but for some reason Munster were playing rubbish rugby in the opening weeks of the biggest season in the team's history. There were injuries. There were lots of excuses, in truth, but Declan Kidney never did excuses.

Neither had he the time to contemplate any such thing, even if it had been in his nature. By October 2006, Munster, whatever their form, were centre stage! Just like Kidney would be at the end of 2006 when he accepted his Manager of the Year award two months later!

Munster, as defending champs, were the poster team at the launch of the new tournament in Twickenham. On the wall behind the top table Ronan O'Gara was to be seen kicking a ball through the twin spires of London Bridge. Declan Kidney would not have dreamed up such a scenario if it had been left to his devices.

Neither would he have chosen what followed. Sky Sports Simon Lazenby asked for Miss London Claire Cooper, and her glamorous assistant to come forward with the Heineken Cup trophy itself. Amongst those beaming with delight on the raised stage was Brian O'Driscoll. But he was not all-eyes for Miss Cooper. Instead, the Leinster hero was enthralled, as was everyone else, to find that the glamorous assistant was Munster hooker, Jerry Flannery. And Fla was not feeling entirely at home in his new role. As for Flannery's coach?

Kidney was all business, and bluntly refused to talk about anything other than his team's first game against Leicester on Sunday, October 22. That was the day when he would have to contend with Pat Howard, the Tigers' coach, the man everyone in European rugby was talking up, and the man whom Kidney would have to unseat if he was to make a successful defence of the Heineken Cup.

Declan Kidney: We've been very busy getting ready for another season. There are more jerseys around the place, more kids looking to play the game. There has been a lot of kids with hurls and footballs around, maybe now they'll come back to us. The season? I'm looking no further than Friday.

(October 11, 2006)

ON THE BIG publicity stage Munster looked sharp and ready. On the pitch, however, in the opening weeks of the season they looked in disarray. 'Second Season Syndrome' had kicked in. They had lost away to Cardiff, Glasgow and Leinster in the Magners League, and a big win over Edinburgh was being asked for in order to get the bandwagon looking something like a ... bandwagon.

Edinburgh visited and won 21-10.

There was no O'Connell, and O'Gara had to leave the field early against the Scots, but nevertheless, Declan Kidney was looking and hardly believing what he was seeing. Munster were a team perilously low on confidence. Their defence looked soft, especially out wide. Against Edinburgh they had to scramble most of the evening and first-up tackles were curiously absent. The general organisation of the team also looked off. Against Leinster, it had really hurt to watch for most Munster supporters.

Especially, the third try scored by Leinster was unforgivable. Leinster went wide. Then they went back up the middle, and then they went back to the left and Brian O'Driscoll sauntered in untouched after a skip pass from Gordon D'Arcy.

Munster were 10th in the table in the Magners League.

LEINSTER, HOWEVER, WERE having their own troubles. And in the middle of the month they had to rein in their own coaching staff. They handed out fines to both Michael Cheika and David Knox, the former seen to be remonstrating with the match official, Simon McDowell at the end of the first-half against Munster. The previous season Cheika was obliged to pay a four-figure sum to the IRFU charitable trust and apologise to the fourth official at the Leinster-Munster match in the RDS.

Tension was in the air in the early months of a new season, to be sure, and it was also alleged that Declan Kidney had gone to the officials' room at half-time in the game against Leinster and talked about Cheika's behaviour. That particular matter was cleared up when Paul McNaughton made it known that he had received a phone call from the Munster coach who had informed him that 'he did not for one moment discuss Michael Cheika with the referee; that he did not and never would do such a thing.'

McNaughton added, 'Frankly I never believed that he did.'

Munster explained that it was quite normal for a coach to engage a referee in brief dialogue at half time.

Everyone just needed to take a chill pill.

BUT, BEFORE THAT could happen, Ronan O'Gara chatted with Duncan McRae in *The Guardian* newspaper, and said so many things that would never have received the Declan Kidney seal of approval. McRae had been the Aussie who, five years earlier, had unleashed a barrage of punches (11 unanswered) at O'Gara as he was pinned on the ground during the contest between the Lions and the New South Wales Waratahs. McRae had received a seven-week ban and a lifetime of infamy for that particular episode. But O'Gara was spectacularly talkative when the pair of them sat down for a chat to be reproduced in the newspaper. Rog made it known that English players only thought themselves superior because of 'where they come from'. Rog reminded everyone that he had been on the winning side in four out of six matches against England. Rog said that Munster and Ireland always believed they could win in England. Rog said that Ireland had better players.

Rog said so much.

Ronan O'Gara: Self-praise is no praise. It wasn't an article about me; I was trying to support my teammates. There's nothing there that I wouldn't back up and say again. If you read it all I don't think there's anything controversial in it. It's just that maybe Irish people, before, haven't backed their own. The only point I was trying to make was to promote my own backline, who have won a European Cup and keep getting criticised.

(October 21, 2006)

O'GARA AND HIS teammates, with Declan Kidney's blessing, had sat down for three hours to discuss what was going so wrong, and why things were not going right in their title defence.

Ronan O'Gara: I back my teammates and I hope the tournament brings the best out in us, and it awakens us, and it has to. I would admit that the intensity we had for the European Cup final as opposed to the intensity we had for Leinster in the Celtic League was poor professionalism by us, and I hold my hand up myself. We weren't there mentally; we thought we could turn up and beat this Leinster team, and they got the result they deserved. That was a message for us.

(October 21, 2006)

DECLAN KIDNEY HAD not been out in public celebrating the Heineken Cup win since the Tuesday after the final. Typically, the head coach had his head down. He knew how hard it had been to win one European Cup. A second? Why should that be any easier, or take any less effort or time? Of course, there were distractions. Three books had been written about Munster's European triumph and needed marketing support. A DVD was on its way. The players had given hundreds and hundreds of interviews. Munster were living and playing at an altitude that they had never prepared at before.

Declan Kidney: There's no guarantee that we'll ever win another one, but the only thing I could guarantee you is that the focus will be every bit as much as it was every other year. And if other teams get better than us, we'll do what we did before; we'll shake their hands, but we just need to make it as difficult for them as possible.

(October 21, 2006)

|||❚❚|||

LEICESTER WERE WAITING, and the Tigers had lots and lots of Irish faces in Pat Howard's ranks. There was Geordan Murphy moving between full-back and wing. There was Shane Jennings in the back row, and Leo Cullen in the second row. There was former Ireland under-21 scrum-half Frank Murphy, hooker Gavin Hickie, out-half Paul Burke, and full-back or wing Johnny Murphy. But Leicester's first home defeat in any competition in 21 months was sealed in the pouring rain, as Ronan O'Gara kicked from 50 metres at the distant posts, and Declan Kidney watched the ball dissect the posts; and the head coach could breathe for the first time in a whole new season.

Ronan O'Gara: If I offended people, I apologise. I've got a lot of respect for English teams; I just said the Welsh and Irish teams were just as good.

(October 23, 2006)

O'GARA ALSO CONFESSED that he had knocked on the ball in the tackle that led directly to the fateful penalty in the 19-21 victory in the closing minutes of a pulsating game. Shane Jennings, instead, was penalised when he played the ball on the ground and, significantly, the home side was penalised 10 metres for complaining. Luck is there for the brave. Munster proceeded to make their own luck and stop mucking about. By mid-December, when Cardiff visited for their Pool Four game, Kidney's men stood on 11 successive victories in the tournament, thereby equalling Leicester's record. Cardiff were defeated 32-18. When Munster set off for Bourgoin a month later, Declan Kidney was facing into his 60th European tie as a coach. He was in exalted company as only Guy Noves and Gareth Jenkins had been involved in as many matches.

Munster continued their winning run, but on a sun-kissed afternoon and under the snow-peaked Swiss Alps they made heavy weather of it before getting home 30-27, and came up just short of a fourth try and a bonus point that would have given them an invaluable four-point buffer when they met Leicester the following Saturday. Munster had reached the knockout stages for the ninth year in-a-row, and their unbeaten run in the competition was extended to 13 matches. However, they had Leicester on their hands.

Leicester, thinking revenge.

And Leicester, all business in looking for their own door to the quarter-finals.

Ronan O'Gara: We don't make it easy for ourselves, do we? We're trying to develop our game in terms of a 15-man game, and at times it looked good, and at times it looked terrible. There were some suicidal passes on out there and I don't know where that came from.

(January 15, 2007)

Declan Kidney: We knew there was no point taking them on up front all day. I think you saw that in the second-half today, because once they got hold of the ball they're not inclined to give it back. So to get a win against what I believe is a very good side the way they played today is a great achievement for us. We pushed it a lot and we made mistakes, but we made mistakes trying things, so depending on your point of view... had we lost today, would we be beating ourselves up? The players are already doing that to themselves. But unless you give a little bit of latitude to try a few things you're never going to improve as a side. And with the way analysis is now, everybody has a fair idea as to how we play... maybe they weren't expecting the way we played in the first-half. It's easy enough when it goes to nine or 10 phases, to hide at the bottom of the ruck, but everybody was willing to look for the ball and eventually Shaun (Payne) and Lifeimi finished off the good work by everybody else.

(January15, 2007)

MUNSTER HAD HOSTED 27 European Cup games in Fortress Thomond. But the old ground had one last opportunity to create further history, and hold it in its famous old hands. The Tigers were in Limerick. It was the Tigers who were given the opportunity to make some history of their own, before Thomond Park was rebuilt and would never look the same again.

It stood like this.

Munster had qualified for the last eight of the tournament. A win would ensure a home tie, against Wasps, Castres, Stade Francais or Leinster. A bonus point defeat might also have been sufficient. If Leicester won by more than seven points, however, they would finish above Munster in Pool Four and therefore send the defending champs on their way to an 'away' quarter-final, most likely against Biarritz or Llanelli. It got more interesting mathematically.

If Leicester won by less than eight points and Munster still managed a bonus point in defeat, the teams would finish level at the top of the pool and the decisive criteria was to be tries scored in the two meetings between the teams, followed by points aggregate. Munster were 2-1 up on tries after their clash at Welford Road. Therefore, Munster needed to stay within seven points of Leicester... and score the same number of tries.

Declan Kidney: I think it's going to be a special day for everybody on the touchlines, and if it's voices or the way we play, or if we've to be carried off the pitch, as long as we're able to look at ourselves at the end of the day, then we'll have fulfilled what Thomond Park is all about, and that's giving it everything. If we do that, we're in with a shout at getting a result. But it's going to be a very tough game because, of all the sides we've played from England, ever since the draw came out it looks to be as if they've been relishing this opportunity.

(January 17, 2007)

THE GUTSY VIEW of life that Declan Kidney had implored of his team had been evident to everyone since the first few minutes of their European Cup defence. On the evening of January 20, 2007, just on the hour mark, Kidney's men declined a near-certain 9-8 lead over Leicester Tigers and Paul O'Connell instead opted for a scrum close to the visitor's posts. It was a decision that would stay with everyone who had been in the ground that evening.

Declan Kidney: We wouldn't be in the blame game here at all really; we'll stand by all the decisions that we've made because over the years we've made decisions on those penalties. When you make decisions on them it takes a lot of courage, and if you do the ordinary thing all of the time you never win anything. In the past we've made them and they've worked in our favour; today was a day that it didn't work out for us and it just goes with the day in hand, doesn't it?

(January 22, 2007)

Robert Kitson (writer): Until Saturday night there were three certainties in Irish life: death, taxes and Munster winning at home in the Heineken Cup. For 12 seasons every visiting side had fallen victim here, reduced to their component parts by a seemingly irresistible force of nature. Leicester's ram-raid in their Pool Four contest was the rugby equivalent of watching the Walls of Jericho come tumbling down.

All records get broken eventually, all great teams get dragged back into the pack. The magnitude of the Tigers' ground-breaking effort, though, should not be underestimated, as Munster were hardly complacent. The bulldozers are about to flatten much of Thomond Park as part of a planned redevelopment, and this was supposed to be a raucous farewell to the rackety old place. Little did the locals imagine that their champion squad would be knocked over as well.

No wonder Leicester's players celebrated into the early hours. Even if they go on to win this tournament for a record-equalling third time, it will struggle to eclipse the satisfaction of beating such highly respected hosts at something close to their own game. The same familiar motto – "To the brave and faithful nothing is impossible" – which has helped propel Munster to 26 successive wins in their daunting lair proved equally applicable to Martin Corry and his team-mates.

(The Guardian, Jan 22, 2007)

BEFORE THE GAME, Tigers' coach Pat Howard had reminded his players and the public that Thomond Park was 'just a field'. And Howard wanted to keep it simple in the minds of his players, right up to the last minute before they left their dressing-room. The loudest message screaming from the wall told Leicester to dominate... MENTALLY

PHYSICALLY

VERBALLY

In the scrum of all scrums on the hour mark, that evening in Thomond

Park, the Tigers tight-head prop Julian White once more saw to Marcus Horan, as he had most of the contest. White bent his back. The home scrum was shuffled backwards. Ollie Smith's try seven minutes later, at the other end of the field, resulted from the same scrum.

Munster 6, Leicester 13.

Game over… unbeaten run terminated.

Ronan O'Gara: It was a relatively easy kick but defensively there was a huge opportunity for a try. I won't go into the specifics of it. You presume you're going to win your scrum ball but unfortunately we didn't and it backfired. You take those decisions on the chin. It's a hard way of losing at the top level, I suppose. It was a great day last May, it's not a great night tonight, but I suppose that's sport at the top. I think the great thing about this team though is that we've done it all together. So let's hope there's a twist in this bad road. I think all of the players didn't play to the best of their potential. We made a few errors. Our start wasn't great. The second-half performance was good but we probably needed to get stuck into them more earlier on. Huge areas to improve on, but it's disappointing for the last game to let down the whole province.

(January 22, 2007)

Pat Howard: They're a good team. I've got no problem with that. Emotionally, we were up for this. We had plenty to play for, and Munster let's be fair, didn't have as much to play for as they normally would, so that may have been a factor. We only won by seven points. Let's not get carried away.

(January 22, 2007)

❙❙❙❙❘❙❙❙❙

OLD THOMOND PARK would be no more. Declan Kidney's European Cup winning Munster team also looked down and out, for a good period of time perhaps, when they came home from Stradey Park two months later, looking the worse for wear; having fought back from a 17-0 half-time deficit, and seeing out the quarter-final to a 24-15 conclusion, but looking a side well beaten at the finish. If they had overcome Llanelli they would have faced either Leicester or Stade Francais, again far home, in the semi-final. As it turned out Leicester would defeat the Scarlets 33-17 in their semi-final, but the Tigers looked tired in the final itself. It was Wasps who took Munster's title, beating Leicester 25-9 in the deciding match at Twickenham.

Munster's brave, but injury-laden season, petered out in the end. Llanelli were full of harder running. They were more aggressive, and they had a higher tempo. That left Munster on the backfoot defensively. There was nothing much Declan Kidney and his coaching staff could do to recover the situation. There were simply too many holes in midfield and outside. They ended up playing catch-up after being stuck on zero points after 60 minutes. They missed the combined force of Paul O'Connell and Anthony Foley. Ronan O'Gara missed his kicks. And three times they had turned down possible three pointers in the first-half. When O'Gara, also captain on the night, moved the ball into the wider midfield channels with skip passes, red jerseys were cut down by the advancing Gavin Evans and Regan King. Alix Popham was a man inspired. Simon Easterby spoiled and spoiled, all evening long.

Eight days later, back in Wales, the curtain was effectively pulled on Munster's season. European dreams had been ended by Llanelli. Domestic matters were brought to a close when Ospreys clinched a 20-12 Magners League victory.

Declan Kidney: You always get a real challenge in Wales and that's how you find out about yourself and there are clearly aspects in our game that we need to look at. We will carry on to the final whistle of the season and tackle each game as it comes. We need to take a hard look at our game, especially in attack. Individual effort and application were there but we need to work on our teamwork.

(April 9, 2007)

2007-2008

'I am not that important at all, or a coach isn't that important at all. You can just facilitate what they want to do. If they want to do it? Ninety-nine per cent of the work comes from themselves, The coach doesn't win the matches. Somebody once asked me what my ambition is in coaching and I suppose my ambition is to be lucky enough to work with players who have ambition.'

– Declan Kidney
(May 6, 2000)

DECLAN KIDNEY COULD try to talk down the importance of the coach in the professional game all he liked, but it was at times like this that nobody truly believed what he was saying. Yes, of course, a great coach was an empty tin can without great players and, more so, outstanding players with outstanding ambition could make the vital difference between a coach being acknowledged as more than great, but actually outstanding. Declan Kidney genuinely liked to bow to his players. And he believed they were everything, but in his 10th year as a coach paid good money to build winning teams there was no hiding from the fact that on both great days and the worst of days, the buck stopped with the top man.

If Kidney had any trouble believing that in 2007-2008, then he just had to watch the star crashing down to earth that was once the glittering career of one Eddie O'Sullivan.

In August, at the beginning of the season, and just weeks before the 2007 World Cup finals in France commenced, his fellow Corkman was recognised as the single most important person in the whole of Irish rugby, a role emphasised by the IRFU speedily signing off a new four-year deal with him. The only worrying talk around O'Sullivan centred on who would temporarily take over the role of Irish supremo if O'Sullivan landed the job of Lions' head coach for the 2009 tour of South Africa? Apart from that, with Triple Crowns more like trinkets, everything else appeared close to hunky-dory.

It wasn't, of course. Appearances were deceiving, even though O'Sullivan had overseen three Triple Crowns in four years, and many sumptuous victories in the Six Nations Championship including a business-like dissection of England in Croke Park the previous February. There were also some big autumn scalps, but on the debit side there were five successive losses to the French, a disappointing 2003 World Cup, no Grand Slam, no Championship title even.

Not that the downside of Eddie O'Sullivan's reign was being discussed in August of 2007.

Philip Browne (IRFU CEO): As yet we don't know the terms of reference for the Lions position. We don't know when the appointment will be made, although we would have a fair idea it's going to be next Spring; there's no point in speculating, so when it arises, if it arises, we (both parties) will deal with it, as we did when Eddie went on the last trip. It's self-evident what he (O'Sullivan) has brought to the game: professionalism, structure, and coaching skills. We have been very fortunate in having him available.

(August 30, 2007)

Eddie O'Sullivan: We all seem to be enjoying what we're doing and doing a reasonably good job at it, so why not continue? If I hadn't the energy or the enthusiasm for another four years I wouldn't be sitting here this morning and accepting that job. I believe I have the energy and enthusiasm for it. I believe the staff around me have, and I've no doubt the players have as well... so I think that's a subjective view about staleness; it's really down to the dynamics of the group around the team and it's worked pretty well up to now... so I'm happy to continue.

(August 30, 2007)

O'SULLIVAN WAS SIX years and 69 matches into his reign, and talked about his desire to lead Ireland out of their group in the forthcoming World Cup and 'into the semi-finals and kick on from there'. In theory, he had two World Cup tournaments and five Six Nations Championships ahead of him as Irish coach and he wanted 'more of the same and what we've been doing for the last four years, which is to try to push the team to as high a level as we can with the players we have'.

All fine and dandy, *in theory!*

O'Sullivan and his team were on the doorstep of another World Cup, but whatever resulted in France did not worry the IRFU. 'We're happy with our decision, regardless of what happens in the World Cup,' stated Philip Browne. The CEO also appeared unflustered that O'Sullivan had come up short of the Union's goals as outlined in their Strategic Plan in 2004 – which was to be consistently ranked amongst the world's top four sides and win at least one Six Nations.

As the coach signed on the dotted line Ireland, in fact, were ranked sixth in the world. The 2007 World Cup would be a complete disaster with Ireland failing to emerge from their group. The 2008 Six Nations would be a shambles with Ireland finishing in fourth position behind Wales, England and France (and with only home wins over the Italians and Scots to boast of), and seven months after signing his new four-year contract Eddie O'Sullivan resigned as Ireland head coach.

The message was clear. In good times and bad, there were no places for head coaches to hide. The IRFU had suggested a Six Nations review but dispensed with that notion and accepted O'Sullivan's letter of resignation after the country's worst Championship effort since 1999. What was there to talk about? The facts were the facts. Ireland's win-loss ratio in the Six Nations under O'Sullivan was second only to France, but in his time in charge England won a World Cup, a Grand Slam and reached a World Cup final; France won two Grand Slams and two titles, and Wales also won two Grand Slams.

The addition to the message: professional rugby was more than a results business, it was a silverware business also.

Declan Kidney's name was thrown into the hat by journalists for Eddie's 'old' job. There were lots of names in the hat. The former Leicester guru Pat Howard, Wayne Smith who was working with the All Blacks, Mike Ruddock who led Wales to a Grand Slam in 2005, World Cup winning South African coach Jake White, and John Mitchell also of the All Blacks.

Heavyweight names, but seven weeks after Eddie O'Sullivan's resignation and three weeks before Munster met Toulouse in the 2008 European Cup final, 48 years-old Declan Kidney was named Ireland's new head coach.

With the rise and rise, and swift fall of Eddie O'Sullivan directly at his back, he knew what he was getting himself into. But there was no fanfare. Unlike the press conference called to announce Eddie O'Sullivan's new 'four years', Declan Kidney sort of slid into the position. He informed his Munster players after a morning training session about his appointment.

He received a round of applause.

Declan Kidney: There is no greater honour for any coach than to lead his country. I have had that privilege at several levels of the game in Ireland from schools and under-19s as well as working with the senior Ireland team and I am delighted to have this opportunity and to be here at what is the pinnacle of my career. I have worked with many exceptional players during my career at both international and provincial level and there is no doubt that we have the talent in Ireland to be successful at the highest level. The challenge going forward for the Ireland team, and Irish rugby as a whole is to continue the growth and the success on the field.

(May 8, 2008)

Philip Browne: The record of Declan Kidney speaks for itself and it was obvious from the very beginning of this process that he was one of the main contenders to lead Ireland to the next rugby World Cup in 2011. His ability to achieve success and develop players in the ever-increasing competitive arena of professional rugby is proven and the IRFU is delighted to have made this appointment.

(May 8, 2008)

BROWNE'S WORDS, AS a ringing endorsement, were not a million miles from the happy-clappy excitement of telling Irish rugby fans seven months earlier that Eddie O'Sullivan had been ring-fenced, for the good of Ireland's game, for another four years. As he penned his words, Ireland ranked eighth in the World, just placing them in the second tier of seeds, above Fiji (ninth) and Scotland (10th). When asked by the members of the press the next day if he was in any way intimidated by taking over his new portfolio Declan Kidney, typically, was disarming in his reply.

He said, 'yes,' and paused… before continuing.

Declan Kidney: You'd have to be…coaching a national side with the way sport is now, and there's so much emotion in the whole thing, and you see the kids wearing the jerseys around the place and knowing that you have the onus to try and represent them the best way you can. If I stopped to think about it, yes, so the trick is not to stop, just to keep going. Thanks for the question but the answer is yes. That's the challenge. It's what I said to the players yesterday. If one of the players came up to me and said, 'Look, I've been offered the chance to play for Ireland but I think I'll stay put,' I'd say, 'You will in your … ear. Off you go. You have to challenge yourself at the highest level'. That's where I've been lucky enough to have been offered that and I suppose that's where I put myself. I'd imagine there's probably 15 better jobs than coaching the national team… and that's playing for it. All I've ever tried to do is help the players I work with to be the best they can be on any given day. I do honestly believe the role can be overstated because it's the players who play the game and the people I have with me who will probably do most of the work.

(May 9, 2008)

‖‖ ▮ ▮ ‖‖

HE COULD POINT at the players on the field all he liked, but Declan Kidney could not avoid top billing in the 2007-2008 season. Close to the end of it he was being hailed as Ireland's latest messiah, tailor-made to lead Ireland to the World Cup quarter-finals and the promised land beyond that point. At the beginning of the same season he was faced with one dramatic head-to-head after another. Coach V's Coach... Genius V's Genius... Magician V's Magician... it didn't matter what title was put on it... one coach, one genius, one magician was expected to deliver over another.

As ordained by the professional game that was gathering pace, and with greed always coming before realism or practicality!

Everywhere he looked at the beginning of the season, Kidney was faced by coaches and geniuses and magicians of all shapes and sizes, and first amongst those was Michael Cheika. It would turn out that Leinster defeated Munster 10-3 in round eight of the Magner's League in Musgrave Park, and the following April Cheika had the opportunity to become the first Leinster coach to record a first double over their arch rivals when Kidney brought his troops up to the RDS for the return fixture. Leinster had won 10 games on the trot and were roaring their way to the league title that would be all theirs.

Leinster 21, Munster 12.

It was a defeat that hurt. And for Ronan O'Gara and Peter Stringer, there was a visit to the hospital to check on respective knee and neck injuries. It was bruising as usual, but afterwards 'Cheiks' and Deccie were very buddy-buddy.

Michael Cheika: They've (Munster) just come back from a very big game, not just physically but emotionally as well, and it's hard to come back again and do it again. But the guys were full of running and playing well and it would have been a brave man to take one of them off.

(April 14, 2008)

Declan Kidney: That's good of Michael to say that but our job as professionals is to be ready for each week and I think that's the challenge for us. We know teams get up for us, but that's what's driven us on to be the side we are. I think that's underestimating his own team's performance, they played very well and they should be congratulated for it.

(April 14, 2008)

Michael Cheika: All around the field we tried to put pressure on them, because if you stand off them and you let them wind up their machine like Gloucester did last week, they'll tear you apart. We gotta play discipline against Munster because they want to talk to you so you've got to be disciplined to steer clear of that. But it's a balancing act between steering clear of that and not backing down. You can't back down but you can't get into it and lose your lot either. In the two games we've played against them I've been happy enough with the discipline bar a couple of penalties, because they're intense matches.

(April 14, 2008)

BUT IN THE late spring and early summer of 2008, it was not the battle of wits between Declan Kidney and Michael Cheika that was enthralling fans. In truth, DECCIE V's CHEIKS was off-Broadway.

On the big stage, instead, was DECCIE V's GAFFNEY, and shortly after DECCIE V's NOVES. Because Munster were on a march of their own. Leinster's determination to win the domestic league was completely in the shadows as Munster went after the very best in Europe. In the Heineken Cup semi-final Kidney had to outwit and outsmart his former coaching colleague Alan Gaffney. And, if he succeeded there, as he did, then he had to come up against the man who was hailed as the greatest of them all, the amazing, the fit as a fiddle, the inspirational, the all-powerful in the town of Toulouse, Monsieur Guy Noves.

Trevor Brennan: This is the moment that coaches like Guy Noves relish. This is why he is here and has been for the last 16 years. He loves a challenge. He loves the fight. I have the utmost respect for him, as a man and a coach. He has a very visible and physical presence on the sidelines when you're on the pitch as a player. He reminds you of what he said earlier in the week or that day. As somebody once said, 'A mediocre coach tells. A good coach explains. A superior coach demonstrates, and a great coach inspires'. Guy Noves epitomises the latter two. No earpieces are required for Guy. Every player on the pitch is aware of his presence. He has a way with words. Before we played Northampton he would wind me up by maintaining, 'The Irish are afraid of the English'. Before we played Munster he said, 'You play against your friends today, you are Irish, not Toulouse'. Always challenging me.

(The Irish Times, April 23, 2008)

TREVOR BRENNAN ALSO placed Declan Kidney in the inspirational bracket, even though he had only worked under him twice as a player, the first time when he had to pull out of a game against Scotland A because of food poisoning and once as a sub against France A in Ravenhill. On the other hand, the former Barnhall and Toulouse star had reinvented himself as one of Europe's premier flankers in the south of France, hanging on Noves' every word and mannerism, but Brennan, nevertheless, has seen enough in Kidney to know that the battle between the two men before and during the 2008 Heineken Cup final would indeed be epic.

Trevor Brennan: At the usual team meeting in the hotel before we'd travel to the game, he (Kidney) sat down, opened a book and started reading from it. The story was about a blazing oil truck which crashed in San Francisco. No-one could get near the fire because of the heat and the mayor offered a reward of $150,000 for the first fire crew that could put the fire out. After a couple of hours comes this little, old fire engine with about 20 firemen hanging out of it, which bounces down the sloping streets of San Francisco and flies straight through the flames, before the boys jump out with hoses and sand buckets and eventually bring the fire under control.

When the fire chief is being interviewed on television the mayor tells him he'd never seen courage like it, and asks him what they'd do with the $150,000 reward. 'The first f***ing think I'm going to do is buy a new set of brakes for that truck.' Declan's point, as far as I can recall, was that when you don't hold back you're capable of doing anything.

(The Irish Times, April 23, 2008)

WHILE TREVOR BRENNAN was enthralled by Kidney's quirks and motivational techniques there were many men in Munster who knew him inside out, and occasionally tired of his leadership ways. They found him ever the schoolteacher; and forever tempting them and enticing them to come up with the answers themselves. Sometimes, quite often in fact, Munster players just wished for Kidney to spell it out. But, repeatedly, training sessions would continue to be stopped by the shrill of his whistle and he would ask the men around him to decide what should happen next? Kidney stepped back all the time from being dictatorial. Players thinking for themselves was far better than a coach having all of the answers. That was his personalised coaching style.

Like Guy Noves, he did not suffer stars. All of his players were equals. And like his opposite number in Toulouse, he lived and breathed the team before him. On occasions, such was his overwhelming respect and love for the Munster team, that he felt compelled to inform those in his dressing-room that they were their own little 'nation'.

The 2008 Heinekcn Cup final would be a battle of Nation V's Nation. It would be a tight battle, tighter than tight, like all of Europe's great finals. Nine of the previous 12 finals had been decided by one score. Two had gone to extra-time, a third should have done so. Two of the finals were won by a single point. In such finals where inches always counted, the wit and influence of the coach sometimes made all of the difference.

In 2008, Kidney as usual, chubby, stoic, would keep his distance from the field, no matter how great the need of his players. Noves, slim, fit, his hair slicked back, his face drawn, would remain as close to the touchline as possible, his breath almost upon his own men and others.

Noves and Kidney were so alike, and unalike.

The Frenchman, a sprinter in his youth and a late arrival into a rugby dressing-room, had been consumed by Toulouse for 15 years, and equally the team by him, as he had patrolled the line.

Guy Noves: I'm not looking to be French coach and as long as nobody offers it to me, there isn't a lot of point in talking about it. I know I have always angered the establishment because I have spoken my mind. I was an international player but at the age off 22, after seven international caps, I said I no longer wanted to play for the national side because the coaches were dishonest. I committed myself totally to Toulouse and never played for France again.

(May 24, 2008)

GUY NOVES, WHATEVER the result in the 2008 Heineken Cup final, was the property of Toulouse for life. Declan Kidney, however, weeks before the game was played, had dedicated his immediate future to Ireland. It was Noves' fifth time to seek to conquer Europe; Kidney's fourth and final time.

It was Declan Kidney's last game as Munster head coach, and he was taking on the most formidable opponent of his career.

||| **I** | |||

AT THE BEGINNING of the 2007-2008 season, Declan Kidney made the most significant signing of his career as Munster head coach. He got his hands on 28 years-old Doug Howlett. It marked a seismic shift in how Munster would play the game in the future. The days of grunt and grind were far behind, and although Kidney had been striving on the training field to endorse a 15-man game the capture of Howlett signaled an official and public intent from Munster. Kidney and his team were preparing themselves to take on the richest and the most talented teams in Europe, and run them off the park, from every position if necessary.

Howlett was unable to join his new teammates until January 1, midway through the season. It was a two and a half years deal, pending a medical and a work permit, but the All Blacks and Auckland Blues winger would quickly become part of the Munster 'nation'. He and his wife and children would fall in love with the place. On the field, the highest try scorer in All Blacks history, with 49 tries in 62 Tests, would deliver with authority.

On the field also, 11 months after arriving in Ireland, he would also help deliver in a Munster jersey one of the most magical, emotional, hair-raising moments – when, in the company of his fellow New Zealand teammates lining out in the famous red, Rua Tikopi, Lfemi Mafi and Jeremy Manning, he stood in front of the remainder of the Munster team and issued an audacious Haka to a visiting New Zealand XV in Thomond Park. A ragtag Munster team would lose the game 18-16, but Howlett and Co had never made Munster feel prouder.

In every sense, Howlett was a sparkling addition.

KIDNEY BELIEVED THAT he never had a stronger hand to play, than the hand he now had at the beginning of the 2007-2008 season. It was just as well. The draw for the European Cup left Munster in the toughest pool they had ever experienced in the competition's history. The pool contained reigning champions Wasps, and it also held Kidney's nemesis from the previous season, Llanelli, and just to wrap it all up in one savagely competitive environment, there was Clermont Auvergne. Additionally, there was the little matter of the 2007 World Cup that had to be played just before the greatest teams in Europe got stuck into one another – a World Cup that would disappoint, and distract, and go down perhaps as the most controversial in Irish rugby history.

Declan Kidney: I think that we have been getting stronger for the last 10 years and bringing young players through has been successful. In a way that is half our job. But being stronger is always relative to what the opposition are doing. Bonnaire (Julien), Smit (John), and Baby (Benoit – three international players who had joined Clermont)… If you look at Clermont, they have two Georgian props, two Argentinians and a South African and that's just their front row. The market has taken a quantum leap. It happens sometimes in football when a team comes along and starts recruiting. You have a player like the Argentinian Ledesma in the squad and then you recruit John Smit (World Cup winning South African captain). We're lucky in that we have players like Jerry Flannery and Frankie Sheahan. But Clermont are clearly one of the teams that are favourites to win the competition this season. Because of the recruitment and organisation over the last two years they have taken a professional decision with a view to winning the trophy.

(November 16, 2007)

UNLIKE THE POWERHOUSES in Europe, as a team Munster had twin objectives according to Declan Kidney. They had to be winners, and they had to aim at winning everything, but equally, ever the schoolteacher, the master wanting only the best for his pupils, Kidney never stopped believing that half of his job was to supply the Ireland team with players who were ready to win in green also. As he awaited the start of the European campaign, with a trip to the home of the defending champs, he was philosophical in his discussions with the Irish media. Twelve of his players were coming home from World Cup duty, all of them with their tails between their legs. Some of them had had their careers rocked on the world's greatest stage. Others, like Ronan O'Gara, had also been dogged with vicious, unfounded rumours that ran around the houses throughout the duration of the tournament.

Ronan O'Gara: I bear no grudge and it doesn't cost me a thought what happened during the World Cup, but I was disappointed and upset for my wife and me. Of course, it upset me seeing how it upset Jess, and I don't think it was good for my parents either because people at 55 and 60 years of age gossip as well, you know. Everyone had their own version of events. But I can't go around telling all the people in Ireland exactly what the truth was and it was never my intention to do that. I was disappointed that the reporters called to my home. I just never saw that day coming when I started playing rugby. But it goes with the territory now and it'll probably happen again. I've accepted now that that's just the way it is and I'm not going to live my life based on what other people think.

(October 5, 2008)

O'GARA WAS CHATTING with the media at the tail end of 2008 as he was about to launch his autobiography. It was a book in which Rog was brutally honest. 'Probably the most comical story was the one where I was supposed to have thrown a Heineken Cup quarter-final against Llanelli in 2007,' he wrote. 'The story goes that JP (McManus) and I backed Llanelli to cover my gambling debts and I deliberately missed shots at goal to make sure Munster lost. The people who spread it and believed it deserve to be pitied for their stupidity.'

IN GETTING HIS men back from World Cup duty, Kidney had much to do, but he did not feel he had to enact the role of psychologist as well as coach. The prospect of heading into the Ricoh Arena to meet Wasps, the best of the best, was simply a good thing.

Declan Kidney: They're good professionals, they're seasoned professionals. They know what they have to do. They've had to get back down to work after the highs of Triple Crowns or European Cups in previous years. You can overstate these things too. They've been good pros. I've always thought that first and foremost they're people. Everyone reacts differently to every situation. We're lucky we know each other very well and some things can be left unsaid… you can over-analyse this too and I'm not going to do that. It was disappointing, everyone put in a huge effort, there was no lack of effort, but sometimes these things happen and instead of trying to over-analyse ourselves, you just get on with it.

It's a great occasion to go to the Ricoh Arena. Ten years ago we'd have given our right arm to go there and play the European champions. I think if you lose the fun of the occasion then you probably limit your own chances of playing to the best of your ability. If we do that we'll be there or thereabouts, and that's all you can ask for in sport. We can not afford as a team, or as a group of supporters, or as a country to get greedy. There are huge challenges there, we're well able to take them but we're basically a light-heavyweight fighting in a heavyweight division.

(November 7, 2007)

MUNSTER WENT DOWN to Wasps in their opening game in the European Cup, though they brought home a valuable bonus point in their 24-23 defeat. They also brought back to Limerick with them a greater belief in themselves than they had the week before playing the champions. Of course, there was a grave danger that their European hopes could be up in smoke before Doug Howlett landed in the new year with the promise of a barrelful of tries, but in the Ricoh on that Saturday evening there was a real buzz from the New Zealand midfield pairing of Mafi and Tipoki. Everyone in the squad believed that if they could stay 'alive' for a few more weeks in 2007, then 2008 could hold a bountiful promise.

O'Gara believed that when Munster were 10 points ahead of the home team, they should have kicked on. They almost had Wasps beaten at that point in the game, but Scottish referee Malcolm Changleng made two critical decisions, both of which hurt Kidney's men. There was the official's decision not to sinbin Fraser Waters for holding onto Brian Carney when he was only yards from the Wasps try-line in the 44th minute when Munster were still in front, 20-13, and then there was the yellow carding of Marcus Horan 12 minutes later for coming in at the side. At the same time Kidney was buoyed by what he had seen from his team.

Declan Kidney: This needs to be our base level now. Clermont present a totally different type of challenge, in the way that they play and the way that they come at you. The way that we attack them… we'll have to vary that too, because of the way they defend. So it's a completely different game of chess. As I said before, it's going to take six cup final performances to be there or thereabouts.

(November 12, 2007)

||||█|||||

MORE THAN ANYONE else, O'Gara found being back in the Munster family reassuring after the tribulations of the World Cup. He was amongst his own, and his confidence was soaring. Five good kicks from six attempts helped to make light of Clermont in a good old 36-13 Thomond Park rollicking. Rog had his coach to thank for helping him get back on his feet in his own time, and in his own way. Kidney had allowed Rog maximum time away from the game before reentering the Munster camp. There was no question of rushing his out-half. He knew Rog better than any of his other players, and he knew he needed to be fully refreshed before taking up his old duties, and the extra responsibility of being the official leader of the bunch in the absence of Paul O'Connell.

Back-to-back games against Llanelli were next up. Two defeats had left the Scarlets seriously wounded, but still dangerous. More than half the job was done with a sweet revenge victory in Stradey Park and, a week later, on a bitingly cold Sunday afternoon in a half-built Thomond Park, Munster were leading 17-13 with 15 minutes remaining on the clock. However, they were facing into the wind, and a full-blown crisis loomed when Horan was shown another yellow. It brought the best out in the team. Denis Leamy and Jerry Flannery lifted the pack, and after an exquisite display of handling a 73rd minute try came courtesy of Brian Carney. It was the first time the Welsh side had ever been beaten in a 'double fixture' in Europe, but Kidney still warned against expectations. His favourite word of the season to date seemed to be 'greed' and he reminded his team and their supporters of the dangers that come with such an urge. 'I don't want to philosophise about this too much,' he told the media, 'but everybody would like everything.'

Still.

Howlett was soon to be handed a red jersey. Munster were only going to get better in the new year, and with Howlett on board Munster found themselves at the end of March, 2008 being named as the top ranked rugby team in Europe. The inaugural ERC list based on performances over the previous four seasons had Munster first on 25 points, one point ahead of Toulouse and Biarritz, and two up on Leicester.

A bonus point earned against Clermont in the Stade Marcel Michelin had helped Munster to get to top spot, but that point also helped them to squeeze into the last eight of the tournament. They trailed 23-6 with almost an hour played, and they had been fairly pummeled up to that point in the game, but they clawed their way back to 23-19 with five minutes to play after Mafi crossed for a try and O'Gara kicked eight points. Munster lost 26-19, but enough was done to make sure that any sort of victory over Wasps in their final pool game would get them through.

A 19-3 win over Wasps on a day that rained and rained brought Munster out of the 'Pool of Death' and into the knockout stages of the tournament for a 10th successive season. In the run-in that followed, Doug Howlett would score only one try – in the 61st minute of a powerful 16-3 quarter-final victory over Gloucester at Kingsholm – but by the time injury forced him to retire in 2013 he would have crossed for 35 tries in total for Munster in 114 games. From the day he arrived, it wasn't about Howlett and tries, it was about Howlett representing everything that Kidney and Munster cherished in their team – hunger and a work ethic to match his teammates at all times.

Howlett was made to measure for Munster. He would captain the team before he finished up. He would also continue to work with Munster with the team after his retirement, and prove himself Munster to the core.

Doug Howlett: I came from one of the best teams in the world, the All Blacks to Munster, which I was going to make my home. There was huge expectation. I was nervous. It took me back to being that 20 year-old kid – having to prove yourself in front of peers and supporters. It was invigorating and it probably gave me a few more years of rugby. Things were getting stale (in New Zealand). It was 10 years doing the same thing. But when I came to Munster and European rugby, it was a real eye opener. There was a major difference coming from New Zealand to Ireland. The Munster team could be world-beaters one day. The following day they could lose to a really poor team. There's emotional rises within the group, but you can't do that every game. You have to be a little more steady with spikes of enthusiasm.

(November 3, 2015)

HOWEVER IN THEIR quarter-final win at Gloucester it wasn't Howlett's try that took the breath away and showcased Kidney's new Munster as a team capable of out-gunning and out-running the very best in Europe, it was one from homegrown Ian Dowling in the 37th minute. It was a try that included everything that was outstanding about Munster, the old and the new. Kidney could not have been prouder of what he saw.

It began with Alan Quinlan spoiling as only the flanker could spoil, and Howlett immediately alive to every possibility. Mafi and Tipoki, as ever, worked a treat before Dowling was released to dart up the wing, before coming inside and keeping the move alive. A dozen phases followed over the course of the following two minutes and 15 seconds, and finally Howlett put Dowling over in the corner. It was the ultimate team try. Everybody had a hand, with O'Connell and O'Callaghan clearing out ruck after ruck, David Wallace breaking three tackles to maintain vital momentum, before

O'Connell carried twice, and Quinlan three times. If anyone doubted that Munster were a far superior team to the bunch that had captured the Heineken Cup for the first time in 2006, this one passage of play quietened them and made them believers.

Furthermore, was there any doubt that Declan Kidney had also grown as a coach? Like everyone else, he had a hand in that try. He would deny it afterwards, applauding only his players, but it was Kidney's hand at work alright.

But, straight away, he had to go back to work to out-think Alan Gaffney. Then it was Guy Noves.

There was one more step before Declan Kidney would play his last game of chess as Munster coach against the man who was acknowledged as the Grand Master of the game of rugby. Toulouse had put Cardiff to the sword, in a four-try 41-17 victory on their home turf, and in the semi-final they went to Twickenham and cautiously, as travelling French teams so often are, they crafted a 21-15 win over London-Irish.

Toulouse awaited, but first Declan Kidney had to devote all his attention to Gaffney, a man who knew Munster 'inside out' in Kidney's estimation, and Saracens. Gaffney had guided Munster to the semi-finals twice in Kidney's absence, and he now had Saracens at the penultimate stage for the first time. The text messages were flying back and forth between 'Gaffers' and his old Munster mates in the days counting down to the semi-final.

Kidney, meanwhile, was making sure nobody around him looked or sounded… greedy.

Declan Kidney: All I know is that we've never, ever beaten an English side in the semi-final or final of this competition. And when you're playing a side coached by Alan Gaffney, you'd want to be a very silly man to think this is going to be anything other than a cup final. There's not many teams that would have lived with them (Saracens) in the quarter-final. I'm glad we didn't play them that day because they were right on the line with everything. The Ospreys didn't get a spare yard. Saracens cut down that space from the word go, they were patient, they were very disciplined on the day, took their penalties and twice didn't get the TMO's call so they could have won by more (than 19-10).

(April 24, 2008)

Alan Gaffney: Well Munster are Munster. You can talk about all of the technical issues and tactics. But you have to front up... when you play a side like Munster you have got to front up. Once you can do that then you are in the game. Munster are a team that have belief, particularly with the pack they have. We have to believe that too. We have to believe that we can match them and beat them.

(April 24, 2008)

NOVES' TEAM HAD made it to the final after a sun-drenched thriller in Twickers. The next day there was sun, rain, thunder and a deluge as Kidney surveyed the scene of his semi-final. It was intense to watch, from the first minute to the last. No inch was given. The first-half was mouth-watering. The second a bit of a mess. Both teams began to flounder in the difficult conditions, and match referee Nigel Owens joined them in a display that was unanimously labelled 'hapless'. Munster took it on the chin early, conceded a try, but dug in and then broke out. Tries by O'Gara and Quinlan had them 15-7 in front at half-time. Only an O'Gara penalty would add to that tally, and Noves watched Kidney on the edge of his seat as Munster hung on for an 18-16 win.

Declan Kidney: Somehow... with a group that's fairly local we've managed to get through to the final and I think that's a huge achievement. This is an exceptionally special time. We had a Celtic Tiger at home that was going on forever and ever, and all of a sudden now it seems to have stopped. This is going to stop too, but if we keep working and if we keep trying hard we'll keep it going for as long as we can, and that's what we'd like to do. Sheer guts and work rate got us through, there wasn't anything hugely technical or tactical. But if you have that and you think back to June when the draw was made... and the amount of effort the supporters put in, we're very proud to represent them.

(April 28, 2008)

NOT EVERYONE BELIEVED that Declan Kidney was fit to face Guy

Noves. Actually, as Leinster back's coach David Knox signed off on three years as Michael Cheika's No.2 he made it quite clear that tying Noves' shoes might be a task for which Kidney was unfit. Amongst other things, 'Knoxy' opined that Ian Dowling's magnificent try against Gloucester came as much as a surprise to their coach, as it did to everyone watching. And he exclaimed that Declan Kidney had no idea whatsoever how to utilise the amazing talents of Doug Howlett.

It was an onslaught that Cheika called 'disappointing'. And when Warren Gatland took his turn talking through the 2008 Heineken Cup final pairing, he showed nothing but the height of respect for the differing perspectives of the opposing coaches.

David Knox: I think he is unproven. Have Munster ever changed the way they play? I've watched them for three years and I don't see anything different. They've always been a famous grinding team… they've always been aggressive and they've always played the ball in the other half, but I don't see any change in their play since. It (the try v Gloucester) was broken field play… they went from one end of the field to the other. Do you think that has been coached… that play? I don't know if that was coached. I don't know if he (Kidney) coaches turnover ball. The main thing that came out of his coaching is that he got the boys to wear blue shirts at training. If I was a coach I'd be ashamed to tell people that… it's not a new move or a tactic or anything. It's getting them to dress in blue jumpers. I don't know if that's coaching… that's more like psychology to me. When I arrived here Brian (O'Driscoll) said he was going to leave Leinster because he hadn't learned anything the whole year under Declan Kidney, who left halfway through the season. Three years later Brian's endorsing Kidney because he's going to have to play under the coach… let's not forget three years ago what he said. I reckon I counted Doug Howlett touching the ball between 10 and 20 times this season. I can not remember him touching the ball off set plays, like Luke Fitzgerald and Rob Kearney and Shane Horgan. I think he has scored two tries and they've both been from turnover ball. This guy is probably one of the greatest finishers in the history of the game. Here he is probably being paid 400 or 500,000 dollars, but are you getting your value out of him? You're in the Heineken Cup and he's scored a try at a crucial time, but that was scored by chasing a kick. I think if he was playing for Leinster, he'd have scored 20 or 30 tries this season.

(May 13, 2008)

Warren Gatland: The match itself offers a contrast in playing patterns. Munster are very accurate, very clinical in most areas and don't make many mistakes. They are a very patient team who have no qualms about spending 10 or 15 minutes trying to work an opportunity or securing field position. They don't panic if it takes a while to get a score. They're content to retain possession, and when the opportunity presents itself take three or seven points with equal facility. Munster don't spurn many chances. A great deal is made of French flair but Toulouse are genuinely an example of what has become a little bit of misplaced generalisation. They can turn nothing into something in a blink of an eye. They offer pace and physique and boast a brilliant offloading game and therein lies the nub of the challenge for Munster: stopping Toulouse's offloading game. During the Six Nations match against France we (Wales) elected to double team ball carriers in midfield, going high in the tackle to stop them getting their hands free. Munster need to win the collisions today, play on the front foot with and without the ball and take Toulouse through lots of phases. They have to offer another 80-minute illustration of their work ethic, mental hardness and willingness to go through the pain barrier and keep grinning.

(May 24, 2008)

Keith Wood: Declan Kidney has always known that Irish teams are woeful favourites. The tag has sat uncomfortably on both the teams and their supporters. In any bar in the country if a pundit on the telly mentions that things are going well, he will be shouted down for putting the kibosh on the team. Winners in sport have always strutted their stuff but Kidney had taken a different tack. His self-deprecating, even bumbling protestations that Munster are lucky to be there at all have taken pressure off his side for years and confounded opponents into thinking they only had to turn up to win. It is a ploy that has paid off in the past but one that is now on its last legs.

(The Daily Telegraph, May 24, 2008)

GATLAND BELIEVED MUNSTER would grin through that pain barrier, and win the European title for the second time in three years. Of course, he was right. Munster would take Toulouse through the phases, Munster would be patient beyond belief, and Munster would work their backsides to a standstill. It was 16-13 at the very end. Alan Quinlan was Man of the Match. Donncha O'Callahan pushed him close. There were many Irish heroes, but the French were unhappy at Declan Kidney's 'happiness' at watching his team hold what they had gained as the game concluded, and hold the ball in their own hands.

The French did not think it was how the game should be played. It wasn't rugby in their view. Exactly what Guy Noves thought of Declan Kidney's 'hold it and win' philosophy remained a secret for a few months, however.

Donncha O'Callaghan: I make no apologies about it. We know it (was ugly) but it was effective for us. I think if you ask them they'll feel like a team beat them playing boring and ugly stuff, but we don't care. I have a medal in my arse pocket. I'm very stiff and sore after that. It was a hugely physical game. To come out on top is incredible. Fellas really dug deep. That's not the prettiest of rugby but it's hard graft to 'pick and jam' for as long as we did. It probably would have been easier or smarter to do something else but that's not how we do things… I think if you are beaten by Munster you could be a bit pissed off because it's not really brains, it's more brawn.

(May 26, 2008)

O'CALLAGHAN HAD SERVED his time in getting into Kidney's best books. For too many early years he saw the coach as an impediment, someone standing in his way, holding him up. O'Callaghan had wanted to break for the finish line as a pup of a professional. Now he had two European medals in his back pocket, and he had Deccie to thank more than anyone else.

Ten years before they had come out on top of the world as a schools team. They had stayed in a town lost in the middle of nowhere in the south of France. The only place to go to pass the time between training sessions was a Champion Sports store and a furniture shop. O'Callaghan and Co turned the latter into their play area. They'd play hide 'n' seek, drive the manager of the shop mad at times. It's not sure who came up with the idea of buying a team rabbit, but they had all watched the *Father Ted* episode where Dougal got himself a rabbit and called it Sampras. But nobody on the Irish school squad thought of buying a cage or any food for the furry little thing, and Deccie was not impressed at first sight.

Anyone who had been near the animal was told to get to the team doc and receive an injection. They bought a goldfish instead. They got their hair cut, pretty much skint. Deccie was still unimpressed. At the end of the next training session he kept the forwards back for 30 minutes extra running... 'Who are the hard men now?' O'Callaghan could hear in his ears as he lapped and lapped in the stifling heat.

The coach kept them on their toes. At just the right time he unsettled a select number, including O'Callaghan, by going out of his way to inform them that he had them in 'his thoughts' for selection. Young lads who thought they were 'sure things' had to think again, and in O'Callaghan's case worry his socks off.

And 10 years down the road, Declan Kidney was at the same business again before O'Callaghan's second European final, telling O'Callaghan, Denis Leamy and Marcus Horan a week out from the game that they were 'in his thoughts' for the final.

All the years he had known Kidney, and he could still never know for sure, for absolute certain, what was in his head.

There was the six-try loss to Perpignan back at the start of the decade. He sent O'Callaghan into the action six minutes before half-time as a replacement for Mick O'Driscoll. Took him off 20 minutes into the second-half, though the coach quickly aplogised twice to the young man for his actions on that occasion. There was a later time in their careers when O'Callaghan wanted feedback, tried and tried again to get some information, and ended up with the coach handing him a tennis ball and telling him to work on his hand-eye co-ordination for the day. Ball off wall... ball off wall... and afraid of being torn apart by the other lads. The time Deccie had to pull him out of the gym and threaten to fine him €1,000 for doing too much work all on his own. No doubt, Donncha O'Callaghan had worked harder on Declan Kidney and their relationship than most.

And vice-versa perhaps?

Trevor Brennan: I stayed on for a good half hour and hardly a single person left the stadium for the ceremony: the closed roof, the lights turned off and *Stand Up and Fight* being played. But even from the stand I could see the disappointment on the faces of the Toulouse players after they were clapped onto the podium by the Munster players, when they had to stand and watch the Munster celebrations. I was delighted to see Ronan O'Gara drag Declan Kidney up. As always, he tried to stay at the other end of the pitch, because he feels it's the players who deserve the plaudits. Credit to the players, they ensured that he had a good send-off. There's no manager or coach who will match what he has done for Munster rugby.

(The Irish Times, May 28, 2008)

DECLAN KIDNEY HAD seen off his toughest adversary. He was Ireland head coach by the end of the same week, starting off on a whole other journey. His final game in charge had been won by an opening 30 minutes of infinite patience, before Denis Leamy crossed for a try and Ronan O'Gara added the conversion, and a penalty, that gave them an unassailable 10-3 lead. It was an advantage achieved against almost impossible odds as Toulouse had dominated that first half an hour and had pinned Munster deep.

Jean Baptiste Elissalde had given Toulouse the lead with a snapped drop goal in the eighth minute. They were hungry for more. But the 'patience' that Gatland had explained was Munster's trump card was crystal clear. And when Munster got themselves in Toulouse territory, they switched gears physically and mentally. The ball was swept wide and Doug Howlett's outside break got them on the front foot, and after Denis Hurley took it on, Denis Leamy tried to reach out from a ruck right on the line and touch down.

The TMO said Leamy had lost control of the ball. Next time of asking, when the Munster pack turned over possession at a scrum, Paul O'Connell led a series of drives and Leamy powered over. O'Gara added the points. Three minutes later he added three more.

It was 10-6 at half-time.

O'Gara edged Munster further ahead after Fabien Pelous was harshly sin-binned for use of the boot. Yves Donguy's try levelled it, but O'Gara won it back, with another true kick. That was the simplest story of the game that ended with Kidney watching his team… 'pick and jam' until the cows came home and eventually the final whistle was sounded.

Declan Kidney: We probably had to lose two (finals) to win two. Some of the lessons we learned then and through the hard times, we put to use this time.

(May 26, 2008)

IT WAS ONLY the fourth of 17 finals that Guy Noves had lost in his years with Toulouse, winning 10 out of 14 as team coach. Six months after the 2008 European Cup final defeat, he talked about it with Gerry Thornley of *The Irish Times* during a seminar organised by the ERC in Druid's Glen golf club in Wicklow.

Guy Noves: There was not much to that match really; that's what I learned. Toulouse could have won the match. We didn't succeed really at the very important points of the match. The missed kick by Jean Baptiste Elissalde. A pass that was a bit too forward. Fabien Pelous got the yellow card too, you know, and that was at a very important point in the match. And let's not talk about the referee. The last 15 minutes were crazy.

(October 11, 2008)

2008-2009

'There would have been a lot of times when I would have read in the paper on a Thursday whether I was playing or not. There's no right or wrong way to tell a player that he is or isn't playing, but I think it's important to tell them.'

– Declan Kidney
(May 6, 2000)

THE MUNSTER BOYS found a lot more ball work being introduced at training sessions, from the very beginning of the new season. There was a new broom at work. Declan Kidney had exited stage left. In his place stood Tony McGahan, his former backs coach. The Aussie was now the new boss in town, and Laurie Fisher was in charge of the pack instead of Jim Williams. Jason Holland was also working with the backs, and Anthony Foley landed in as assistant forwards coach. McGahan talked about his 'new, fresh, younger management team' to the media, and that was one thing, but when Paul O'Connell yapped on about Munster going 'up a notch' in their preparations it was made pretty clear... 'The King is dead... Long live the King' or something of that general view on life had taken a hold in Declan Kidney's former 'nation'.

O'Connell spoke specifically about Kidney always looking to gain a psychological edge before every big game. He said that that had worked in the past, but that the team needed to move on. Mature, if you like, as a group of rugby footballers.

Paul O'Connell: Previously there needed to be an edge. There needed to be something… a chip on the shoulder. While we'll never lose that, I think we've drifted from it a small bit in that we've become more performance-orientated no matter who we're playing, no matter what the competition is, no matter what the motivation is. It's actually a hard thing to do for teams. It's a hard thing to master. It's something we've definitely got better at. If you look at our performance against The Dragons a few weeks back, very often against those teams in the Magners League we've done just enough to win and we've been caught once or twice because of it. But I think there was a great desire from the boys to keep pushing, keep pushing. I think that's a good thing for us. This year our pre-season training went up a notch on other years. I think it was something that consciously needed to happen. We won it last year so we needed to take a step higher and I think we did that. I don't know if we did it two years ago. We were inexperienced then with how to deal with having won it. No doubt we tried our hearts out but I'd say there was a lot of wasted energy too in a lot of what we were doing.

(October 9, 2008)

O'CONNELL, KIDNEY'S FORMER captain, was right to talk of the future and to talk up Tony McGahan, but in doing so he did appear to downgrade his former coach as a tactician. McGahan himself seemed a mite more sensitive.

Paul O'Connell: He'd (McGahan) be more into getting your job done. You know, technically, and making sure no matter how emotional or how much passion you bring to a game so long as you do your job technically well and aggressively it shouldn't make a difference.

(October 9, 2008)

Tony McGahan: It's been built over a long period of time. It's been built with a lot of hard work, a lot of tears, a lot of laughs at the same time, and success at the back end of this period. Really we need to continue the work that's been ploughed in over a number of years and this year we have an excellent group of core senior players who are extremely keen to do well. Look, we've put a lot of work into our attack this year, we've put a lot of work into our catch-pass drills, and we have some very good players. So we feel that we're playing to our strengths and we'll play to that. But we certainly still hold the ability to play cup rugby when we need to, or when we need to close down games or to up the tempo. Hopefully, this year, we'll have the ability to do both.

(October 4, 2008)

A WEEK EARLIER, Munster had taken the train up to Dublin and trotted out onto the field in the RDS and given Leinster quite a trimming. No wonder O'Connell and McGahan had their tails up subsequently in chatting with journalists. It was 18-0. After Felipe Contepomi had missed three kicks in-a-row, Ronan O'Gara had put Munster into a 3-0 half-time lead. He added a second penalty in the third quarter, and then McGahan watched his boys move up a gear and finish the home team off with tries from Justin Melck and Doug Howlett. Yep, it was pretty comprehensive in the fourth week of the season, and all the more heartening since Michael Cheika started both of his new arrivals, CJ can der Linde and the powerful Rocky Elsom. It was all systems go.

But, what happened next is hard to explain, unless of course Munster's failure to defend their European title, and subsequent fall from grace entirely, can be set in the context of all empires shaking in their boots when an emperor of long standing passes on.

When Alex Ferguson departed Old Trafford as manager in 2013 there was no reason to fear that the glory years would run dry. Manchester United was a winning machine. In Fergie's 26 years at the club he won 38 trophies, including 13 Premier League titles, five FA Cups, and the Champions League twice. How could a run of that magnitude come to a shuddering halt? But David Moyes, one of the most respectable managers in the game of football, lasted less than one season in Fergie's old shoes. Louis van Gaal, one of Europe's greatest football minds followed and lasted two seasons. Neither won a thing. Jose Mourinho was next up and won nothing to shout too loud about either in his first year.

In the European Cup semi-final in Croke Park, at the end of his first season as Munster coach, Tony McGahan watched Kidney's old team get stuffed by their greatest rivals. That defeat to Leinster was noted as a passing of the baton in Irish rugby and Leinster would subsequently best Munster's total and claim three European titles. In the 2010 semi-final Munster lost to Biarritz. In 2011 they didn't make the quarter-finals. The following year they did and lost to Ulster. Year after that they got beaten by Clermont in the semi-final. They lost to Toulon at the same stage in 2014. The next year they again sank in their pool. Same again in 2016. And then in 2017, after McGahan had been replaced by Rob Penney, who was replaced by Anthony Foley, who was followed by Rassie Erasmus, Munster were well beaten in the semi-finals of the European Cup one more time.

As Paul O'Connell warmed in the autumn of 2008 to preparing and playing at a higher 'notch' with Munster in the future, he had no idea what was to behold. But, on reflection, all the talk by so many people about fancier tactics and reinvention would seem a bundle of tommyrot.

|||**■**|||

IN THE SUMMER of 2008, Declan Kidney was on a watching brief as Ireland quickly toured New Zealand and Australia. Connacht coach Michael Bradley took interim charge of the team, while Kidney looked on. It was a decent double performance, going down 21-11 to the All Blacks and 18-12 to the Australians. If Kidney had been in charge he might have been quietly pleased with himself. Those amongst the Irish party who were happy enough included Brian O'Driscoll, who was in a bit of a hurry to find out if he would remain Ireland team captain.

O'Driscoll decided, once the tour concluded, to make a beeline for Kidney and find out for himself. In August, when he did so, he found a man stronger within himself than the man who had once been Leinster coach. O'Driscoll was aware of Kidney's man-management skills. He understood he was someone who saw players as people, and not just pieces of meat packaged in different coloured jerseys. O'Driscoll decided to tell Deccie about a little hot water he and some of his friends had got themselves into with the police in New York while on a break. Deccie appeared unflustered by that, but he did suggest that O'Driscoll should perhaps hand over the Leinster captaincy. He also advised him to start enjoying his career, and his life, more.

Ireland?

Deccie added that they would talk about that down the road. It was more than a reasonably good first meeting between Ireland's greatest coach and Ireland's greatest rugby star.

IF MCGAHAN AND Co in Munster were looking to improve things in the autumn of 2008, then so too was Declan Kidney. And he was not altogether complimentary about the fitness levels of the players at his fingertips on the national stage.

Declan Kidney: Some of the little things we've noticed, talking to Les (Kiss) and a few others is that fitness standards need to be up a touch, so they're allowing the players to be a kilo or two lighter if that means their aerobic fitness is better. The passages of play are going on for so much longer. There was one passage of play in a Super 14 match that went on for six minutes where a three minute passage would have been considered very long (previously). We can expect more of those in a game now, it's going to put its own demands on the players.

(August 8, 2008)

KIDNEY, HOWEVER, DESPITE challenging himself at the highest level in European club rugby still had a lot to learn about the trade at national level. For starters, all of his talk about the players being the only really important people, was not going to be swallowed by too many onlookers. Though, Deccie did try in his opening weeks to take that big step back.

Declan Kidney: If the coach is feeling any different to the players going out onto the pitch then he probably shouldn't be there. The coach's job is done between now and the time they step onto the pitch. What you want then is to organise it in such a way that the players feel confident enough and responsible enough to take the job on from there. The final whistle goes and the coach steps in again. Obviously, the coach has a bit of influence during the game in terms of substitutions; maybe a few pointers he can give at half-time through his co-coaches.

(August 8, 2008)

KIDNEY REMAINED A puzzle to Irish rugby fans, and Irish people generally, despite being in the public eye for over a decade and becoming one of the most recognised men in the country. Any old guff at media briefings would no longer do once he was Ireland head coach. It was a whole different stage. A sharper spotlight. More eyes and ears around every corner. He seemed to realise himself that he needed to talk more directly to sportsfans, and in October he gave his most revealing interview of all to Gerry Thornley of *The Irish Times*. There was some of the same Kidney modesty at the beginning, talk that the influence of a coaching staff is about 10 per cent, that the players do the rest, that he had already done a large part of his job by building his coaching team. But then, Kidney was disarmingly straight up, starting by explaining that he thought there was very little wrong with what Eddie O'Sullivan had being doing. Kidney and Thornley talked in the semi-darkness for the second half of their interview in the offices of the Connacht Branch. Did that help the coach express himself more openly?

He also dropped a little clue about how Ireland might proceed to actually win an historic Grand Slam very soon indeed.

Declan Kidney: We can still have great fun over the next few years and if you're having fun then you never know what's achievable. But we have to get rid of the word 'should'. The only thing we have to do is give it our best shot. If we do that, then anything is possible. If we don't do that, that's not right. You'd be as nervous as hell (about starting the job). You'd have sweaty palms and that was me. You wouldn't be ready if you weren't nervous. But then you have to tell yourself you can only be like that for so long. You have to front up and if you're asking the players to believe in themselves then you have to believe in yourself too. That comes easier to some people than to others; it doesn't come that easy to me I suppose, but I'll give it my best because I know that's all I can do. When I started off in Munster I was a schools coach. I'll learn in this job too but there's no point in taking it on if you're not willing to learn. I'll make my few mistakes – but that's alright. There's the genuine errors but we'd hope to get more things right than wrong.

(October 22, 2008)

KIDNEY TALKED TO Thornley about risks, for instance, his belief in not playing it too safe. He revisited a story from his youth when he played out-half for Pres and Munster schools but missed out on an Irish jersey to the brilliant Paul Dean from Leinster. He talked about losing one Munster schools senior cup final when he took a quick throw to himself, but failed to control the ball, and Christians grabbed a match-winning try as a result.

'It went the five yards, I caught it, I got tackled, I passed it back,' he explained. 'It wasn't a poor pass or whatever, but they scored a try and we lost. Yeah, it's like all slagging in Ireland. 'Holl' (Jerry Holland) always slags me about it too. Among my peers it doesn't matter what I do, it'll still always be there.' He promised that he would not stop any Irish player from thinking on his feet as well.

Declan Kidney: If the thing is right, they should go for it. Rugby is a game of decisions; that's why it's important you create an environment where players have to make decisions. They'll still have to make decisions, but if they're use to making decisions Monday, Tuesday and Wednesday, they'll make decisions on Saturday. That's not just on the rugby pitch; that's in life in general. It's easy to spot genuine mistakes, but I think it's relatively easy to spot a mistake where a fella didn't bother his arse to cover a part of the pitch. If a fella doesn't work hard and a mistake is made, that's a totally different matter.

(October 4, 2008)

‖‖▌‖‖

AT THE TAIL end of 2008, Declan Kidney was back in a place he would have done anything to avoid. He was Manager of the Year again, a prize that was always going to be his after his second Heineken Cup victory. 'Dream year?' he responded to MC Des Cahill, '… every time I wake up it is a dream day!'.

There were brilliant men in the room, looking at him on stage and this was perhaps one time in his rugby life when Kidney's passion to underplay his own achievements might have been allowed. Brian Cody who had won the All-Ireland title with Kilkenny for the third time in-a-row was sitting there. Close by him was Aidan O'Brien, the sensational training wizard and a winner of 23 Group One races in the season. Tyrone football manager, Mickey Harte who had led his county to a third All-Ireland title in the decade was present, and so too Billy Walsh and Pete Taylor, the respective coaches of the Irish mens' boxing team and world champion, Katie Taylor. Quite a field, indeed. And Kidney mentioned his fellow coaches by name, one by one, acknowledging their special gifts, and calling his selection above all of them as 'extraordinary'. He also went out of his way to enforce with his audience the absolute importance of not dwelling on success.

Declan Kidney: One of the things you learn in Munster is that you can't afford to think like that because then you get deflected from what is happening. We have had to cut ourselves off from it. In an hour's time when I am away from here I will have to cut myself off again because the time for looking back is when we're finished. Right now, it's the next match.

(December 12, 2008)

TRUTH WAS THE next match was never more important to the new Irish head coach. The opening months of his reign were not spectacular. His team looked down in the dumps, and played like a team playing from a bad memory. He had been back in his beloved Thomond Park for his first game as national coach on November 8, when Canada visited. The November internationals against Canada, New Zealand and Argentina were not just significant because they were Kidney's openers, they were doubly important because of Ireland's perilous world ranking. Ireland were eighth in the list, barely above the Scots. Any slippage, and desperate times awaited Ireland in seedings for the 2011 World Cup.

The Canucks were routed 55-0, despite the freezing cold wind and rain, and the ball resembling a bar of soap, and Kidney could feel proud as he sat in Thomond's expansive new stand. It had been 24 weeks since he had taken charge of a rugby game. In his third game as Irish coach, in a fiercely bitter duel with the Pumas, Ireland secured a second tier ranking in the world after a 17-3 win. But a lingering hangover from the 2007 World Cup remained, and afterwards Kidney struggled to come to terms with the team psyche as he spoke to the media. 'They have won three Triple Crowns but we just seem to knock that fact,' he explained. 'They should be full of confidence, but they're not.'

In between these two wins, Kidney had watched an Irish team have a 21st tilt at the All Blacks, and had heard encouraging words from his opposite number, New Zealand's Graham Henry.

Graham Henry: I have had a little association with him (Kidney) over the years; a hell of a good man. He has been the Munster coach and won a couple of European Cups. Obviously the Munster boys played for him and I'm sure the Irish boys will do the same. I think change sometimes brings the best out of a team; it happens early. There are a lot of examples of that. Although Declan is a new coach at this level, most of the players he's coaching he has coached before. It's not as though they don't know him. I don't think the transition will be too difficult for him. It might be very stimulating.

(November 12, 2008)

Declan Kidney: Graham is in this line of work a lot longer than I am so it is nice of him to say that. I dunno. I'm obliged to Graham. I think it was about seven or eight years ago when he was in charge of the Lions he was good enough to let me into a few training sessions in Australia. Not the meetings, but I got to see the training sessions. It's a bit like coming up against your former teacher in lots of ways. He is a good man. His record is excellent. What way we'll play? I wouldn't try to describe it. I won't try and bracket it too much. The lads will just go out and play the way they play. It will be up for someone else to bracket it.

(November 15, 2008)

THE PLAMASING COMPLETED, Ireland bent a knee one more time as the All-Blacks cantered to a victory in Croke Park that was far more total than the 22-3 scoreline suggested. On their previous visit to Dublin the New Zealanders had romped home 45-7, and the totality of their superiority was no different three years later. Kidney's men were confined to two long range penalties over the 80 minutes. The 3-0 try count for the visitors was also misleading.

The bottom line at the end of November, as the coach himself had observed, was that Ireland was not a happy team. They were not content within themselves. There was a moodiness. Too many men were out of form in a green jersey. They went back to their clubs and hit the Heineken Cup road, but before the end of the year Declan Kidney wanted a conversation. He did not want to talk with his players, not especially; he wanted them to talk to themselves. A three-day training camp in the Johnstown House Hotel in Enfield in County Meath was probably the last thing the players would have chosen, but it turned out Kidney chose wisely, and the camp would go down in history as the most telling get-together in the history of Irish rugby.

Kidney asked his senior players, O'Connell, O'Gara, O'Driscoll and Co to be in Enfield four hours before the rest of the squad. He wanted to chat with them first of all. He told them that talking would come first, training after that.

More than anything else, Declan Kidney wanted to know what was on the minds of his players? He felt in his heart the team was dawdling and he wanted to find out why such a talented group were prepared to let their careers wander in that direction. To help, he and team manager Paul McNaughton had asked Padraig Harrington to visit them, and the Open golf champ would do so and he would remain for two hours, chatting about the years in which he was chasing a major, and how he then changed things around. Harrington discussed the two sides of his brain: the organisational side and the artistic side, and he let his audience know that he might have never made his breakthrough unless he stopped being too methodical, and allowed his game to become more instinctive. How Declan Kidney loved that message!

If there were boils to be lanced, Kidney did not want anyone waiting around the place wondering where to start. At the team meeting the evening of their first day he broke the squad into three groups; front five, middle five, and back five, and a fourth group comprised the coaching team. Paul

O'Connell and Rory Best were two of the facilitators in each group. The third was Ronan O'Gara. But none of the groupings were certain what they were suppose to be talking about.

Kidney visited O'Connell's struggling group after a short period. They asked him what they were supposed to talk about? What had he got in mind?

Kidney told them to talk about exactly what was on 'their minds'.

The groups remained huddled for an hour. And another half an hour. They were showing no urgency about breaking up. In the group being facilitated by O'Gara was Rob Kearney, a junior in the squad, just 11 caps to his name, but plucky enough to ask his master out-half why Munster players seemed to have a spirit that appeared to only manifest itself fully when they wore a red jersey.

O'Gara reported back to Kidney and the whole squad – the genie was out of the bottle! Only one coloured jersey could fully dictate a man's worth when he judged himself at the very end of his career. It was time to put Ireland above everything. No second prize. No safety net.

Even though there was still a Six Nations Championship around the corner where the team would have to do their real talking, Ireland was a happier squad. Everyone felt it. And Declan Kidney, more than anyone, glowed in the sense of happiness. He had always put a happy team above all else. When the team met up before the Championship in their training base in Killiney Castle Hotel, he sought to further sharpen the sense of who they all were and with the help of Paul Pook, the team's Strength and Conditioning coach, he saw to it that the gymnasium in which the players would spend so much time potentially bored out of their skulls would be a very different place. The bare walls were filled with posters and pictures. In a flea market Pook had come across an old print of the Irish Grand Slam winning team of 1948.

Pook had it framed. He put it up on the wall in one corner of the gym, and when Kidney came across it on his next visit he suggested to Pook that they write something above the photograph.

'The Greatest Irish Rugby team – So Far'

IT WAS SEVEN years since Ireland had beaten France, and as team captain Brian O'Driscoll later remarked they 'owed the French' one. A spectacular Jamie Heaslip try had Ireland 13-10 ahead at half-time. Ireland were smooth and sharp. They were building phases, and breaking down the visiting defence. Further tries from O'Driscoll and D'Arcy, and Ireland win 30-21. Afterwards the captain and the coach kept the emotion down to the minimum, despite the relief at finally overwhelming the French. Others were more effusive.

Donncha O'Callaghan: I feel that player-wise there is great clarity in our game plan now. We know exactly what we're about. That's not making excuses for poor performances in the autumn. We know what Les (Kiss) wants in defence; we know what Gert (Smal) wants in the forward play, and the way Declan wants us to play. There would have been little grey areas there in the autumn internationals but now there is pure clarity. You know when we hit the wide channels what we are trying to do, when we hit midfield the same. Of course it takes a bit of time to bed it in with the coaches. Like I said I'm not trying to look for excuses with regard to past performances but that extra time has been important. There was a great feeling among the team. There was a great will to get off the ground after you made your hit, get back up on your feet and make another tackle. I think Tomas (O'Leary) bullied the forwards brilliantly, shouting and roaring at fellas. That's all we need; a bit of direction. He gave that to us. When you can get the likes of Stephen Ferris, Haysie (John Hayes) and Jerry (Flannery) screaming at you to get off the ground, you wouldn't be long there. We have a saying… 'no logs lying on the ground'… you just heard fellas shouting that today.

(February 9, 2009)

THE WIN OVER the Italians that followed shoved Ireland up to sixth place in the world rankings. In a numbers game, as professional rugby was now becoming, a 14-9 half-time lead was simply not big enough. Tries from David Wallace, O'Driscoll and Luke Fitzgerald ended it at 38-9, and 14 of those points came in the final five minutes of the game. How absolutely crucial those 14 points would be when by season's end, with a Grand Slam and Championship on the line, and Ireland had to visit Wales' Millennium Stadium with a 13 points differential. But, that was far down the road. Ireland were two from two, and England were coming to Croke Park on March's opening weekend. It was a crossroads in the 2009 Grand Slam winning season. Martin Johnson, England's inspirational World Cup winning captain, was less than a year into a coaching position that was proving just beyond his capabilities. If Ronan O'Gara had brought his kicking boots to Croker the English might have been easy meat. Instead, a 14-13 victory was the order of the day, and after a tight first-half (3-3) O'Driscoll made the decisive breakthrough when he received a pop pass from O'Leary two metres from the line and saw two big men, Nick Kennedy and Julian White, between him and the line. He went in low and hard. O'Gara made it a two score game with a penalty, and just as well as an Delon Armitage try was converted by Andy Goode in the final minute of the game.

Declan Kidney: I'd have to say an awful lot for Ronan today. You miss one or two penalties and all of a sudden you can go into your shell. He didn't. When we needed a conversion to put us up, or a penalty, he was the man who stood up. He never shirked it. Today was one of Brian's better days and I'm delighted for him. But I always look on the fella who's not having a good day; it's how he digs in that could be the deciding factor. We're having a bit of craic, that's an important part of it. There's a lot of experience in the team, they've been down different roads before and we want to try and put that to good effect with some of the younger fellas coming in. But there's nobody like Scotland to disturb a party.

(March 2, 2009)

Jamie Heaslip: The amount of times that Rog has slotted over so many kicks, you are not going to hold that (two from six) against the chap. He tried to put his hand up in the changing room and no one was having it. I don't believe in putting any sort of pressure on him. He has enough pressure. He has enough pressure as the main kicker so I don't believe any sort of extra pressure is positive at all. Everyone's chasing records. I don't exactly think he's thinking of Jonny Wilkinson's record when he steps up to take a kick.

(March 2, 2009)

Declan Kidney: I'll go to my golf; what if they lip out? Two of them came off the post. Right? We had to take a little from the chasers. Right? How much courage to stand up and take that conversion at the end. Right? We do have a back up plan but part of it is my belief in Ronan. If things are going over it's an easy game. It's when they are not going over, to have the courage to stand up and to put in the tackle he put in today. He had a different type of game. Not the one that other people see but he did an awful lot of good work. They were coming down his channel all day and he stood up to it time and time again. You cannot coach that. That's something that comes from within himself.

(March 2, 2009)

‖‖‖∎‖‖‖

THROUGHOUT HIS COACHING life Declan Kidney never tried to hide the fact that he hated breaking the worst news of all to his players. It appeared that such conversations knocked as much wind out of the coach as the man standing in front of him. Two games divided Ireland form a first Grand Slam after 61 years of waiting, however, both of them on foreign turf, Edinburgh's Murrayfield to begin with, and then the Millennium Stadium in Cardiff. Ireland were on a winning run. Everyone was happy in camp. There was no need at all, on the surface level, for Kidney to get to work on the one job that tested his stomach.

But he made the decision to remove four players from his team for the first trip. The whole team was shocked when word started to filter through. O'Driscoll later confided that he had picked up a vibe from O'Gara, but nobody thought it would be four.

Flannery, Heaslip, O'Leary and Wallace were the four men. 'I didn't want to wait until we lost before I made some changes,' Kidney eventually confided in his team captain. They were still four tough conversations for the coach. The four easier chats were with Best, Leamy, Stringer and D'Arcy who were back in the team.

Paddy Wallace had been idling in the team room when Kidney asked to have a word with him outside. When Wallace left the room he found the other three, Heaslip, Flannery and O'Leary in front of him. Kidney told them straight. He said they were not being dropped from his team. Neither were they being rotated. He explained it was something that he felt deep down needed to be done. It was the Monday evening before the game against Scotland. Rocked that little bit by the decision making, the whole squad needed a little extra cheer later in the night. It was good timing that Christy Moore had been asked to drop into the hotel in Killiney to play a few songs for the lads.

The game was always going to be tight. The statistics did not lie, and the Scots were in fighting form. They had completed the most off-loads (42) in the Championship up to that week and also the highest number of passes (545), and it so happened that Ireland, curiously, were bottom of the table in both categories with 10 and 380. On the following Saturday, Ireland looked constrained in the first-half, as though the level of expectation had chained them down. It did not help that South African referee, Jonathan Kaplan and the Irish team, as in the past whenever they shared the same pitch, appeared to be on different pages with regard to the rules of the game and their interpretation. Kidney watched his men play as though they were indisciplined, which he knew they were not! But seven of the 12 penalties they conceded on the day came in the opening half. When Brian O'Driscoll decided to speak to the referee, he made sure to begin every sentence with the word… 'Sir…'

But Kaplan gave him short shrift. O'Driscoll had been penalised for seemingly trying to free ruck ball with his right boot three times. The Scots' scrum was on top, and they were winning the collisions. Chris Patterson had his eye in with his boot as well, and there was a hill to be climbed in the second-half. The home team could have been 10 points ahead by that stage in the game, instead of a 12-9 scoreline after Patterson and O'Gara had traded penalties. But David Wallace had stopped Thom Evans in a breakout. Tommy Bowe and O'Driscoll had made try-scoring tackles. Ireland needed to get back into their dressing-room more than the Scots. On reappearing, Ireland's intensity shifted up a gear. O'Gara and D'Arcy led the line up in defence a lot harder. O'Gara also began to take the ball flatter from Stringer. Clear-outs became clinical in nature. O'Connell and the lads were getting to grips in no uncertain manner with the Scots in the lineouts.

The game was turning, and it completed its move in the 51st minute when Heaslip, a 30th minute substitution for Leamy, took the offload from Stringer and went over for the game-winning try, 22-15. It was a moment Heaslip wanted the Ireland team management to remember, but some showboating, and a little wave to the crowd before touching the ball down one-handed, did not endear him to his teammates who just wanted the points on the board. The win left just the Welsh in the wings, waiting to be accounted for, but the game in the Millennium Stadium would be the fastest turnaround fixture in the entire Championship. Kidney had no worries for his players. 'We've gone to the well a few times with these lads,' he informed the media in the hours after the game, 'but they're still good and thirsty.' Especially so, since nobody knew what the coach might have up his sleeve in his next team selection.

With the Welsh in the wings, of course, was their coach Warren Gatland who forever it seemed would have a strained, twitchy relationship with the Irish after his forced departure from the job now held down by Declan Kidney.

Warren Gatland: It's a long time ago now. For me, it's in the past. When there has been that expectation on (Irish) players to perform in the Six Nations tournament and World Cups, they have sometimes faltered a little bit so it will be interesting to see how Declan is going to handle that and the players handle that this week. Win the game is first (for Wales). Win the Championship, the Triple Crown and deny them the Grand Slam. Then see what position we are in and hopefully start thinking about the points. We are confident we can come up with a win and who knows what will happen if we can get ourselves ahead in the game and that Millennium Stadium factor begins to kick in. There is obviously a lot of pressure and expectation on Ireland.

(March 18, 2009)

WALES HAD TO win by 13 points to lift the Championship trophy. There was no hiding from the numbers game, once more, and Kidney and his team management felt a responsibility to go through the range of numbers with their players. They needed everyone to have processed decisions in advance. What if Ireland were 15 points down with three minutes to go?

Harder still, what if Ireland were six points down and there were three minutes to go? And we get a penalty?

They had talked through all sorts of scenarios, but six points down and three minutes left on the clock was the one set of numbers that stuck most with O'Driscoll and Co.

O'Gara stated bluntly and decisively that there was no way that they would kick the penalty. Kidney was in complete agreement with the decision of his players, even if such a decision might lead to a Welsh try at the other end and cost Ireland absolutely everything – the Championship, the Crown, the precious Slam.

IT WAS THE longest week in the lives of the Irish players. And Monday was the longest day of all. A week earlier four players had been axed from the team for the Scotland game. Kidney could couch it in as many ways as he liked, to a player it was… an axe!

And one they needed to avoid at all costs, and so they looked at their phones and looked again, and again, reassuring themselves that the coach had not asked to see them. Even eye-contact with Declan Kidney was being avoided by some, just in case they read something into it, or offered the coach an easier opportunity to call them to one side and spill the bad news.

A phone ringing.

A screen flashing.

Deccie's name popping up.

That was the nightmare scenario all through Monday. Normally the call should come about an hour before the team sat down for their dinner, in or around five o'clock. The four players who had received the nod for the Scots' game, and the four players who had been told there was no room for them on the team were on tenterhooks. But everyone was nervous. After all, a coach never, ever changes a winning team, but Deccie had done just that, and not just one little tweak! He'd made four of the hardest decisions. They all feared he would make more.

Like everyone else, Jamie Heaslip knew how often Declan Kidney spilled out the word 'honesty' to his squad. Honesty was the core of the whole caboodle. Heaslip had 'honestly' told Kidney how he felt about being dropped for the Scots' game. Kidney had told him that he wished to reward the lads who were training well, and who were showing extra for their provinces. Heaslip told him he was not happy. But Kidney had resolved that he never needed to justify a decision with a player; he preferred to just give his decision, and then give the player all the time in the world in his company. But no withering explanation.

That was the way to do it. Even if it left some players flummoxed. Best to tell a player that he 'didn't have a start' for him. On Monday, it was good news for Heaslip, and Flannery and O'Leary. Not so good for Wallace.

EVERYONE KNEW IN their gut that the kicking games of Stephen Jones and Ronan O'Gara, more than likely, would have the most decisive bearing on everything! The Championship, the Crown, the Slam, but nobody could have imagined just how dramatic and dangerously edge-of-the-seat it would actually be in the final minutes and seconds in the Millennium Stadium. O'Gara's sensational drop-kick? Jones' aching penalty kick that followed so fast? Nobody could have written it down in advance of the contest. Though Jones, perhaps, went closer than anybody else when chatting with the media before the game, and the Scarlets kicker with 79 caps and 678 points to his name was unflinching in laying down the gauntlet to Ronan O'Gara, who at 32 years of age had played 92 times for his country and racked up 912 points. O'Gara had numbers that were there to be chased by others, and Jones was an admirer, but Jones went through the O'Gara game in such minute detail that it did appear that he was searching for a weakness – or perhaps simply raising the pressure on his opposite number by way of over-the-top adoration?

Stephen Jones: A great kicker of the ball, O'Gara is a great kicker of the ball. The kicking battle is going to be interesting. Look at the stats and whoever wins the kicking battle wins the game. It's about the variety of kicks, when to kick, and when it is best being clever, isn't it? That's the way I think Ireland will go. I think they will probably put the ball up the park. They have got a very good defensive lineout haven't they? You play to your strengths. How many years has O'Gara been at the top? He's been brilliant hasn't he? He dictates things well, a very, very good tactical kicker. He complements that pack well. He keeps them going forward. He keeps them on the front foot. Distribution game is good. He bounced straight back (after missing four against England), didn't he? How good is that? He did his job well. He's mentally tough. He's proved that time after time. We'll obviously try to put pressure on him defensively because we can't allow him to dictate things because he does it well. And that's going to be a challenge for us. You look at where Ireland is strong. They are very good up front, aren't they? They want to play forward as much as they can in the game. They are very efficient. The fact the lineout is very good, I think they will probably be direct and obviously with O'Gara and O'Leary they will probably try to kick. O'Leary kicks more box kicks. We have got to up the tempo, throw the ball around. But kicking is a huge part of our game. For us, it's trying to get that balance right. That's the big challenge we've got.

(March 19, 2009)

ON THE THURSDAY before flying over to Wales and getting settled into their Hilton Hotel, whatever pressure the Ireland squad was feeling, and however the likes of Stephen Jones and others poked at the squad to test how they were bearing up under such pressure, there was time for some relaxation. It was time for the players to order around Declan Kidney and his coaching staff. Geordan Murphy and Donncha O'Callaghan wanted a sprint race for the old lads.

It was a handicap race, naturally, and the really old lads, like Alan Gaffney and kitman Paddy O'Reilly were only running 45 metres. Gert Smal was running 55 metres. Kidney had 65 metres to run. Team manager Paul McNaughton, a former Irish centre, was on 70 metres. Then less Kiss was on the 80 metres mark.

They all whinged.

Everyone wanted to claim an extra five or 10 metres.

Murphy and O'Callaghan would have none of it, and the whistle sounded. Deccie was going well. Smal began to leg it, even though he had complained louder than anyone pre-race about the state of his poor knees. With 10 metres to go Rala O'Reilly was winning, but his legs went completely. Deccie and Small hit the line together. The South African claimed victory. Deccie seemed as happy with silver position.

Les Kiss: It's quite a good feeling when the boys sit around in that circle with Declan in amongst them. The rest of the staff sit behind them. None of the players said anything. Declan picks his little themes, and to make sure that we didn't leave anything for when we look in the mirror afterwards.

(March 28, 2009)

IT WAS A game that flew by, and then stalled and allowed everyone to watch as Jones and O'Gara stood up to kick it to the death.

The game plan had been simple enough, when delivered by Kidney to his circle of players one final time before leaving their hotel. It centred around field position. The more minutes they spent in the Welsh half the better. It was about hitting the corners. Putting the ball up high. It was so much about O'Gara's boot, as Stephen Jones and the Welsh knew it would be! Pressure, pressure, pressure.

But Ireland were 6-0 down at half-time. Back in the dressing-room, Kidney spoke first. Then Kiss. Then the team broke up into their individual units.

Back on the field, Ireland crashed into the game for the first time all evening. Leamy. Horan. O'Callaghan. Wallace. O'Connell. All of them tore holes in the Welsh defence, until Ireland were one foot short of the line. O'Connell let the ball go to O'Driscoll and he made it in, just about. Referee Wayne Barnes checked with his TMO Romain Poite.

It was a try. And soon it was 14-6 Ireland, after an O'Gara chip into space bounced just perfectly for Tommy Bowe's line that put him in straight between the posts. Stephen Jones brought it back to 14-12 Ireland. Wales got Jones in the pocket for a drop goal.

15-14 Wales.

There was four minutes and 40 seconds left on the stadium clock. After Jones kicked the ball out on the full, Ireland get a lineout. O'Connell and everyone else saw only one play. They needed to get the ball to Rog. His drop kick was true and straight.

17-15 Ireland.

There were two minutes and 15 seconds left on the clock.

With 50 seconds remaining Paddy Wallace competed for a ball in a ruck inside Ireland's half. Wayne Barnes blew his whistle. Jones prepared to kick Ireland's Grand Slam dream to oblivion.

In the Ireland coaches' box there was shock and disbelief for a few seconds. Kiss could not bear to sit down and watch the kick. He and Gaffney stood up.

They went to move to the rear of the box but Kidney told them to sit back down. When the cameras turned to the Ireland box all was calm. Everyone was seated around Declan Kidney.

The game then ended.

17-15.

The count had finally stopped at 61 years.

Declan Kidney: Honesty, trust, hard work, willingness to go the extra little bit. It's like what I said earlier, nobody was blaming anybody. We had none of that, no cliques, no nothing. We gave it a go in the best way possible. You can't overestimate honesty.

(March 23, 2009)

Paul O'Connell: Jose Mourinho used to do a lot of it with Chelsea, taking the pressure off his players. You need a big ego to do that which he (Gatland) seems to have from his recent success as a coach. Perhaps he needs to get his feet back on the ground now. A lot of the stuff that came from Warren Gatland's side this week, you wouldn't see an Irish coach doing that, or an Irish person doing that. We were very honest in everything we did and that's a big part of our trait, a big part of Munster and a big part of Ireland as well. Did the good guys win in the end? I don't know about that. But we won and we're happy.

(March 23, 2009)

Declan Kidney: When November was over, we sat down. I have a brilliant bunch of team leaders, Brian, Rog, Paul, Rory. We sat down with Paul (McNaughton) and we had a good frank discussion. We opened it up, asked the players what they think? 'Let's put it out on the table, lads!' It was nothing hugely scientific. I'm not a management consultant or anything like that, but it was just saying, 'Let's be honest with one another now… what are the (wrong) things?' You'd be surprised that by talking about it, and a little bit of slagging, all of a sudden a whole lot of doors were opened, and we just have some craic now. I'd be a believer that you don't ever own a jersey, you don't ever nail down a jersey. You have it for one afternoon, and that's your chance. You leave your DNA in it. Hopefully today the lads have added their little bit to it, so that whoever fills it in our next match in May, they'll feel that onus on them to represent it.

(March 23, 2009)

Ronan O'Gara: I'd an awful lot of time to think about it (the drop goal). I was roaring for the ball for 30, 40, 50 seconds, I don't know how long, but then Strings showed great composure. I think he knew what he was looking to do. I took about 15 yards from Strings, they obviously got a running start. No way the ref was going to give a penalty; they were well offside. So I had to concentrate on getting the ball up rather than driving through like a normal drop kick.

(March 23, 2009)

Stephen Jones: I can safely say I've never been involved in such an emotional and dramatic last five minutes. It was amazing and I experienced the whole range of emotions from when my drop goal went over up to the final kick to win the game... it was mad. It was bitterly disappointing for me. I did not strike through the ball and got under it, which was frustrating. When you are out there, you just think of the process you need. I knew it was a long kick but I was happy with the way I was striking the ball. In hindsight, maybe I should have given it to Gavin Henson. But you have to back yourself in those situations. It was going straight.

(March 23, 2009)

Ronan O'Gara: Crack under pressure? I've won two European Cup finals under pressure, no one of those Welsh fellas have played in a European Cup final. What are they basing this on? They've won Grand Slams maybe. They talked the talk this week but they didn't walk the walk. I'm particularly happy in that regard.

(March 23, 2009)

2009-2010

'There is a huge pride and a huge onus, and we've mentioned that. We've talked about that and we know the onus that is on us to perform to the best of our ability, but we also believe that the true sportsman in the country knows that if we do that people will stay with us. That's more important probably than the result, that we go about our job in an honest way, and that we use our resources wisely, that we plan for the future, that if the economy is teaching us anything now: deal with the present, but don't be that greedy.'

– Declan Kidney
(November 7, 2009)

THE SCALP OF South Africa was claimed in the autumn, and Ireland finished a whole year unbeaten. Eight games. The team remained unflinching and heroic right to the end, and by December Declan Kidney would, once again, be Manager of the Year and right on the heels of Jack Charlton who had claimed the title four times in his decade as Ireland's supremo on the soccer field. Ireland had nothing to fear. Although Kidney reminded everyone as he held his award that there was a perilous fixture list directly ahead in 2010 – with games against the English, the French, the All Blacks and the Australians, and all far away from home. However, Irish rugby had the broadest of smiles on its face as it turned into a new year. Who cared that the last time Ireland had won in London and Paris in the same year was in 1972? Or that the last time such a lofty 'away double' in these two cities was achieved prior to '72 had been in the slam year of 1948? Ireland was top of the tree, and unofficially top of the world tree into the bargain as the win over Pieter de Villiers' Springboks had been in a seismic meeting between northern hemisphere Champs and southern hemisphere Champs.

We had it all and, therefore, Ireland also had so much to lose in 2010.

But, win or lose, Kidney had already warned the country, in addition to his own squad of players, of his intention to have 'honesty' guide him in his decision-making, and neither would he fail those around him in refusing to 'plan for the future'.

It was not a time to be soft or sentimental, not when a team was balanced at such a height, and Kidney would be true to his word. He decided to stick with Brian O'Driscoll as his captain, but the role of Ronan O'Gara as his on-field general indefinitely was already in some doubt. O'Gara had shown indifferent form despite finishing the Six Nations on such a thrilling note in 2009, and an unmemorable Lions tour of South Africa that followed on its heels was considered to have left him psychologically wounded.

O'Gara had been doing the business on the field for Kidney for 16 years. But the stakes in the autumn of 2010 were never higher.

Declan Kidney: We're now more of a target in other people's eyes, we're now more analysed, more so more of our failings will be spotted, more of our warts will be attacked. So, can we get stronger within that? Look at how we play. Do we change it just for the sake of changing it, no? But we look to change it to bring out our strengths a little bit more. We must play like an Irish team, we must just play smart. Because if we go out and say 'Well, this is our game and we're good enough to beat anybody playing this way' we're going to get hammered.

(November 7, 2009)

LESS THAN A fortnight after those words were spoken, Ireland drew (20-20) with the Aussies in Croke Park, thanks to a magnificent scrum move straight off the training ground that saw Brian O'Driscoll score his 37th try for his country in the final play of the day. O'Gara converted. But 24 years-old Jonny Sexton got a start in the 41-6 win over Fiji in the RDS less than a week later, kicking seven from seven, and a week later back in Croker Sexton kicked five from seven in the brilliant 15-10 win over the South Africans. Kidney, before the Springboks game, had gone to some length in attempting a mixed-up explanation for opting for the younger No.10.

Declan Kidney: I thought Ronan was going well. He played well against Australia. We know that. Jonathan got a chance last Saturday (against Fiji) and he did okay. As a side we need to grow. When do you give him a go? I'd like to be playing Ronan. I'd like to give Jonathan a go but I can only have one. This time I've given it to Jon. There were a multitude of things behind my thinking. Last week the only reason that Ronan didn't play against Fiji was because we had to try and find out what would happen if he wasn't around.

(November 25, 2009)

AGAINST THE 'BOKS, Kidney and the Irish public saw something more from Sexton, in his second Ireland appearance, than perhaps they had expected. At the higher altitude of world rugby he still had a steely quality to his game, same as he showed in guiding Leinster to European glory a few month before when, out of the blue, he jumped into Felipe Contepomi's boots. He looked at home too in a more stifling pressure game. He kicked one huge penalty from over 50 metres to trim the visitor's lead to 10-9 and three minutes later steered Ireland in front with another difficult one, from a tough angle 40 metres out. By the end of the month, Sexton was a suitable alternative to Ronan O'Gara any day of the week perhaps, if Declan Kidney so decided. Also, by the end of the same month, Kidney was IRB Coach of the Year.

Kidney professed mostly happiness with his month's work in November of 2009, but his honesty with his players and his determination in planning for a greater future for Irish rugby would leave him looking to get to grips with the final few seasons of Ronan O'Gara's career.

That immensely tough task, unfortunately, would also be a long-running sub-plot to the last four years of Declan Kidney's coaching career too.

Declan Kidney: I said that I wanted to give him (Sexton) a go to see what he would do and how he did. I thought he went okay. It was that sort of game where the forwards and the number nine had a huge say in how the game went. He slotted a few penalties, that's different to how you play at out-half, but you know there were one or two that went astray and maybe Ronan would have kicked some more. What I'm really hoping is that we don't go down the road of just giving one a rough time. It's just a blessing that we have both and we're going to need both of them.

(November 30, 2009)

SIXTEEN LONG YEARS.

Indeed, since their days as schoolteacher and pupil in Pres Cork, Declan Kidney and Ronan O'Gara had been mostly inseparable. But that was to change. Kidney had made up his mind. He needed to be as clear-headed and unemotional as he possibly could be – and he was! Right to the very end, when he cut O'Gara from his Irish squad entirely in 2013 and thereby ruled out one final emotion-filled day with the Irish fans for Rog – a day that would come Brian O'Driscoll's way when he reached the very end, and a day that would also be spared for Paul O'Connell.

O'Gara was also a giant of Irish rugby. One of three giants – but Declan Kidney would decide that affording everyone fairytale endings was not part of his remit as Irish coach.

By February of 2010 O'Gara was back in the green No.10, but because Sexton was carrying a 'dead leg' nobody knew for sure whether Kidney had been of a mind to recall the man who had served him longer and more assuredly than anyone else. With the Italians in Croke Park for Ireland's defence of the Championship title, O'Gara kicked four penalties and two conversions in a 29-11 win, but before the game Kidney had left him in no-man's land as to his inner thoughts. 'You learn in this job you never make a decision until you have to,' the coach said, smiling broadly, when asked by journalists as to whether O'Gara was getting the nod in the first place. It was O'Gara's seventh successive campaign to start as Ireland out-half, and his 31st consecutive Championship match, but his days were still counting down as a no-brain first-choice. A week later in the Stade de France Ireland's hopes of retaining 'everything' were blown sky high into the Paris air. It was 33-10. A proper thumping, and an indentikit scoreline to Eddie O'Sullivan's last match in charge against England two years before. It was, however, after a long unbeaten stretch, a very sobering result for everyone involved in the Irish team. The Irish players trooped off the field, beaten up, and their heads bowed. Kidney was one of the few stoic people in the ground after the game, though some of his words were old and unhelpful. He talked about only failing if a team failed to pick itself back up after such a misfortune. It was not what the Irish public, or his players, needed to hear at the end of a 12-game, 15-month unbeaten run. Instead, a very definite path to recovery and a quick return to winning ways was what the Irish public had in mind. The members of the IRFU could be included in that number.

It was two weeks to Twickenham, and the English, but not for Ronan O'Gara who was denied a personal salvation when the team was selected. Sexton was back in. Kidney, once again, was at pains in explaining himself.

Declan Kidney: To leave someone like Rog out of this match is not an easy call on him, with the wealth of experience and knowledge that he has. I just felt it was right to give Jonathan this go. He's been training well, and that's the type of squad we want. If we didn't have that squad then we could be caught badly.

(February 24, 2010)

IN THE LIST of great Irish victories at the home of English rugby, the win in the spring of 2010 did not top the list. It was a smash and grab away performance, as Kidney's men lived off scraps and more scraps, but still won on the scoreboard (20-16) and had three tries to one to show over Martin Johnson's men. Ireland's hunger in the tackle was the chief characteristic of the afternoon, as demonstrated by 99 tackles. There was only one missed in the 80 minutes. Kidney also emptied the bench and O'Gara got game-time and slotted a conversion, but against the Welsh next time out he was back on the bench – and only took the field for the final two minutes to replace Keith Earls. Sexton's kicking in Croke Park was not of the highest order, but a 27-12 win left everyone involved in Irish rugby an awful lot calmer and more content about the general direction of the season. It was also nice to hear Warren Gatland say a big sorry to everyone in Irish rugby after his bullish and cutting remarks a year earlier.

Warren Gatland: We have nothing but a huge amount of respect for the Irish coaches and players, particularly for what they've achieved for Ireland, but also for what Munster and Leinster have achieved as well. But that respect doesn't mean that we don't want to desperately beat them or that our players don't desperately want to win. It was a huge achievement (2009). I have a huge amount of respect for Declan in terms of what he's achieved as a coach, not just with Munster and Ireland, but Dolphin, the Irish schools, the under-age team, the Ireland A's. He has a fantastic track record and I admire what he's done in sport.

(March 12, 2010)

A TRIPLE CROWN was possible, but not for long. The Scots put an end to that presumption in Croke Park, with Dan Parks kicking more than Johnny Sexton and Ronan O'Gara combined in a 23-20 victory. O'Gara replaced Sexton after 52 minutes. And Declan Kidney may have been delighted to have the pair of them in his squad, but there was no certainty that Sexton was the better man. Or that O'Gara should not be allowed to grapple with his form and, as he had done so often in the past, put himself and Ireland back on the correct course.

In the three-match tour of New Zealand and Australian in June, Ireland still lacked a true general on the field. O'Gara started against the All Blacks and with a round total of one dozen Internationals (John Hayes being the last to fall because of a virus, and be replaced by Tony Buckley) unavailable to Declan Kidney, Rog's chances of performing some miracle were vastly reduced.

Ireland lost 66-28 in a nine-try rout. Jamie Heaslip was embarrassingly red carded. O'Gara himself was yellow carded. It was all fairly horrid, all told. Kidney did his damndest to explain it all. He asked for 'positive motivation'.

Declan Kidney: I thought we showed reasonable skills in the second-half that we can play the game. Everyone thought that we were a bunch of muckers, we showed we're not a bunch of muckers in terms of our skill. But the first-half is what I keep going back to, because that's our job, you don't hide away from that fact, you just put your hands up and say 'We made a mess of it, we need to learn and learn fast'.

(June 14, 2010)

O'GARA WAS OUT, Sexton back in. Ireland lost to the Maori 31-28 in Rotarua. Australia awaited. Ireland had not won a Test match in the southern hemisphere since beating Australia in 1979 in the 'Ward-Campbell saga' and the Suncorp Stadium in Brisbane was a last opportunity to break that duck before Kidney's men returned for the World Cup the following September. It was a big game, and one that Ireland were up for, only losing 22-15. Sexton kicked Ireland's five penalty goals. O'Gara, who had been named on the bench and also left sitting on 99 caps, did not appear at any stage. Before the game Kidney had agonised in public over his difficult choice.

Declan Kidney: Yea, yea, yea... it certainly is (a tough decision), but he'd (O'Gara) be the last person that would want emotion to come into the whole thing. You have to do what you think is right. To leave John Hayes out after what... 102 caps, and there's probably only been 105 in that time. But yea! I remember talking to Tom Kiernan one day and he was just saying that he doesn't know how Rog has done it, performing at that level in that position, that consistently, over that period of time, is an incredible achievement. But I'd like to think that there's more than 100 in Ronan. That's what my belief is, when the 100 comes, it'll come, but to do what he's done to date, and to keep doing it, we are in that lucky position.

(June 23, 2010)

IT WAS THE 24th consecutive defeat to one of 'The Big Three' south of the equator. And it was the end of a season in which Ireland had fleetingly sat on top of the world. It was also the end of a season in which Declan Kidney had slowly begun to come to terms with Ronan O'Gara's future retirement, but repeatedly stepped back from making the biggest decision of his magnificent coaching career. Every time he spoke, his loyalty to O'Gara and his admiration for the man, shone through. However, those words of golden admiration for O'Gara sometimes also surely blinded Johnny Sexton's eyes at times.

In a six months period, an unbeaten Ireland had lost five times in eight games. There had been no sign of Ireland, as Grand Slam champions, as Europe's greatest rugby team, progressing. The words of support from one of his old coaching colleagues, Jim Williams, now within the Australian management, were badly in need as Ireland limped home.

Jim Williams: Surprisingly enough now I'm not with him, you certainly understand how he went about things as a head coach. You learn to appreciate the decisions he makes and what he does and why he does things. Declan's very good at seeing the bigger picture. I'm a technician and that sometimes narrows your focus a fair bit. But, with Declan, it's the bigger picture and moving forward and the team dynamic – being able to get the players up, get them in the right frame of mind. They know what to do. You look through the team. They're all class players. Their skills are good. They know how to handle situations on the pitch. It's just creating the right environment and then bringing them together to make sure they're all on the same page. Once I left Munster and looked back, you understand how Declan did things the way he did. It's an understated way. The passion's there, it's the way you get the message across. And they're so good at timing when they need to be up, in the dressing-room – that's when the passion rises, that's when the intensity rises. And Declan's very good at doing that, and getting it moving throughout the Test week, so that they get to the point where they need to be when the ball's kicked.

(June 24, 2010)

2010-2011

'I suppose it would give encouragement. But I think too much of them just to let them away with that. Then we go into the old things like, "It was a great performance". We're too good a country to buy into that. We need to work on things ourselves. I don't want to sound like a broken record. It's in our own control, if you look at the turnovers, just getting a few simple things right. We put our defence under a lot of pressure. You guys probably know the stats better than I do. Was it 70:30 possession? We need to make it 50:50.'

– Declan Kidney
(November 22, 2010)

Matt Williams: If Eddie O'Sullivan or Warren Gatland had produced these numbers and results the collective media would be clambering for blood. Kidney has won a Six Nations Championship and two European Cups, which is why this has not occurred. But, to paraphrase Harry Truman, the buck has to stop somewhere and in my experience it is always with the boss. Quite frankly, the national team are under-performing. They know it and we know it. The tide needs to turn.

(The Irish Times, November 27, 2010)

MATT WILLIAMS WAS the first to ask the big question of Irish head coach Declan Kidney in the late autumn of 2010, just over 18 months since the Grand Slam. It was a brave move from *The Irish Times* columnist because Kidney remained Mr Popular in Irish rugby, and throughout the country. He was still the smiling, usually happy-faced messiah in people's eyes. Belief in him, and in his methods was still rooted in sporting minds. But, soon enough, others would follow Matt Williams. Some of them would be Declan Kidney's peers; a few of them his former players in Munster's sacred red. The coach continued to preach his belief in a more expansive, adventurous game, and he also made it clear that it was owed to Irish rugby to build for the future with a broader number of international players than ever before.

But, results were results... and whatever the future held, too many defeats were coming hard and fast for the liking of most rugby folk.

The November series just finishing had sparked the big question in the mind of Matt Williams. It was a series of games that were played in the newly opened Aviva Stadium (or the old, completely rebuilt, and soon to be forgotten Lansdowne Road). The ground opened its arms to Manchester United and also Lionel Messi's Argentina in early August, and it had the look of a magnificent new home, and potential fortress for Irish football and rugby teams.

Everyone wanted to sample the turf – as Kidney's men had South Africa, Samoa, New Zealand, and Argentina visiting in the month of November – though some would have to wait in the wings longer than others, including Ronan O'Gara. The Springboks made sure that the first of those games was a true homecoming for the Irish team, and waived their right, if there is a clash of colours, to ask the home team to change to an 'away' strip. Unlike his summer of sick certs, when up to 15 players were unavailable for one reason or another for the tour down under, the Irish coach had a full hand to play. He chose Johnny Sexton at No.10.

Brian O'Driscoll: It's a hugely exciting prospect being back home, and as much as we loved playing in Croke Park, this is where we belong. It might look vastly different from the last time we played here, but essentially this is the home of Irish rugby.

(November 6, 2010)

THE DAY HOWEVER would turn out rather grim. Suddenly the Grand Slam and all of those 82,000 full houses in Croke Park seemed even more distant in the past, as the official attendance at the Aviva only reached 35,517 on a damp, grey afternoon when Irish rugby fans showed their displeasure at the IRFU's ticketing strategy that was considered 'ill conceived' by most commentators. Out on the pitch, there was no great cheer either. For starters, the players' commemorative jerseys were ripped apart in the first-half and the Irish team needed a change at the interval. A repeat victory over the world champs was denied (23-21) and the bravest of efforts from O'Gara, who had come onto the new field 13 minutes from the end – and became the third Irishman and the 16th player all told to reach a century of Tests appearances – to draw the game also was denied. His last gasp conversion kick rebounded off a post.

Ronan O'Gara: I think it's easy being an expert and sitting on the sideline. It's very tough for boys out there. I've been there before. Coming off the bench, sometimes your impact can be overemphasised and that probably happened today. It just felt like there was probably an intensity missing and I felt probably 'Strings' (Peter Stringer) and myself and Donnacha Ryan ... you just have to add to it and give it a lift. I was so pumped there was probably a little bit of draw on the ball. It rattled off the post as opposed to hitting the post. That just shows how pumped up you are. The ball didn't move. It was a true kick and that's all I can ask for. Sometimes they scrape in...sometimes they go wide... today it hit the f***ing post.

(November 8, 2010)

KIDNEY'S THIRD SEASON in charge of Ireland moved fast through the month of November, and never really slowed down. It was not until the final game of the season, against the English back in the Aviva Stadium, that the performance the coach was repeatedly requesting of his players actually presented itself and in so doing stopped Martin Johnson's team in its tracks – and stopped them just short of a Grand Slam.

The errors – there were 29 turnovers against the South Africans – kept adding up in huge numbers in the first eight games of the season. Only on the last day did Ireland look like a team that had full, deep-seated knowledge of who they were and what they could achieve out on the field. What all of this had to do with a rotating No.10 shirt, who knows? But O'Gara was back for the 20-10 victory over Samoa, and grabbed a try as well as kicking a brace of conversions, and two penalties.

Gert Smal (Ireland forwards' coach): This is just my personal experience but there is a lot of negativity around the team at the moment and a lot of things being said about their confidence, but I really don't feel it being in the team environment. This is where composure comes into it because what you don't want to have is too much fear and you don't want to have too much confidence, so you have to get that balance. Playing against the number one team in the world there will be plenty of motivation. The players will also back themselves and there is a lot of confidence that we can take them on.

(November 17, 2010)

A WEEK LATER the No.10 jersey was handed back to Johnny Sexton, and he played the full 80 minutes against the All Blacks in a 38-18 loss. O'Gara came on four minutes from the end to replace Rob Kearney. And for the final game of the month, Kidney stayed with Sexton in the 29-9 win over Argentina, O'Gara getting 12 minutes at the very end. It was a disappointing month. Ireland won the two Tests they could not afford to lose, but lost the two that really mattered in everyone's eyes. Before the All Blacks match, Kidney had appeared relaxed with his team selection, and even a little giddy. After the game, he was back to his old self, trying to offer his listeners some comfort in his beliefs, his vision even.

Declan Kidney: It's a factor (selecting the Leinster partnership of Eoin Reddan and Johnny Sexton) without being overly significant. We need to try different combinations too. International football does not allow you, like provincial football, to be chopping and changing all the time. We need to find out a few things. In this particular case, it wasn't a case of, 'If he's playing, the other guy has to play with him'. I'm quite happy to mix and match. It's a factor, but it's not one where if one plays, the other has to play with him. If that didn't excite you (Ireland looking for a first win over the All Blacks in 105 years) you shouldn't be here. It's a huge challenge but you can either crawl under a rock or you can look at it, take it on and see how we go. That's what we'll do. My background has always led me to believe from schools that you have who you have and who's to say, if they win…I'm not sure what's above a Golden Generation… but when they win on Saturday that will make them platinum.

(November 19, 2010)

IN THE FIRST 40 minutes against the All Blacks it was possible to trace every score Ireland conceded to a mistake of some kind when in possession. Ireland played quite well. Some observers considered it the best performance in 12 months, and with Kidney pointing out that for much of the game four of his tight five had only 47 caps between them, there was a lot to be said about the home team's resilience. But Ireland got beaten by 20 points – pretty much the exact number the All Blacks put on the board in a 10 minute period either side of the interval. When they made their minds up, the All Blacks had blown Ireland away and had ended the contest long before the final whistle. What they did was out of this world, but it was also clear to see. The All Blacks never allowed carriers to get isolated. They always had quick fire ruck ball. Dan Carter always had multiple choices. And with only the smallest number of players committing to each breakdown, the visitors produced wave after wave of Black power.

Declan Kidney: On the pitch, they're getting more comfortable making decisions and understanding that if they make a decision they won't be castigated for making the wrong one. That's a positive and a negative… in my perverse way I see the negative as a positive. Imagine when we start getting our lineouts ticking and kick-off receipts ticking and we don't allow ourselves to get counter-rucked, then that's how many balls (lost)? Looking back, the first 40 minutes against South Africa put us under a lot of pressure to try and win that one. Had we got a win in that one we could have relaxed things a little bit more. If we get the first 40 minutes right against South Africa we'd be in a happier place now, even though we did have a 20 point defeat against New Zealand. But, like I say, with New Zealand, the more often we play them the better. We're okay, but I wouldn't get overly excited about it.

If we go and try to play the way we did two years ago, whereby you set two targets inside your own half and kick it down, you end up defending all day. So I don't think there's a choice really.

I think to say that we're playing a new game… I wouldn't feed into that. I know there might have been talk of new ideas and stuff like that, but there wasn't any vast change in plan. We're adapting to the change of law emphasis rather than just trying to do it, because we still have to work to our skill levels.

I think part of that is getting the balance of decisions as well. So the players do have the licence to make decisions. But I suppose I've always felt it's a players' game.

(November 30, 2010)

THE SIX NATIONS swept by even faster than the month of November. A third season was over. And Declan Kidney kept explaining himself, and explaining was not a profitable thing for a Grand Slam winning coach to be doing with his time.

Declan Kidney: You're not going to win every game every year, but if you say that (the Slam was a pedestal to be knocked off) then Padraig (Harrington) made a mistake winning his three majors. I'm happy that some of the foundation stuff has been done. Ireland will win another Championship. Ireland will win another Grand Slam. When? Who Knows? Would I like to be around? Of course I would. Any excuse for a party, and you want to represent people very well. I can't say I know, but I have an understanding of what way things are in the country and I take that very seriously. If there's ever a time to win, there's even more reason to do so now, but we can't carry that burden. We have to accept the responsibility of who we're representing and the times that we're representing everybody in. We would love to win for everybody even more now. I believe that we have a skills set that is Irish and what we need to do is to adjust the plan to that. If we try and copy Australia and New Zealand… anybody who copies anything the best you're aiming for is second. We're Irish. We should never be willing to settle for second, right?

(January 29, 2011)

DECLAN KIDNEY NEEDED Ronan O'Gara to save his neck on the opening day of the 2011 Championship. Rog replaced Johnny Sexton with 14 minutes remaining in the 13-11 win over Italy in Rome. It was a game Ireland should have won comfortably, but instead grasped at the death. At times Kidney's men looked magical, and midway through the first-half the depth and width shown in one of several multi-phase attacks had Ireland looking, if not like the All Blacks at their very best, then looking better than any Irish team had ever looked on the field. But there were also mistakes. And O'Gara's dropped goal, in truth, saved everyone's neck.

Brian O'Driscoll: I sound like a broken record but those things are in our control. It's just a few individual errors of turning ball over unnecessarily and there are the fine lines between winning and losing Test matches. It's difficult to take. Guys have to go back and look at their individual performances, errors that were made. The more pressure that is put on guys who are in the starting 15 from other players… you are going to have to up your game or be replaced. They're the blunt facts of the matter.

(February 14, 2011)

IRELAND OUTSCORED THE French three tries to one, but lost 25-22. Sexton started. The next day against the Scots, O'Gara was back in. Kidney explained that he was rewarding O'Gara's form. 'I think Jonathan has come on,' he said. 'He was a very good player before we ever met him and I think he's improved no end. But this was a game I just wanted to give to Ronan.' O'Gara was 13 points away from becoming the fifth player to reach 1,000 Test points and heading into the Scots' game he was six points adrift of Jonny Wilkinson as the Championship's all-time points scorer. But anyone thinking that the Irish coach had drifted into a decision based on sentiment or old loyalty was not taking a close look at Declan Kidney. He was making hard decisions.

He was ready to make hard decisions all of the time.

Ireland defeated Scotland. O'Gara was Man of the Match, but Sexton came in cold at the end and closed it out very effectively. For a brief period of time, it appeared that the balancing act between the two No.10s was perhaps profiting the squad, however, there were still so many mistakes happening all over the field which showed up Ireland as either an ill disciplined group, or an extremely nervous bunch of men who might be happier with one man occupying the out-half position, full stop! Halfway through the Championship, Kidney had watched his team outscore the opposition on tries 7-2, but their two wins either side of a defeat were by two and three points. The penalty counts remained a dagger to the team's heart – 13-5 against Italy, 10-8 against France, and 12-4 against Scotland.

O'GARA WAS STILL two points away from the glorious 1,000 mark. He started against the Welsh in the Millennium Stadium, Sexton replacing him after 50 minutes, but only after he had converted O'Driscoll's try and kicked two penalties. Ireland lost 19-13. Generally, Ireland's kicking game was brutal, with slices and miscues from O'Gara, and also Sexton and Paddy Wallace when they came into the action. Ireland had led 13-9 at the break. Sexton, when he came on, sliced his first kick out on the full and offered the home team the chance which they took to score a try. Sexton then missed with an easy enough penalty chance. He had relaxed by the end of the game and settled the team, and against the all-conquering English in the final game of the Championship was handed back the No.10 shirt.

That afternoon there was another cameo only for O'Gara.

Ireland recorded a seventh win (24-8) in eight games over England, brutally ending a Grand Slam ambition, and embarrassing them further when it became known that the English players had recorded a Slam video with Nike's help – and that 5,000 Slam t-shirts were in the hands of fans.

It had been a long and frustrating season for Ireland, however. The perfect team performance, and the dovetailing of Sexton and O'Gara, had been a long time coming. And while everyone celebrated and forgot in the throes of their celebrations, the truth was that seeking out the end note of the Championship had been not only hard work, but punishing work, and sometimes confusing work.

How happy, in its heart, could Ireland be that they had really evolved, or even arrived at a place more secure and profitable than the place they had occupied three years before? Was it months and months of arduous planning that resulted in bundling over the English?

Or was it Ireland, happy in the role of underdogs, and mostly disrespected, mounting one hell of a performance against the one team that had always brought the best out of them in the professional era?

Nobody, not the coach, and not his players, wanted to think it was the latter. They could not afford any doubts. The World Cup was less than six months off. It stood as an imposing mountain. One that had conquered and left Irish coaches, as well as Irish teams, beaten and bemused in the past, and always appeared to spotlight the self-doubt hiding away in Irish rugby squads.

Declan Kidney: It was always in there, but it was a balance between trying to get a lid on the fear factor and trying to lower the anxiety levels. There was nothing they did out there that surprised me. We had better field position; we were a bit more patient and played with a bit more ball, until the game went to 24-3. Then we got a little bit loose and gave them balls inside our half and let them come back into it. It's thin margins. Today went our way… other days didn't.

(March 21, 2011)

Johnny Sexton: I literally haven't watched a TV or opened a paper since (the French game). At times the Mum and girlfriend will be giving out about certain people and you're like, 'Just leave me out of it… I don't want to hear about it'. But sure you know it is all part of it and I'm sure it will continue. It was brilliant (receiving a standing ovation as he left the field). I have said it before, it was for Ronan as much as myself. It was great to get an ovation like that. There is a lot written about the two of us and said about the two of us. We are fully aware that at times when one plays well the other gets criticised. That is how it should work.

(March 21, 2011)

2011-2012

'I know its unconventional to have different half-backs at different times but sometimes it depends on how you look at that... is it an area of strength or something you hide away from and just put your eggs in one basket. But when they've all been on the pitch they're brought their own bits to it. When Jonathan came on the last day, Italy were attacking and he was hugely strong defensively for us. Eoin (Reddan) robbed two great balls for us as well, so leaving them out isn't the easiest thing in the world then either. But Conor and Ronan have gone quite well for us earlier on. I just think we're in a lucky situation.'

– Declan Kidney
(October 5, 2011)

SEVENTY-SIX DAYS before the opening Pool C match in the World Cup against the United States, Declan Kidney brought his 43-man training squad together in Maynooth's beautiful Carton House for their first get-together. A month later, the IRFU signed up the head coach, and three of his assistants, Gert Smal, Les Kiss and Mark Tainton (Alan Gaffney deciding to return home to Australia after the World Cup) for two more years. It was a vote of approval from the Union, which had also learned its lesson from four years earlier when Eddie O'Sullivan had rashly been handed 'four more years' on the eve of the tournament in France.

It was all systems go.

A first semi-final in the World Cup after seven brave, but ultimately clumsy attempts was the single mission on every single mind in the Irish camp. To sharpen a vital edge to the team, it was decided that Ireland would play more games (five in four weeks) than any other nation in preparation. There was Scotland, France twice, England, and then a quickie against Connacht in between all of them.

Paul O'Connell: There is probably a balance alright. But winning is a habit. I'd like to be winning them and I'd like to be playing well too. But there's going to be four tough games and they probably won't all be pretty. People will jump up and down at times if it isn't pretty. For us it is important to realise that being dogged is a big part of winning competitions, winning games when you are sometimes not playing well, and when you are playing well putting teams away. Hopefully we can strike that right balance. We are in a very good place going into it. We know how good we can be. But the Six Nations showed both sides of Ireland. We also know how bad we can be when we are not right mentally, physically, and that's a good place for us to be. We've been successful in the past when we have just taken one game at a time.

(July 16, 2011)

Alan Gaffney (Irish Backs coach): We have to get the balance right to make sure they are sharp by the time the World Cup comes around. We are probably looking at two and a half to three games maximum per person. If that can be done, that is the optimum. It's going to be difficult to achieve across the board. The balance is very, very important, but in each game we'll be going in very, very strong.

(August 2, 2011)

IT TURNED OUT the month of competitive action was not so good. The four Tests were lost. It was pretty much a disaster as feel-good, happy, conscientious, morale-building preparation goes. Johnny Sexton kicked two penalties as the Scots won 10-6 in Murrayfield on the opening weekend of August. A week later O'Gara kicked four from five in State Chaban-Delmas in Bordeaux as France won 19-12. Paddy Wallace kicked four conversions in the six-try 38-3 win over Connacht but when the French came to the Aviva a few days later, in a game that Kidney and his men needed to win far more than they cared to admit, there was another kick to the stomach. Sexton started, France won 26-22, and before he handed O'Gara back the No.10 shirt for the visit of England Kidney had to sit down face-to-face with 13 of his players (one had to be informed over the phone) and tell them the fairly awful news that they were not being brought on the World Cup journey possibly of a lifetime for some. O'Gara kicked three from four against the English. Martin Johnson's team grabbed the game's only two tries, and enjoyed a well deserved 20-9 win, although Kidney watched his men win six lineouts inside the English 22, in addition to one scrum, and come away empty-handed on each occasion.

Donal Lenihan: Losing all four warm-up games was never on the agenda and not something anybody anticipated. Having finished the season as Europe's highest ranked side (fourth), Ireland have now plummeted to eighth in the IRB rankings. When the Irish squad sit down to review the events of recent weeks they will see that a failure to capitalise on point-scoring opportunities against the French and English cost them dearly. When playing against opposition of that calibre it is imperative to score when the opportunity comes. That was evident in Bordeaux when Ronan O'Gara opted against going for the corner despite being in the ascendancy with Ireland trailing by a point. Unfortunately he missed the kick but it was the right option at the time. This was in marked contrast to the events of the last two weekends in Dublin when eminently kickable penalty opportunities were wasted in favour of quick taps or kicks to the corner. In those instances, Ireland failed to register any points. Not only that, but in both games the opposition was energised even further by their defensive efforts in keeping their try-line intact.

(Irish Examiner, August 31, 2011)

Tommy Bowe: We didn't attack with the same sort of flair that we normally do. We are well renowned for having a world-class backline. Attacking off first phase we are normally very dangerous, but we weren't as accurate as we could have been. We are obviously going to want to score a lot more tries and to do that we have to be more creative.

(September 6, 2011)

Alan Gaffney: We have been doing a lot of work on micro-skills and plays in the last couple of weeks, basically fine-tuning, because all it takes is a split second to run a move and one wrong line and all of a sudden there is a hole left. I don't want to see a World Cup being dominated by teams that aren't playing exciting rugby, but that puts the onus on us not to go back into our shells. We want to play exciting rugby, but we have to have the ability to play 10-man winning rugby as well.

(September 6, 2011)

Tony Ward: So what would constitute a successful World Cup? As articulated best by Brian O'Driscoll before leaving Dublin, nothing short of a semi-final for the first time in seven attempts. Irish rugby demands something heroic from this group, who are charged with the responsibility of providing that feel-good factor over the coming weeks. While good performances are obviously a bonus, Kidney will know better than anyone that, from here on in, they will be judged on results alone.

(Irish Independent, September 6, 2011)

Brian O'Driscoll: Pre-season games are very different to World Cups. People just expect you to pick up after having a four-week holiday and a pre-season and it doesn't happen like that. You have to play your way into form. Very rarely do you see any team in the world in their first match together just playing brilliant rugby. Only people who have been there can understand how difficult it is to build your way into things, that it isn't just about flicking a switch in the green jersey and being back to where we were against England in the last game of the Six Nations.

(August 31, 2011)

Declan Kidney: It's not so much evolving. That was last season. This season has been about trying to get up and going. I felt, 'Let's go in at the deep end… against the teams that we know are going to be knocking on the door for the title'. While we're disappointed with our losses against England and France, I'd like to think that if we had to play them again in five or six weeks' time we'll have learned from this experience and we'll be the better for it.

(August 31, 2011)

A GLASS ALWAYS half-full was to Declan Kidney's liking. But, definitely, there was needless pressure imposed on the entire squad after those four losses in August, and even though that dispiriting month seemed far behind them when they set up camp in Queenstown, in the fun- and adventure-capital of New Zealand, Kidney's team had left themselves open to minute analysis before they had played even their first game of the tournament against a US Eagles team in New Plymouth coached by Eddie O'Sullivan.

Self-analysis was also peaked in that first week in the Land of the Long White Cloud. What could Kidney's men do differently, to separate themselves from the dismal Irish record in 25 World Cup games up to that point?

Five of those games were against Tri-Nation teams, and all of them lost – Australia ('87, '91, '99 and '03) and New Zealand ('95).

Six of them were against other Six Nations teams, another five of them lost – losing to Wales ('87) and beating them ('95), losing to Scotland ('91), losing to France ('95, '03, '07).

There was one win against Argentina ('03) and two losses ('99 and '07). And then there were the wins, all against teams that were also-rans – Tonga ('87), Canada ('87), Zimbabwe ('91), Japan twice ('91 and '95), Romania twice ('99 and '03), Namibia twice ('03 and '07) and Georgia ('07).

Ireland's record at World Cups was simply one of serving up a complete injustice to itself as a strong, credible rugby nation. Training under snow-peaked mountains in Queenstown in September of 2011, old World Cups were entirely irrelevant, of course. Nevertheless, the Irish coach seemed a little too relaxed perhaps.

Declan Kidney: There won't be any lockdown. It would be awful to come to Queenstown and not see it properly. It's a smashing spot. The way our matches are, this World Cup is more like a tour. Queenstown is as good a place as any to start. When we landed and were hit by that reception, we knew we were in the biggest rugby tournament in the world. It was a special occasion. The backdrop we were training against today is not something you see too often... it was pretty spectacular.

(September 3, 2011)

BEATING UP ON the minnows was no big problem for Ireland at the 2011 World Cup. The Eagles were taking out in the first game 22-10 and Russia were done in 62-12, and there was one of those rare World Cup wins over a Six Nations opponent which could not be sniffed at – the Italians getting a proper spanking 36-6. It wasn't all the prettiest or the most spectacular of rugby, but it was historic because in between Ireland also turned over a Tri-Nations team for the first time in the tournament, taking Australia 15-6 in Auckland's Eden Park with a performance that was inspiring. It meant that Ireland had stepped out of its pool unbeaten for the first time in a World Cup. Confidence was sky-high. Higher still, as top place in Pool C sent Ireland to Wellington where they got to meet the nearly always beatable Welsh in the quarter-final.

Up front in Eden Park the Tri Nations champs who were without their inspirational flanker David Pocock and first choice hooker Stephen Moore came a distant second, with Cian Healy especially doing a number on poor Ben Alexander. But Kidney had to be just as pleased that all of his dreams of getting the very best out of Sexton and O'Gara became a reality with the latter coming on in the second-half as a replacement for Gordon D'Arcy and taking over the kicking duties – and nailing two vital late penalties. Sexton had kicked a penalty in the 16th minute and had left the teams level at the interval with a dropped goal. He was just wide with another penalty attempt from 45 yards out just before half-time, but on the resumption Stephen Ferris and Sean O'Brien continued to blast big holes in the Australian defence, and the Aussies creaked, cracked, and Sexton kicked Ireland in front 9-6, and was agonisingly close with another that hit the woodwork. It was a brave man who would hand the kicking duties to O'Gara, but Declan Kidney was unflinching and did exactly that. He believed in Rog who, while disappointed not to get his start against Australia, had been saying so many of the right things in the weeks leading up the biggest ever victory by Ireland on the world stage.

Ronan O'Gara: I'm enjoying my duel with Johnny. It's reinvigorated me big time and I'm enjoying the challenge. We both have big importance to the team. The most important thing is that Ireland do well and I'm sure that we both have key roles to play in that. The fact that this is my last World Cup is important. I've had a good career and made an impact at European level but this is the elite level. It would be hugely fulfilling if I did have a role at world level and that's a goal of mine. Until you perform at a World Cup you shouldn't talk about it because you haven't done it. For years at Munster we were unlucky not to win the Heineken Cup but then when we did win European Cups we earned respect.

(September 6, 2011)

AFTER THE GAME, however, a visibly emotional O'Gara chose to rock the team by saying he'd be 'done with Ireland in a few weeks'. Declan Kidney and his management team were as surprised as Irish TV viewers. While O'Gara may have considered 1,039 points in 113 games for Ireland as good as any crossroads at which to make a big statement about his future, the management was not buying it. Neither were his teammates who goaded him with the fact that he had contract with his name on it that still had two years to run. 'Ronan hasn't talked formally to us about it,' team manager Paul McNaughton explained, before adding, 'He's a very, very important part of the set-up here.' A week later, O'Gara would win a Man of the Match award against Russia and, while still remaining a touch melancholy, and no doubt aware that the replacements' bench was still awaiting him in the near future, spoke in a more considered manner.

Ronan O'Gara: I'm just about playing rugby now with a smile on my face. I felt an awful lot of pressure for 10 years of my career but at this stage I don't read too much into it, get on with it and realise that there is much more to life than rugby. This is the be all and end all, obviously, but I think when you have kids or when you have a family you appreciate that you have to find a balance. I really enjoy it. People probably felt there was pressure on me for a big performance but I didn't think it. I was disappointed not to start against Australia but I know I have an important role to play in the squad and you soon get over that. You can have as much of an impact in 30 minutes as you can in 80 minutes. My head is in a really good place.

(September 26, 2011)

THE WHOLE IRISH team was in a place that looked so good, and somewhere nobody thought them capable of when they boarded the plane in Dublin a month before. There was only one angry note, and that came after the victory over Australia when remarks in new newspaper column by former Aussie centre Tim Horan got right up Declan Kidney's nose.

Tim Horan: 'CLEVER IRISH FAKED WAY TO VICTORY'. Ireland had a deliberate plan to fake injuries each time there was a breakdown in play last Saturday, so they could slow the game down and frustrate the Wallabies. How can I be sure? By talking to Irish assistant-coach Alan Gaffney in the dressing rooms afterwards. If James Horwill was more experienced as a captain, he would have blown up about it to referee Bryce Lawrence and really created a scene – there is no way Richie McCaw would have stayed silent if a team used the same tactics against the All Blacks.

(Herald Sun, September 19, 2011)

Declan Kidney: What I can tell you for definite is that the reporter (Horan) was never in the dressing room… that the coach in question never spoke to him, so I can only let you make your own inference as to how he feels he can quote something that was never said. I think it's incredulous and slightly scandalous that he would try to bring one of his own fellow countrymen into something that is totally untrue. But that's for other people to have their standards in life.

(September 24, 2011)

Tim Horan: After the game, I went down just outside the dressing rooms and onto the field… and Alan Gaffney was there. I know Alan Gaffney very well, we were Wallabies selectors together. I had a great chat to him, applauding him for the tactics that they used: I thought that they were wonderful tactics in the conditions. Yeah, I definitely spoke to him.

(The Irish Times, September 24, 2011)

Declan Kidney: Like I said, it's for other people to have their standards. But I think it's important that if we got something wrong, we'll hold up our hands, but when we don't get something wrong we'll defend ourselves and we won't be shy of doing it, as I'm sure every other nation would be. I don't think I was that strong (in response to Horan), I just stated the facts really. To be honest, I wouldn't be losing any sleep about it. I'm sure it's possible that you could make a story out of it and I know that it's difficult to try and get stories. I'm sure you're sick of the sight of us and we're only here three weeks. But I wouldn't be losing any sleep over it myself.

(September 24, 2011)

IRELAND WERE IN their fifth quarter-final and looking stronger than any Ireland team before them. Newspapers in New Zealand were applauding Ireland and presenting Kidney's men as everyone's 'second favourite team' in the tournament. The *New Zealand Herald* screamed 'IRRESTIBLE IRELAND TAKE SPOILS AGAINST ITALY' and there was no doubt that putting their neighbours, Australia on their backsides endeared Kidney and Co to the general New Zealand population.

Hayden Meikle (*New Zealand Herald*): Otago Stadium turned into an Ireland paradise tonight. The 40th and final Rugby World Cup pool game saw the $200 million venue turn almost completely green, and everyone's favourite second team launch into the quarter-finals with a fourth consecutive win. They have backs with real zip and a loose forward trio, led by the classy O'Brien, as good as any.

(New Zealand Herald, October 3, 2011)

THE OTAGO STADIUM was a standard-bearer, and Ronan O'Gara had passed with impressive colours. He had a six from seven 16 points haul against the Italians, in a stadium where so many kickers, including the miraculous Jonny Wilkinson, had struggled to stay strong. O'Gara was standing on 16 from 19 kicks in the tournament – and two of those misses had struck the upright. The long-range forecast for Wellington on the evening of the quarter-final against Wales was for rain and wind. Coach Kidney was left to work out the maths, add in what Sexton offered in defence, take from that what O'Gara brought with wit and wisdom...and make exactly the right choice for Ireland.

He chose Ronan O'Gara for the biggest day in Irish rugby history... possibly? And, after all of his deliberation over the No. 10 jersey, it didn't really matter anyhow, as Ireland went down with a massively inferior performance against Warren Gatland's Wales. It was 22-10 at the end.

Declan Kidney: You get a sense how much people are feeding off it and you really want to go well for everybody. Not just yourselves but for everybody at home and all the supporters we had out here which was magnificent. That just makes the hurt all the greater when you're trying to give somebody something. Should I phone the Samaritans or what should I do with your questions? I don't believe that they (owe us anything) but I'm especially disappointed for them because they'll see it as their last chance. A lot of them will wear the green again but in terms of World Cups, they were more than anybody looking to try and finish off this World Cup on a high in terms of their career.

(October 10, 2011)

THE QUESTION HANGING in the air was simple enough. If a group of players that included O'Driscoll, O'Connell, O'Callaghan, and O'Gara, just to mention four from a Golden Generation, could not reach a World Cup semi-final what hope was there for Ireland in the future? Add to that... if such a group of footballers were led by Ireland's greatest living coach Declan Kidney and came up short ... what the hell?

But the story of the defeat by Wales was also enlightening. Kidney was out-coached by Gatland. Wales fought with greater hunger from the very beginning. They targeted O'Gara and his defensive frailties, but Gatland also refused to expose Shane Williams to Tommy Bowe's aerial threat and, simply enough, switched George North to the left wing. It did not take genius! Neither was it beyond belief that the Welsh coach would look at Ferris and O'Brien, and decide that at the first opportunity Ireland's primary ball carriers should be chopped down.

Declan Kidney: They're a good side. Battles with Warren have always been nip and tuck. We've had a few in the past. We've won a few, he's won a few but it's not about us, it's the players on the day. They came up with a good game. Credit due to them for that. They picked their scores when they came their way. It was 7-0, then 7-3 when we took one under the posts. They defended well and then they got a penalty on the halfway line and it goes over on a windy day. That makes it 10-3, they're nice and comfortable but we get back in and you think 'happy days'. But the nuances are tiny when you're discussing it afterwards. We know we coughed up the ball, missed a few tackles but that's going to happen in every game. They got the momentum on the scoreboard and they did very well with it. We said all the time... we'd try and build a squad. The squad wasn't just for this event. We have to have fellas coming through and the provinces are so important for guys coming through. We know where the challenges are and that lie ahead in making sure Ireland is as strong as possible and we need to feed off one another. We have an Irish set-up that has stood us well in the past and I'm sure it will stand us well in the future.

(October 10, 2011)

WALES HAD WON three tries to one to earn their semi-final place, for the first time since 1987. Shane Williams squeezed over for Wales' opener. Keith Earls replied for Ireland after the break, but scrum-half Mike Phillips and centre Jonathan Davies burst past Cian Healy settled it for Gatland. In the kicking game, Rhys Priestland added seven Welsh points to Ronan O'Gara's five. Johnny Sexton was on to replace O'Gara after 55 minutes, but there was no magic from the Leinster No.10. Whenever Ireland threatened, Wales had enough numbers to cope. The Welsh lineout was able to match O'Connell and O'Callaghan, and the Irish scrum was neutralised. In midfield, O'Gara and O'Driscoll were also counted out by their opposite numbers. It was a thorough job done by Gatland and his coaching staff. For Kidney and his helpers, the future looked sort of dodgy. They had a big squad, but an ageing elite, and in addition in the Six Nations down the road and the three-Test tour of New Zealand that would be hot on its heels, there was going to be no patience or understanding, as a country demanded a winning team.

Before all of that, however, there was the little matter of the Lions head coach – a position that had Declan Kidney's name in the hat once upon time. The appointment was set to be made a month after the end of the 2012 Six Nations, but in newspaper circles Ian McGeechan taking charge for the fifth time did not seem such a bad idea. The job, of course, would fall to Warren Gatland in the end and he would, once again, stamp on Irish hearts by removing Brian O'Dricsoll from his final winning selection against Australia.

Some time before then, Declan Kidney would be Ireland's former head coach.

Andy Irvine (Lions manager): Geech has not ruled himself out entirely. I have spoken to him. He is an option. The head coach will have to be free of other commitments. He has to be totally unencumbered in the season leading up to the tour. I think the current head coaches of Ireland, Scotland and Wales (Declan Kidney, Andy Robinson and Warren Gatland) would be available, but the person we choose will not necessarily come from the hone unions.

(November 29, 2011)

|||■|||

IRELAND FACED A first Championship campaign without Brian O'Driscoll since the old Five Nations of 1999. Surgery on his shoulder meant a new No.13 (Keith Earls), a new captain (Paul O'Connell), and an Irish team that no longer would hold a magic wand in its hand during the toughest of games.

It was a Championship in which Ireland needed to knuckle down, and be as smart as their coach always asked them to be. It was also a Championship in which Declan Kidney finally made up his mind and selected Johnny Sexton in five out of five games, and sent Ronan O'Gara in as a replacement for Gordon D'Arcy in the third quarter of every game – with Sexton reverting to inside centre and allowing O'Gara to see the game down the straight.

In some ways it worked. Sexton settled down after his hit 'n' miss World Cup and his kicking boot rewarded Ireland against Wales (four from seven), Italy (seven from eight), France (three from four), Scotland (five from six), and England (three from three). O'Gara did not take a single kick.

Johnny Sexton: I beat myself up a bit at the time (after the World Cup). It's probably something that I've struggled with a bit. But you learn a lot with setbacks. Obviously I place-kicked poorly in a couple of games. That can happen to any place kicker. Unfortunately it happened to me on the world stage in the two biggest games of my career. It still doesn't sit well with me... that it happened then, something I'd been building up towards for a couple of years. It still hurts but I've tried to move on. That's life. You move on from it. I've a lot of good people around me. That's the fact of the matter. Now I want to play in the Six Nations and to do well. I don't think I've played a game for Ireland without Brian at 13. But we're going to have to get used to it. He's not going to be around for the Championship. We haven't spoken about it. It's different without Brian there. But we all have to up our game and make up for his absence.

(February 2, 2012)

THE 2012 CHAMPIONSHIP was Declan Kidney's fourth campaign. After the Slam in 2009, Ireland had finished second to England the following year (winning three from five), and they had the same winning return in 2011 but landed in third place in the table on the same tally as France but with an inferior points scoring difference. Ireland needed to be on the move, upwards, in 2012, without or without the man called BOD. It wasn't like any outstanding team had a stranglehold on the tournament. There had been four different winners in the four preceding seasons. Ireland's claim was as strong as anybody's, and a failure to move from mid-table could only be seen as a failure.

Thanks to having the Italians served up on a plate seven times in total, Ireland had won 10 of their last 11 opening Championship games. But in February of 2012 Wales were on that first plate. Wales, and after that it was supposed to be France, though a frozen turf at 9.0 pm local time in Paris would put paid to that game when it was called off as the Irish team were putting on their tracksuits in their dressing room and preparing to take the field.

There was no hiding place against the Welsh.

They had floored the World Cup dreams of Kidney and his men only a few months before. Now they were coming to the Aviva. Revenge was called for, in whatever shape or form… didn't matter really, Ireland just needed to win.

Warren Gatland: I think Wales have two extremes. We're incredibly dangerous with our backs to the wall or incredibly dangerous when we're playing with a lot of confidence, and at the World Cup we were playing with a huge amount of confidence at that stage of the tournament.

(February 4, 2012)

THE GAME ENDED in controversy, and it did so with Leigh Halfpenny kicking an 80th minute penalty, after a harsh call by referee Wayne Barnes on Stephen Ferris for a tackle on Ian Evans, which steered his team to a 23-21 win that was a tad fortunate in the end, but one that was also mostly deserved. Gatland was big hearted afterwards and said his team were 'lucky' though the Welsh coach was definitely being a touch magnanimous. Wales had carried the ball through a dozen phases in marching 50 metres up the field and putting themselves in a position to claim the victory. They also won the try-count by three (Jonathan Davies two, and George North) to two (Rory Best and Tommy Bowe).

Warren Gatland: I don't think we played as well as we could. When we get it right we're going to be good. To come here and be under a bit of pressure and down to 14 men (for the last 15 minutes), I think we showed a lot of character. They are the pleasing things. The displeasing thing was a lack of discipline which could have cost us on another day. We got out of jail.

(February 6, 2012)

Paul O'Connell: We conceded a lot of momentum in the first-half and didn't defend with our heads up. Our scramble defence was really good but we got caught on the short side. They carried hard but you can't give a team that length of time with the ball in hand. You just put yourself under pressure.

(February 6, 2012)

Declan Kidney: That's the nature of it. Three teams are going to have their Grand Slam finished and three teams are going to work on for it. There is a Championship still to be won and that's what we'll work towards. What we can solve ourselves... we'll try to solve... field position... they ran the ball out of the 22. How they made such in-roads there... we'll take a good look at what we can solve ourselves. We'll work on what we can work on. Look, we're a lot better than that, okay? We put ourselves under a lot of pressure defensively. We had to defend for 60 per cent of the game and if you do that you're asking for trouble.

(February 6, 2012)

Paul O'Connell: I don't think it (Ferris' tackle) was the winning and losing of the game. I missed a tackle myself for their try late in the game and we probably gave them a lot of ball early on we shouldn't have. If you're going to leave it come down to one decision, pick out one player... then you are not operating well as a team. There was a disappointment. I think we put ourselves in a position to win the game and we conceded eight points in that five minutes and that's what cost us the game, not that one incident. I think we conceded a lot of momentum in the first-half and gave them a lot of belief. We probably didn't defend with our heads up as we should.

(February 6, 2012)

WHAT HAPPENED NEXT?

Hardly mattered where Ireland finished in the Championship table... second, joint third, or worse? All that truly mattered was that a Welsh side that Ireland believed themselves superior to – and whom Ireland had lost to in the World Cup quarter-final – went on to win the Triple Crown and Grand

Slam in 2012. Warren Gatland and his men took it all back home with them.

Ireland beat Italy (42-10), drew with France (17-17) when really they should have beaten them after holding an 11 points lead at the interval after two Tommy Bowe tries, thumped the surprisingly cocky Scots in the Aviva (32-14) with four tries, and then got thumped themselves by England (30-9) at Twickenham to sign off on a Championship that was annoyingly inadequate rather than dispiriting.

Ireland finished third in the table, behind Wales and England.

Warren Gatland effectively won himself the Lions job.

Declan Kidney remained in no-man's land as Irish coach.

Declan Kidney: It's different from three years ago. This is not the Grand Slam side of three years ago. There's seven or eight changes in the side now and we're having to learn a few things along the way, and we didn't panic in the second-half (against France) which I was happy with. We did a lot of things well, and the more you do well the more disappointing it is when you don't close it out. They're the bits we need to work on. In the first-half they were inclined to go wide, in the second-half (in the rain) they put it up their jumper and with the laws the way they are now that's an area we'll take a good look at and see what technique we can use to get the ball back to us.

(March 5, 2012)

Vincent Clerc (French winger): It was annoying. It's difficult sometimes to have players who slow down our ball and are always playing to the limit of the rules. They're not always sanctioned so all the better for them. But it's true that after that it was sometimes difficult to put pace into our game and to cause them trouble. It's a shame because we were able to destabilise them in the end. We were often in their 22 but we weren't able to take some decent chances.

(March 5, 2012)

Declan Kidney: You don't lose players of the calibre of Brian and Paul (O'Connell who was ruled out for the rest of the season after sustaining a knee injury against the French) and just rock up. After the match I wasn't so much congratulating them about the result (defeating the Scots), which was great, but the way they conducted themselves right throughout the week. We know we have another huge task next week (against England). It's the first time ever I think that we've had four of those matches on the trot, but we're enjoying one another's company and let's work on it and long may it continue just the way it happened today. You don't just rock up to Twickenham and say 'That was great lads… we'll do the same again'. You have to prepare properly and diligently for it and so that's why we have to knuckle down and do that.

(March 12, 2012)

Andy Farrell (England assistant coach): Those boys aren't frightened of anything. We are up for any type of challenge. We don't know fear. You couldn't get a harder working or more humble group of blokes than the side we have here. Rightfully so, they (Ireland) have a good record here, but that means nothing to this England group. Only a handful of these players were involved in any of those games.

(March 17, 2012)

Declan Kidney: Look, today hurt. It hurt a lot and if it didn't hurt we shouldn't be here (in Twickenham). Everybody will walk away from the last 20 minutes of the game and that's the bit that will really hurt us. But we have to take a look at the first 60 where we turned over the ball so often that if we got a few scores then all of a sudden it changes things around. Now that would have been difficult today because you have to have a platform and we didn't have it obviously at scrummaging time.

(March 17, 2012)

LOCKED TOGETHER IN the memory bank of everyone with even the faintest interest in Irish rugby was the 2011 World Cup and the 2012 Six Nations Championship. This mass of games formed one gigantically sized disappointment. It was heavy and immovable. And the next campaign to be quickly locked onto that troublesome load was a three-Test series against New Zealand in the summer of 2012. In truth, it was the very last place in the world Declan Kidney needed to be bringing a soul-searching Irish team.

2012-2013

'The three things that I try to do as a coach are to enjoy myself, to help players I am working with to improve, and to win. But not necessarily in that order.'

– Declan Kidney
(December 18, 1999)

ON THE AFTERNOON of Sunday March 3, 2013, only a few hours before his squad was due to meet up in Carton House outside Maynooth, Declan Kidney was determined to have a private word with Ronan O'Gara. He didn't know that O'Gara was eating pizza and ice cream in Luigi Malone's in Cork city centre with his wife, Jessica and their four children. Or that O'Gara and family were then hightailing it to the Cork Opera House to catch *The Gruffalo Child.* The evening before, O'Gara had played well against the Ospreys and was happy in his own head that his form was decent. His gear was in Carton House. As normal, he was going to hook up with Donncha O'Callaghan, after both men packed in some personal time with their families, and get to the Irish training base by 9.30 pm.

When O'Gara took his vibrating phone out of his pocket in the Opera House and saw Kidney's number he chose to ignore the call.

He knew it was not good news.

Halfway through the production, O'Gara brought his son JJ to the toilet. His phone went off again. It was Kidney once more. O'Gara chose to ignore it a second time. It was only when the show was over that he decided to return the call.

Kidney quickly explained that he needed to meet up and chat.

Ronan O'Gara: Sometimes the management stay in Carton House because they're so busy, but Deccie was in Cork. He bent over backwards to try and meet me but I just said, 'Deccie, it doesn't make any difference to me what you say to me, whether it's over the phone or to my face, I'm not going to look upon you any less as a man. It's obvious you've got something to say'. I've learned over the years that the key with Deccie is not to speak too much because that's what he loves. He's happy to leave 40 second silences on the phone if you let him.

(November 2, 2013)

KIDNEY INSISTED THAT he wanted to meet. He did not want to talk over the phone. He had the toughest conversation he ever had to have in front of him, and he wanted to look Ronan O'Gara in the face. He had to tell the man whom he had spent a lifetime with, and whom he admired and believed in more than any other player perhaps – since making him captain of Pres under-14s – that he was axing him from the Irish match-day squad for the following weekend.

It was the most gut-wrenching conversation of Declan Kidney's coaching life. It had to be face-to-face, however.

O'Gara told him, as Kidney hummed and hawed, that he was ready to hear what had to be said. 'I'm not f***ing stupid,' he added, 'I realise what's going on.'

Kidney spilled his beans.

O'Gara said 'Ok'.

Kidney wondered if O'Gara wanted to ask anything?

O'Gara asked why?

Kidney said he did not think his form was 'good enough'.

O'Gara snapped and asked if he had seen the Munster game against the Ospreys the previous evening.

Kidney said he had been at the game.

'How do you think I went?' asked O'Gara

Kidney replied that he went well, but it was the first time in 14 years that Ronan O'Gara would not have his name in an Irish match day squad. It was a seismic moment in Irish rugby. O'Gara was gone.

There would be no final farewell for him in a green shirt.

Neither would Irish rugby fans have the opportunity to gather together and formally thank the greatest out-half in Irish rugby history.

Gone!

It was all over. Declan Kidney, only a few weeks later, would also be told that it was all over for him as well.

O'Gara deserved better.

So too did Kidney.

But the pressures and demands of the professional game would have both men being pushed over the cliff edge.

||||∎|||

TECHNICALLY, A SEASON that began with a warm-up match against Scotland in Murrayfield on the first weekend of August (2011) would end on the last weekend in June (2012) when Ireland had played their third Test match (and their 17th Test of the season) against New Zealand. It was simply too much. Ireland did not have the depth. They would lose Paul O'Connell and others (Mike Ross, Stephen Ferris, Tommy Bowe and Luke Fitzgerald) before starting into the virtually impossible task of breaking the All Blacks down for the first time in over a century of trying. Typically, Declan Kidney preferred to be up-beat.

Declan Kidney: For some of us it will be the only time we will tour New

Zealand in our careers. Imagine going through your career without doing that. Simon (Zebo) is the youngest at 21. If he is still there (in the Ireland team) at 33 he'll be doing well. Gee... not to go down there would be like having a hole in your CV.

(May 31, 2012)

IN THE FIRST Test in Auckland, the home team with a new coach in Steve Hansen, had a matter-of-fact 42-10 victory.

Declan Kidney: We took a good look at things on Monday with the players and saw where we went wrong so the focus this week will be 99 per cent on ourselves... we need to get ourselves right and not be concentrating on the others.

(June 14, 2012)

IN CHRISTCHURCH, WHERE New Zealand were playing for the first time since the earthquake in the spring of 2011 that resulted in 185 deaths, Ireland caught their hosts on a night of high emotion and came agonisingly close to a momentous result, losing 22-19, but only after the game was balanced on a pivotal 76th minute scrum that resulted in Nigel Owens penalising a dominant Irish scrum for wheeling. Before the game Kidney wished to put sport in perspective. After it, he had to bite his tongue about the match officials. Later still, however, after the third Test, when Ireland felt the full ire of their hosts and collapsed to a 60-0 defeat, he let it all pour out. Ireland had been lulled into a false sense of self-worth by the All Blacks and then they had been thoroughly humbled, before being cold-bloodedly embarrassed by the finish of the same game.

Declan Kidney: It's a very difficult thing to put into words what you see around you here and to try and express your emotions. Fair play to the people of Christchurch that they've done what they've done to get themselves up and going again. We're absolutely delighted to be here and to be the first

International team in here since this. Every country goes through its different crises and you can just feel this one, can't you? When you see the energy of everybody and what everybody had put into it... that tells you all you need to know. We played New Zealand last Saturday night and we've after-shock from that ourselves (referring to a 4.2 shock the previous Monday evening). We were obviously disappointed about last Saturday night in a rugby context but this puts it all into true context. That was just a game. This is real life.

(June 14, 2012)

Brian O'Driscoll: When you turn over the ball you have got to ramp it up again... not think or pray that the referee is going to call a scrum. They don't want any scrums... they want to play. And when they turn the ball over, that's a great attacking option for you too. You've got to stay with them, stay with them, stay with them... and take your chances when they come. We don't have to play with any concerns, we've been written off over here already so just play with, not wild abandon... but controlled abandon, as such.

(June 15, 2012)

Steve Hansen: We beat an Irish side that probably played as good as it could have... and we haven't played great, but we showed a tremendous amount of character.

(June 18, 2012)

Declan Kidney: It's like a game of chess. They'll look at new areas to come at us so we have to be wise enough. We'll have to look at areas to go after them and we've done a lot of defending the last few weeks. It's going to be very important to freshen up so that we can look forward to the game in Hamilton. It was a tight call (the contentious scrum). That was what he had to do. It's gone against us. Not a lot I can say. The reaction? We're obviously disappointed. We had them in those two scrums and then in that one we had them turned in towards touch. They were corralled in there, and their scrum went around a bit. Was it 90 degrees? We got a nudge on, but he deemed it to be us wheeling. Us wheeling it... but not holding it up. I'm sure it's an area they will look to improve on next week. Right now that is all we need to concentrate on… getting ourselves right for next week.

(June 18, 2012)

Johnny Sexton: I thought we had it. Even at the end I thought we were going to get another chance. We put everything into it and we probably made a couple of mistakes at key times, like straight after half-time, to let in a soft try. We are very proud of our effort, but it seems to be the same story.

(June 18, 2012)

Les Kiss: We were just saying the other day we'd love another five games in a row here. That would just be Heaven as a coach, because we know we would keep improving. You don't make promises, but I know the hard commitment is there by the guys to make sure that they do what they have to do to get there. And again we haven't left a stone unturned in terms of coaching. Anything and everything is possible and I think we'll be fine by what they've done so far this week.

(June 20, 2012)

Declan Kidney: We won't try and hide from it. We were hammered (60-0) and it's unacceptable and we need to learn from it and improve… and I've absolutely no doubt that we'll do that. Absolutely, absolutely (in accepting the word humiliation)… I can't say anything other than that. You don't get into it for games like this. But you're the coach… you're the one that has the responsibility to rectify it.

(June 25, 2012)

Keith Wood: It is very easy to call for someone to lose his job, which again I am not in favour of. I think Declan had a good selection at the start of the tour. He picked a good squad. I think he has made some big errors in it and I think he is under proper pressure now, without a shadow of a doubt. I think he has made a chunk of big errors and the defensive game-plan is the biggest one in my view. I know Declan pretty well. I would hope he sees the criticism. He knows it himself, as every player does who plays badly. Anthony Foley reminds me at every available opportunity that I disgraced the nation by playing for Ireland against Argentina in Lens when we lost in '99 (World Cup). I don't need any reminding. We were awful. Those things happen and they stay with you. Do you walk away from those things totally? Do you get a time for a chance at redemption or do you actually redeem yourself? So Kidney gets an opportunity, unless the IRFU say, 'Ok, we have enough... you are gone'.

(June 28, 2012)

IT WAS EMBARRASSING, and also a little confusing. How could an elite team in world rugby put ridiculously good and ridiculously bad performances back-to-back? In Christchurch the team had been level (19-19) with 10 minutes remaining. Two minutes later the host nation lost Israel Dagg to the bin. With 27 seconds only on the game clock, Dan Carter kicked the dropped goal to win it. But one week later in Hamilton the All Blacks had run in three tries in the opening 18 minutes. In his autobiography *The Test* Brian O'Driscoll admitted it was 'hard, mentally, trying to see a way back when they're in fourth gear and you're stuck in first'. The Irish captain rated his own performance 2/10. 'There are bad passes, balls down, system errors in defence, and almost no positives to put up against the negatives,' he wrote, further admitting that at 41-0 he wanted it all to end, but there was still a half an hour left on the clock.

'That was fun out there today!' exclaimed O'Driscoll's opposite number, All Black leader Richie McCaw. While that summation may have appeared insensitive, there was no point anyone in green feeling sorry for themselves at the end of a series in which the other team triumphed 15-2 on the try count.

⫶⫶⫶█⫶⫶⫶

THE IRISH MANAGEMENT team had a full season to run in their contracts but, undoubtedly, they were being pushed closer and closer to the cliff edge with every single defeat. Certainly, there could be no more forgiveness. The World Cup exit at Welsh hands still hurt, as did the sight of Gatland's men claiming the Grand Slam. The shock of the horrific 60-0 defeat in Hamilton was not going away either. The past cast a deep and chilling shadow over all of the earnest work Kidney and Co were doing in completely rebuilding an Irish team.

South Africa, Fiji and Argentina were up in the November series, but a full month before then journalists felt entitled to openly present Declan Kidney with the 'big question'.

Declan Kidney: We're talking about my situation? My situation doesn't matter, the only thing that matters is that we do well. That's been the only pressure I've been under from day one. Coaches are the same as players... you're here for a while so you make the most of everything. We've a fantastic occasion coming up so that's the only thing I worry about. The other stuff that goes along with that doesn't matter. I'm not important in this. All that matters is that Ireland go well. The results are not the way we would have wanted them. We've learned a huge amount from that. I've been in this long enough to know that out of that, great things can come... it all depends on how you approach it. You look at other sides like England who went through the same sort of thing... then a couple of years later they were winning all sorts of things. We'll make no promises. Where Irish rugby stands in world rugby has been, traditionally... we've gone from third to eighth... ninth... since rankings came in and we've got to fight for every ranking point we get and that's what we'll look to do in November.

(September 26, 2012)

Les Kiss: We have got to get to a point where we are consistently excellent in our preparation and New Zealand was an eye-opener for a lot of them in terms of what is required at the highest level of Test rugby. The silver lining to it, along with the second Test which when we go here we know we can be great, was that we had three Tests against them in-a-row which not many people have done and that gives us a really good baseline. We know where we need to get to. Sometimes you think you know where you need to get to but those guys have had it right in their face and from the most experienced guys in the team like Brian to the youngest they said they had never experienced anything like that before. At Test level you don't have the breadth of error rate or the margin of error in terms of your accuracy. You can't just be off the boil a little bit, particularly against the highest ranking nations.

(September 26, 2012)

WITHOUT LEADERS LIKE Paul O'Connell and Brian O'Driscoll, both out injured, and with Ronan O'Gara spending more time off the field than on it, it was only right and proper to fear the worst in November. Ireland bounced back in the first-half against South Africa with a new captain in Jamie Heaslip and led 12-3 at the interval in a bad-tempered affair. Early in the second-half Ireland conceded important field position, and both sides lost a player to a yellow card, though in Ireland's case it was a double blow in that Heaslip had to make the long walk to the sideline. JP Pietersen also went for 10 minutes but the game was scoreless in his absence. When Heaslip's back was turned the Springboks scored 10 unanswered points and swivelled the scoreline from 12-2 to 12-13 in their favour. It finished 16-12.

Declan Kidney: So they definitely haven't forgotten how to win… they're still confident in what they're trying to do… it's just a frustration. And I know they're going to click. We have had ourselves in some situations like that alright and they've gone against… but you just have to stay the pace with it… because then you know it will turn. It's a learning process… it's a tough one, but like I've said before … I've been down this road before and I know how it twists, but they have to twist it themselves.

(November 12, 2012)

Jamie Heaslip: When anyone mentions pressure this week, I keep hearing Cian Healy in the back of my head saying… 'pressure's for tyres'… for us to be honest, all of the outside pressure and chat… we're just letting it wash off us as best we can and just focusing in on us and what we have to do because it's a tall challenge that we have.

(November 23, 2012)

THE NEW CAPTAIN spoke after Ireland had turned over Fiji 53-0, and a few days before overwhelming Argentina 46-24 in a six-try walloping. Everyone in the Irish squad could breathe again, though only for a few weeks. Kidney was especially relieved at seeing a new Irish team step forward.

Declan Kidney: We'll assemble again at Christmas. I'll fight… no I won't fight, but I'll try to get whatever time we can together. It's a new squad. When you're in school, you're used to having different squads all of the time, year on year… but to have so many… like somebody just counted out that of the 32 we had in training this week, we had 17 new guys compared to the World Cup. That's a monumental turnover. If you look… the bench had three one-cappers. I think four of the pack together had 21 caps… two or three years ago if you had 21 caps you were a novice. Now all of a sudden there's 21 caps between four of them. I think that's why there's a lot of talk about Craig (Gilroy) but I suppose wingers are a bit like goalscorers in soccer aren't they? They get all the glory.

(November 26, 2012)

Gordan D'Arcy: We're definitely on the start of a really exciting group of players who are bringing their own unique brand to the Irish jersey. And I think you can see a definite Irish way of playing that's kind of different from all the provinces. The management have done a really good job in basing a game-plan around the strengths of the players. They'll have learned a lot from what they've seen. From the South Africa game, having to be mentally tough in a tough environment. And then today how pressure, pressure and pressure can create opportunities. Two different learning curves but both very important and hopefully they can combine for us going into the Sx Nations.

(June 28, 2012)

║║║■■║║║

THERE WAS NO going back for Declan Kidney.

He had watched his work come to fruition at the tail end of 2012 and it would have been foolish not to believe that he had also viewed the future of Irish rugby. He had made the No.10 jersey Johnny Sexton's property, and next was the Irish captaincy. He had to have a talk with Brian O'Driscoll.

He asked that they meet in the Four Seasons Hotel in Ballsbridge. O'Driscoll felt something was up, and coach and team captain were not meeting for some cosy pre-Championship chinwag. Kidney asked about O'Driscoll's ankle and the surgery? O'Driscoll said his ankle was good and it felt good to be back.

Once they reached the privacy of his room Kidney did not hold back for long before declaring his intention to take the captaincy from Ireland's most decorated player. He said he wanted to stick with Jamie Heaslip. O'Driscoll accepted the decision, but was unhappy with the explanation given, that Kidney wanted O'Driscoll to concentrate on himself.

O'Driscoll would later write about his 'disappointment and hurt' and also admitted unhappiness with Kidney's offer to allow O'Driscoll to explain to the Irish public that it was his own decision. O'Driscoll was about to turn 34. He had led Ireland on 83 occasions, since captaining his country for the first time when winning his 31st cap against Australia in November, 2002, before taking over the team officially two years later when Keith Wood retired. Declan Kidney would tell the Irish rugby public that O'Driscoll might someday be back as captain.

Brian O'Driscoll doubted that.

Vincent Hogan: Declan Kidney ran a lot of red lights on Thursday evening to get away from the Brian O'Driscoll question. When Declan is rattled, he has a tendency to finish his sentences with the word 'okay?' It isn't so much a question as a warning. A kind of shorthand invitation to desist from whatever line of questioning is being pursued. Kidney would have known that stripping the captaincy from Ireland's greatest rugby player two weeks before the Six Nations commences would light a small firestorm of speculation, yet he seemed remarkably ill-prepared to face it. If anything, he sounded like a man just pulling over the shower curtain to find TV cameras at the bathroom door.

(Irish Independent, January 19, 2013)

Declan Kidney: It was not something Brian was ever going to give up, or felt he should give up. Maybe sometime in the future but he wouldn't have felt that the time would be right now. Sometimes as a coach that's what your job is, to make the calls you feel are at the right time for the player even though the player mightn't agree with you. That's basically the job... there's not too many ways of saying it, but it is very tough. None of us are here forever, so if you're not disappointed when something is taken from you, then you're not human. It's a word that describes how you feel... it's not a word that describes how you act.

(January 18, 2013)

THERE WERE ONLY weeks remaining in Declan Kidney's time as Irish head coach. He would make more big decisions in those weeks and not back away from being bold and brave, even when those same decision, like for instance putting a barrelful of faith in 21 years-old Paddy Jackson at the same time as he said adios to Ronan O'Gara from his squad, did not stand up and deliver for him. In March of 2013, with days left as coach, he was asked how he was sleeping?

Declan Kidney: Great. I seem to nod off okay. There's different things in different lives. I take it very seriously. I wouldn't try to be glib one bit about it. This is not so much a job as a lifestyle but what you have to do... if you don't sleep you're not going to make decisions the next day. Sometimes you sleep on your decisions and then you know when you're sleeping well you wouldn't be too far off the mark. So thanks for the concern about my health.

(March 1, 2013)

IT WAS SOME surprise to everyone who knew him, when the coach welcomed into his camp Enda McNulty, the former Armagh footballer who had built up quite a reputation as someone helping teams and individuals with the mental side of the game. A number of Irish rugby players were already amongst his clients. Now McNulty was part of the Irish set-up, but being there personally for his players and aiding them in their psychological preparation had always been considered Kidney's strongest asset.

Maybe everything was up for grabs?

Ireland needed to get their Six Nations campaign off to a flyer... and remain airborne, but it was the dastardly Welsh and the grimacing Gatland who faced them once more in their opening Championship fixture in the Millennium Stadium. A fourth successive defeat to Wales was a chilling thought, especially with England to follow that, but the game went to plan right from the start and remained completely in Ireland's control (leading 30-3 early in the second-half) and then was almost stolen from the team's grasp. It ended three tries each in a 30-22 Irish victory. When O'Driscoll touched down for Ireland's third it should have been lights out for the home team, but instead Kidney watched his players kick the ball back to the Welsh rather than retain possession. Wales began to go through their phases at a higher tempo. Ireland struggled to retain their fast defensive line speed. Poor discipline at the breakdown earned two yellow cards. They also lost the penalty count 13-8. A good day in the office had a sting in its tail.

Ireland also had a long and worrying injury list in the making. One that would stretch and stretch over the coming games, starting with Johnny Sexton who suffered a grade two hamstring tear in the 31st minute against England. O'Gara looked rusty when replacing him. England won ugly, 12-6 and did so against the odds.

Stuart Lancaster (England coach): Ireland were in the ascendancy and then we lost James (Haskell) to the bin. The way we managed that period and to end up 12-6 at the end of it was great. I thought our technical discipline was good. We really pride ourselves on our discipline. We were pleased how we managed that but I guess it was composure in the heat of battle really.

(February 11, 2013)

Andy Farrell (England assistant coach): A huge win simply because we came to Ireland and we're playing against a hell of a good side. These days are made for players like Ronan O'Gara and Brian O'Driscoll, their experience… and they know how to get through these games. The way we composed ourselves and finished the game stronger… the way we were able to put the ball into the corner in the last 20 minutes was a master class really… to go on and win the game.

(February 11, 2013)

LOSING TO ENGLAND was the tipping point.

Kidney had to choose between 21 years-old Paddy Jackson and Leinster's Ian Madigan as understudy to O'Gara for the trip to Murrayfield, most observers reckoned. Jackson was two years younger, lighter in the body, and had inferior kicking statistics to Madigan.

And Kidney duly defied everyone's though process and named Paddy Jackson in the No.10 jersey against the Scots, with O'Gara still on the bench.

It was a call that left the nation breathless. Ireland were already down seven first-choice players and even though 12 years had passed since the Scots had managed back-to-back Championship wins (they had just taken the Italians 34-10), it did not appear to be time to take any additional risks.

At half-time in Murrayfield, it looked worrying that Ireland had only managed to make 80 per cent possession count for a 3-0 advantage on the scoreboard. Jackson had only managed one from four in the half. O'Gara would come on and take him out of his misery midway through the second period, but Ireland's performances by that point was mystifyingly poor. There was lack of variation in the play. Shots at goal were being declined. The Scots were having no trouble with one-off runners. Discipline began to slide. Even O'Gara lacked composure, with one cross-kick slicing off his boot and landing in no-man's territory. And, finally, there was an implosion at the end and a 12-8 loss.

The Irish team, and Declan Kidney, had finally been tipped over.

Declan Kidney: It's hugely disappointing. This isn't what you get into it for. To have got into those two matches… you have to close out tight games and that's what we need to learn how to do. We won't make excuses, we all know that's not going to get us anywhere and so we just need to work ahead and look how to finish off those. Had we taken one of those try-scoring opportunities it would have been a completely different day today. There were so many of them (chances) really. You go into the game to try and create them, and we managed to do that, and then you just need to finish them off. The penalties that we gave away that gave them their 12 points… I thought that two of them were very soft from our point of view to cough up. We probably got into three… four lineout positions inside their 22. Had we won them that would have put more pressure on them too and more points could have come from that. We had a couple of line breaks… obviously the place kicking as well then too.

(February 25, 2013)

BUT KIDNEY SOUGHT to defend, and protect, Paddy Jackson from the defeat. He said the general play of his out-half was very good. 'He helped to get us a few line breaks,' he continued. 'I thought his kicks down the line off penalties put us in good field positions and he had the courage to go for those which is a good thing.' He also forgave Jackson his missed penalty kicks.

A few days later, Brian O'Driscoll was asked about the position of the Irish coaching team. He was asked straight up by journalists… no apologies, no lowered voices. There was no hiding from the biggest question in the room, and nobody bothered to hide from it.

Brian O'Driscoll: We haven't collectively gotten together and said what we do and do not want. The IRFU will make the decision. That's their role… it's not the players' role to do that. We know that Declan is certainly contracted until the summer tour and all the management that are there are going to be involved for the next two games at least, so let's go about trying to win both of them. Beyond that… it's not in my control. It's about trying to stop a little bit this two-game rot and get back to consistency of performance. I don't have to answer that, because I don't have a say in it. It doesn't matter what my opinion is one way or the other.

(February 27, 2013)

AFTER O'GARA WAS dropped from the squad before the next game against France, O'Driscoll was surprised. The test message from Rog shocked him. 'After 128 caps he deserves better,' O'Driscoll wrote in *The Test*, 'He has earned the right to a proper farewell, but he's not going to get it'. Paddy Jackson and Ian Madigan were Kidney's chosen No.10s for his second last match as Ireland's head coach.

Declan Kidney: These calls have to be made. That's the role of the coach. You can avoid them… it was a very tight call but when you have to do your job… you have to do your job. It's not about bringing anything down on myself. It's about doing my job. That's the way I see it. The easy thing at this time is to make no decision.

(March 6, 2013)

Alan Quinlan: It's a shame the way his (O'Gara's) Ireland career ended and we'd all have liked to see him getting an ovation from the Irish fans as he walked off the pitch for the last time. But life goes on and when people talk about him in years to come, nobody will remember this week. They'll remember all the other weeks. It is a pity that this will be the way it ends for him and Declan Kidney. They've known each other for so long and have been a part of each other's lives for decades now. It's a big call and Declan knows that by making it he's going to draw a lot of attention on himself, which he doesn't really like doing. In the end, Declan made his decision believing in what's right for the team and by his own admission Ronan's form has been patchy. Their relationship has always been interesting. I think in the beginning people assumed that because they knew each other from the time that Ronan was a schoolboy they must have been very close. But that wasn't always the case. They sparked off each other plenty of times over the years and although I don't believe they've finished up on bad terms, I do think it was a shame it wasn't handled better.

(The Irish Times, March 6, 2013)

Mick Galwey: At this stage, I think we should be getting behind the team. We are facing a French side who are coming off the back of three defeats next weekend and they will be fighting for a win at the Aviva. But whatever decision Declan makes, I think we should respect and support the team. We have to remember that Declan has done an awful lot for Irish rugby and even though it's time for him to go… in the middle of the Six Nations you can't change the coach. We have to stick with what we have for the next two games.

(March 3, 2013)

IRELAND AND FRANCE would end up side by side, at the bottom on the Six Nations table, both of them on three points, both losing three games. It was Ireland's worst Championship performance since the Five Nations Wooden Spoon of 1998. When they met in the Aviva Stadium they also drew 13-each, an early try from Heaslip being neutralised by a late try from Picamoles, Jackson kicking three from five for Ireland, and Michalak and Parra between them kicking three from six for the French.

Ireland were at bits and pieces, physically, and by the end of the draw with France Kidney had Ian Madigan in the centre, a clearly injured Brian O'Driscoll outside him, and hooker Sean Cronin had come in for Eoin Reddan who had broken his leg. Ireland themselves limped to their final game against Italy. They were without so many... and so many leaders. No O'Connell, Ferris, Sexton, D'Arcy or Bowe, for starters, and Keith Earls and Luke Marshall would also be in the treatment room in Rome midway through the first-half. O'Driscoll got sin binned – his second yellow in 130 Tests, both of them against the Italians – and then Luke Fitzgerald came off as damaged goods. Kidney moved Peter O'Mahony from flanker to the wing. Paddy Jackson survived the carnage and kicked five penalties from five but it was not enough as the Italians totaled 22 points in one of their most famous of victories.

It was a calamitous ending.

Six weeks before all of this, Ireland had led Wales 30-3 five minutes into the second-half of their opening game of the Championship and Gatland was unable to stop his team meeting with an eighth defeat on the trot.

But Ireland would end up losing to Italy, and Wales would beat England 30-3 to retain the Championship.

All hard to stomach, or fathom ... or adequately explain.

Declan Kidney: I know what I can bring to it. I know what I brought to it over the years. I know that I've been in holes before like this and I know how to get out of them, but I think now is the time to sit back and reflect and let's take a look at things. I'm a bit like a broken record there now, but in terms of the doom and gloom, and there'll be a lot of that, in a strange way over the coming years we'll benefit from what we've gone through here with the fellas coming through and that's what we must remember.

(March 18, 2013)

IN APRIL THE IRFU began their search for a new coach. Les Kiss was asked to step in as the interim head coach for the summer tour of the USA and Canada. The full-time job would soon fall to Joe Schmidt. The IRFU in a statement thanked Declan Kidney and said their goodbyes.

Later Philip Browne would add that Kidney would 'have liked a new contract' but that they had a difficult decision to take. 'Declan has been a huge part of the professional coaching structure in Ireland for the last 15 years but we went through a process looking back over the last 18 months and looking at what we felt was needed to take the team forward,' explained Browne. 'And obviously one has to take into account the injury profile in the Six Nations as well, but at the end of the day we have to take decisions which are in the best interests of the Irish team in the long term and our view was that it is the best time to change the coaching structure. It was a difficult decision and he was disappointed but he understood.'

It was a formal last word on Declan Kidney's career, but words which were more powerful and pertinent came from Ronan O'Gara, who had turned 36, and was about to commence his own coaching career and would decide to join up with Johnny Sexton in Paris, as assistant coach at Racing Metro. He had learned so much from Declan Kidney, once his 'Master' in Pres Cork. He had started off getting his first official fitness programmes from Kidney that, even in his schooldays, were legendary. They were excellent and 'savage', in O'Gara's eyes, in equal measure. O'Gara and his friends would train for Kidney on Christmas Eve, St Stephen's Day, round the clock if asked to, and at lunchtime and during breaks the pair would meet up and talk about games in private. Kidney would draw a rugby pitch out on the A4 folder in his hands and then he would ask all the important questions of his chosen out-half.

'What would you do here?' Kidney would ask and point his pen at a portion of the field on the A4 paper. 'What would you do there? What would you do off this scrum? Off this lineout?' The out-half would later be handed his first IRFU contract of €15,000 per year and receive a sponsored Rover from Cork Constitution, and no longer have to belt it up to Limerick for

Munster sessions in his mother's Mini Metro. Declan Kidney, even then, though their schooldays together were long over, was still The Master.

As a young pup on the European stage, and doing the business in the Heineken Cup, the English media had begun touting O'Gara for Lions representation, but Kidney knew it was too much too soon. 'O'Gara did okay, but it will be another two or three years before we see the best of him,' Kidney replied when asked his opinion. In his memoir, O'Gara reflected that the coach knew him so well.

He explained that Kidney had seen his 'cocky side' and while he understood it was a vital part of O'Gara's game he also knew how vital it was that this characteristic did not go unchecked in his earliest years.

O'Gara and Kidney did not always agree on things. He could take it or leave it when Deccie played *The Lion King* to his squad. The Master had been his coach since he was 14 years-old. There came a stage when he thought that there was nothing new that Deccie could say. They disagreed occasionally. Also, they had a deep and underlining respect for one another that was an immovable object.

Ronan O'Gara: I was omitted from the squad a few weeks ago and that's really, really disappointing, and then Deccie got his news yesterday and I'm sure he's hugely disappointed. I know the man really well and he's been there for my whole career so it would be remiss of me not to compliment him on what he's achieved. The last few years haven't been great but the Grand Slam has been a masterstroke… really.

(April 4, 2013)

Declan Kidney: If you want to make God laugh, tell him what you're doing tomorrow.

(Many days… many years)